FORTY! Schmorty!

...life keeps happening

Conversations with Mattie and Eve

Mattie Mills **Eve Selis**

Published by:
Anybody Wanna Peanut? Publishing

ME! Enterprises
4653 Carmel Mountain Road, Suite 308-406
San Diego, CA 92130

www.fortyschmorty.com
info@fortyschmorty.com

First Edition

ISBN-13: 978-0-9786247-6-7
ISBN-10: 0-9786247-6-9

Printed in the United States of America

Book Design: Tom Gulotta
Cover photo: Jonothan Woodward

DEDICATION

Mattie: This book is dedicated to my husband Troy, my wonderful children, Gia, Gabby, Nathan and Morgan, and to my sisters, Margie and Kay.

Eve: I dedicate this book to my children, Megan, Jake, Sarah and Henry, and to my husband, Tom Gulotta, for his continued belief in my crazy life adventures!

CONTENTS

ACKNOWLEDGMENTS

This book would not have been possible without a dream, a phone message and a lot of hard work. Mattie and Eve would like to thank Mike Nottoli for taking the time to meet with two crazy forty-year-olds, for hearing us and believing in our dream. We appreciate all the phone calls you took and computer questions you answered as well as introducing us to Shlomi Ron; the guys at Gorilla Soapbox: Ty Mabrey, Mike Evans and Andrew Schultz; and Teresa Jache.

Shlomi Ron: Thank you for your marketing expertise, taking time to meet with us at Starbucks or Skype and *all* your website/blog input!

Gorilla Soapbox: Thank you for recording and co-producing our thirty-nine *Forty Schmorty!* podcasts, available online at iTunes and gorillasoapbox.com. We appreciate your patience and humor and all the long hours you spent before, during and after each shoot!

Teresa Jache: Thank you for believing in our vision and sharing your soulful "Ghost Weaving." Your encouragement and continued enthusiasm and support for this project have been a constant reminder that we have a right to write the way we wanna write!

A special thank you to our extra editing eyes: Stella Clemens, Anita York, Susan Francis and Barbara Fandrich, as well as everyone else who took a gander at our work in progress.

And to Judy Epstein, a world of gratitude for your wisdom and support.

HOW TO READ THIS BOOK

Imagine yourself as a fly on the wall listening in on a conversation between two best friends discussing life as they see it in their forties. Don't be surprised if from time-to-time they end up speaking to you and bring you in on the conversation. We recommend you find a comfortable spot to read, and bring the following:

- box of tissue
- cell phone (you will want to call your girlfriend)
- snack
- bottle of water
- favorite cup of tea
- highlighter
- pen

We also give you full and complete permission to "dog ear" any pages you wish as a quick reference find—just in case.

So put your feet up and take a load off! Start at the beginning and enjoy our journey. It's a fun, fast and easy read. If you've got an entire yummy hour or just a few minutes before the next grocery run, enjoy being **Forty** right now—it's only here for a short decade and then it's on to the next adventure because...Life Keeps Happening!

FORTY Schmorty!
...life keeps happening

PROLOGUE

The following is Mattie leaving a cell phone message for Eve
(February 14, 2006 at 5:06 p.m.)

*Okay, here's my first idea and thought. As I'm scrubbing my
kitchen sink with Soft Scrub, inhaling the intoxicating fumes of
cleanliness, listening to my Alan Phillips CD serenade Morgan and
myself with very cool African music, I think about us and I keep
wondering what could we do? I am always telling people, "You
need to write a book." Well, I think we need to collaborate on a
book. We could get Tom to be our ghostwriter 'cause I ain't never
written a book before, have you?*

*A book about celebrating motherhood and being forty, but with
a twist because we're musicians. It would be about friendship.
It would be about two different lives merging and encouraging
others in our particular predicament. A book about not being so
disappointed when things don't come to you in life. A book about
how we should celebrate the journey. Oh my God, what did I just
say? I know it seems like a long endeavor, but it doesn't have to*

take as long as it took to get to this point. And if we were to lock ourselves in a room with a tape recorder we could have a ten-book series! We could include a CD of songs that you've already written about life and encouragement. And if that's not enough, we could probably collaborate on one together. I don't know – maybe it's the launch of our 20-to-the-second-power magazine?

Eve, you've gotta call me. My brain is EXPLODING!! Okay, back to the Soft Scrub. Love ya, bye!

FORTY Schmorty!
...life keeps happening

INTRODUCTION

con·ver·sa·tion: (kôn´vêr-sā´shên) noun

1. The spoken exchange of thoughts, opinions, and feelings; talk.

2. An instance of such exchange: to hold a long tête-à-tête on the subject.

Mattie and Eve here and this is our first time getting together so we're probably going to be a little unorganized. We didn't have a chance to get online and gather our thoughts before we got together and started to write so pick and choose, as you will.

Eve: This whole process started for me with a quote from Albert Einstein. It says, "We can't solve problems by using the same kind of thinking we used when we created them" and it really got to me. I mean, all day long I would say to myself, "Change your way of thinking, change your way of thinking." Then Mattie and I are calling each other up on the phone back and forth, going through this...well, we're both going through this transformation right now in our lives. What do we want? What are we doing? How did we get here? What the heck? We're just going through it.

Mattie: We're looking back at our lives and now we realize we're in our forties and we had both set out with some very powerful dreams in our early twenties, and we really have fulfilled a lot of those dreams to a certain level, but not to a major degree. But yet, there's still something more out there. I think with the experiences we've gone through, and our friendship together, we definitely know now that it's come to a point where we both feel we've got a lot to give back. Because of what we've been through we have a lot to give people in their forties. I guess we're baby boomers of sorts or "after-the-boom babes." We feel that collaborating on this book is not only about helping others, but also to help ourselves because we can't afford therapy! We're thinking that if we just sit down and talk about what we need to talk about and get it down on paper, we'll help other women who are right there with us.

Eve: Yeah, I think you've totally touched on the path we've chosen. I was talking with my friend, Kim, about this very thing months ago. I was asking, "What the heck am I doing, why am I still striving for this dream of wanting to sell records and pursuing a major record deal? I'm still at it and here I am forty-two and all these eighteen to twenty-year-olds are the only ones getting deals with major labels." And Kim said, "Eve, just because we didn't choose the same path Madonna chose, doesn't mean our path is any less valid or that our journey hasn't given as much as her journey has. Her journey has been before an audience of millions and our journey has been before an audience of hundreds!"

Mattie: Thousands! So, I guess what we want to do is encourage women and moms of all walks of life because this is a very "of the times" book. This is where we are now. How can we grab what we have now and move forward to make things better? It's all about making a contribution to better our world and ourselves. Helping people change their way of thinking from tragedy to elation, from depression to wonderment and happiness, and keeping it there! How do we help each other get there?

Eve: We've been talking back and forth about what we're going through in our everyday lives for the past two months now. Every phone conversation with Mattie has been a lift. Even if the next day I wake up and say, "What am I doing?" Just talking about it really helps. Mattie and I have been talking about getting together to start this book and now we're doing it. We're so excited! But, you should see the e-mails we have. "Okay, tomorrow I've got to..." Mattie lists seven things and then I start to say, "Okay, I've got seven things, and when we've got time, let's try to get together."

Mattie: This could be considered the introduction to our book, "Conversations with Eve and Mattie" because that's what this is. We're gathering all our thoughts together and creating new catch phrases and "isms" to throw out there like multi-level marketing, calling this idea of ours "multi-level motivation." We start our little motivating synergy and then pass it on to a woman who decides to read this book and she passes it on to two other friends who pass it on to five other friends. Eve and I are ready to do this, give back. We believe we are at this point in our lives where we can make a difference.

Eve: We're grabbing quotes from everywhere. For example, Einstein's quote about the power of change. I was recently performing at a general session (corporate meeting with entertainment, PowerPoint presentations and lectures) for Century 21 Realty in Las Vegas. They are now called "Agents of Change." You can see their commercials on television and they are actually very good. The reality of their business is that everything is going online now and people are bypassing realtors because they can do it all themselves and they don't have to pay a fee. Realtors have to look at their business and say, "Okay, we have to overhaul this or we're out of business!"

These are the "top of the top." These are the companies bringing in millions of dollars! I think this whole concept, as with Einstein's power of change, is great for them. But what does that mean to us? What does that mean to two moms who are carpooling their kids to school and trying to get doctor appointments scheduled and paying bills and oh yeah, I didn't have enough work in music this month so kids we can't eat for the next week, sorry. So, it's time to go through the CD collection and sell some CDs so we can eat or pay the bills!

So, let's talk about ideas for chapters because I've already got my first idea for my chapter about Mattie. The first time I met Mattie she was three months pregnant and wearing size 0 jeans and I knew I hated her. That's my first sentence! Then it says, "Just kidding." But I knew I wanted to be so much like her. I envied her. I looked up to her. I knew I needed to find out who this person was. I had no idea, but I think I knew deep down what a huge influence she was going to be on me. I had no idea that our friendship would grow to what it is today. So that's just something I need to sit down and think and write about, and get my thoughts out. That would be part of our friendship chapter.

Mattie: My first recollection of meeting Eve goes back a little bit further. She was performing in a club in Pacific Beach and was wearing this black and white horizontal striped top, not P.B. Café but this other club across the street; it had bands...

Eve: José Murphy's?

Mattie: Yes! José Murphy's! It's where Dee Dee, the bartender, used to work. She would slam those bottles around, and it was really cool! I remember I was in that club, but I don't remember whom I was with. I remember being introduced: "Hey this is Eve," and I recall looking at her. Her eyes were beautiful, stunning brown, and her hair was perfect and she had a really cool gig. It was funny because she had a lot going on that evening. It was just a "Hi, nice to meet you" kind of thing and that was it! The next time I saw her was at the

NAMM (National Association of Music Merchants) show.

Eve: My God, you have the memory of an elephant! I don't even remember meeting you at José Murphy's. But those were the 80s; it was a bad decade, for music anyway.

Mattie: At the NAMM show I passed right by her and I thought, "Oh yeah there's Eve," but she didn't see me so I didn't want to say anything. So I didn't. Later, I did see Eve perform in Solana Beach at the Del Mar Café. That's where I saw her play and I thought she was a cool singer, beautiful, sounds great, has it all together! That's when she was established in my brain. Then we met again as her name came up as a possible singer to join me in the band The Heroes. I was thinking, "Yeah! She would be great!" We did a couple of gigs together before she left with the group to go to Europe. I stayed behind because I was pregnant.

Eve: We did just a few gigs. I joined in November so we had some December dates and I'll never forget. Unbelievable, here I am single, I have no kids, I have expendable time, I'm living in Los Angeles and I drive down for these gigs. I meet Mattie who is three months pregnant and she has more energy and more stamina and more enthusiasm on stage than I did. I remember the first couple of gigs with her. I was exhausted and sore for a week because I had not done anything like that! The fact that she was so much farther along than me I thought, "Okay, time to step up!" I couldn't complain because I wasn't even pregnant. Damn! Unbelievable and still wearing size 0 jeans, her second pregnancy!

Well, the other thing is that at that time of my life, I wanted kids so badly. I wanted to have a family. I always had the challenge of wanting to pursue my career and wanting to have that fame and fortune and also wanting the family life and the stability of the everyday changing of diapers and loving a husband and cooking a meal and all that. It was such a pull for me in my life, and then I finally meet someone who had it, who did both and was going crazy trying to find a sense of balance.

Mattie: And that was only part of the story. So here we were two female singers in San Diego, California, who made the career choice of singing in bands for a living and taking our talents and pulling them forward and that was our choice. It was our choice to become performers in San Diego and eventually we moved up from there. We were just starting to get out of the club scene and working more into the private parties, weddings and corporate functions and it was at a great time for corporate events because economically things were great.

Eve: And of course I was only going to be in the band (in my mind) for six months till I got discovered, then I'd have to go on my world tour. Eight and half years later, I finally quit the band and moved on to do my own thing. It's so funny the plans you make and then, life.

Mattie: But you had your plan, you had your goal and you set out, then of course there's a diversion of some sort. So, that's where we started.

Eve: Our friendship has gone through so many different phases from the awe to getting to know someone and the friendship part and then being there for someone and then you start having your ideas of what's going to make them a better person and make them happier. Then comes the conflict of "Wait a minute, don't tell me what..." We really have had a relationship like sisters. We really have. We've been through the fire and come out better for it. We want to share that.

Maybe we should just do an overview. Real specifics in the beginning and not touch on all those details because we don't have enough time in our book to get to all the rest if we do that.

Mattie: Or enough Kleenex.

(Tape stops for a moment.)

Eve: We just had a good cry.

We did want to talk about chapters. Friendship will be one, marriage another and since we've both had two, that's four marriages between us. Children and career will be other chapters.

Mattie: So, friendship, kids, marriage, career...

Eve: Faith?

Mattie: Faith, finance.

Eve: Yep.

Mattie: Finance and then parents, right? Talk about being parents, or our aging parents and how they've influenced us today and always. Support system. A support system of friends, people.

Eve: Friends, family. That brings us to the Internet. Maybe the support system on a website idea will come together, because we would like this book to be a resource. I just wrote this down, "A resource of ever expanding change in the universe of our life." You know what I mean?

Mattie: Wow! That was good!

Eve: But finding the support systems. Hopefully what we'll end up accomplishing through writing this book is obtaining information that helps us. 'Cause I think the bottom line is we want to help each other. I love Mattie, Mattie loves me; we want each other to be happy and we want each other to continue on whatever road it is we're on and finding things that are helping. She leaves me a message on the phone or a quote or "This is what happened to me" and it makes me feel better. Having that on a website always being updated so people can go online...oh, we have to do a cleaning chapter too, sorry.

Mattie: Cleaning.

Eve: Mattie is *the* cleaner of all cleaners!

Mattie: Yeah, right on, put it in there!

Eve: But you know, what is the column in the paper where people write in about cleaning? There's a very famous... What's her name?

Mattie: Right in the *Currents* section?

Eve: Umm, umm...

Mattie: There's a section and I didn't know about that?

Eve: Yeah! They write in ideas and say, "Sometimes when I get ketchup on the carpet I put..." you know...

Mattie: Heloise?

Eve: Heloise, it's Heloise! Okay, we got the website, we added cleaning...

Mattie: Dreams and hopes is a good one. We also discussed a chapter called "Just Trying to Matter." I think a good chapter to put in would be "Diverted Plans."

Eve: And some of these might end up jumping over into other things. Like we're talking about dreams and hopes and diverted plans. They may be part of the same chapter.

Mattie: And I think there should be one on anger and happiness.

Eve: Okay, good idea.

We were just talking about how here we are 42/45 and we're both asking, "Did we think this was where we were both going to end up?" I mean, I used to dream when I was younger of all the things a young girl would dream of; Prince Charming, white horses and living happily ever after. I remember a friend of mine, Julianne, she and I used to say, "Some day we'll have kids and we'll meet at Souplantation and we'll talk about our lives." We did that once or twice. But how did we get here and are we happy? Is this what we wanted? This is when we were young and carefree and didn't know what broken hearts felt like when it came to a relationship. We need to add a CD of inspirational songs written by both us and other people.

Mattie: The other thing too is that you just can't ignore the kids. There's Julie Clark from Baby Einstein. She has this mega industry where she has touched children's lives. I think down the road we should record a children's CD.

Eve: I definitely would like to record a children's CD. Also, Mattie and I had started on this idea about fitness for kids over ten years ago. Statistics have come out since then, that there are more overweight Americans than any other country in the world and there are 70 percent more obese kids now than when we were kids. So, we were way ahead of our time!

Mattie: Yeah, that show is all in a box in my garage.

Eve: Since Mattie and I don't have set schedules we're going to try to get together each week and work on this. Maybe it'll end up being a situation where we get inspired like Mattie did at two o'clock in the morning to answer her e-mail the other day. It's the only time she could do it!

Mattie: Yeah, we'll see how it goes. Actually, this is pretty exciting, what we're doing this second in time!

Eve: No matter what, this is going to happen!

FORTY Schmorty!
...life keeps happening

1
FRIENDSHIP

Mattie: In this chapter my thought was "How do we correlate friendship with being forty?" First though, I should disclaim that everything you read in this book is purely our take on each particular subject. We're not professionals by any means, just experienced.

Eve: And one thing I'm hoping we can keep as a thread throughout our whole *Forty Schmorty* book is that when people read each chapter, knowing this is simply our opinion, they can get a positive feeling from what they've read. I'm hoping the entire book will make people feel hopeful even when we're dealing with very serious matters.

So, I found this quote and I'm not sure who wrote it but I thought it was perfect.

> *Even though we've changed and we're finding our own place in the world, we all know that when the tears fall or the smile spreads across our face, we'll come to each other because no matter where this crazy world takes us, nothing will ever change so much to the point where we're*

not all still friends!

Wasn't that nice? I went online and searched Albert Einstein's quotes on friendship because I'd like to keep him involved. Remember his initial quote, "You can't solve problems by using the same kind of thinking you used when you created them."

Mattie: Well, I found a quote as I was searching online, but before I did, I decided to look up the word "friendship." I found a few things I thought were interesting. "Friendship" in *Roget's ll Thesaurus* is described as follows: "**Friendship** *noun* the condition of being friends: chumminess, closeness, companionship, comradeship, familiarity, fellowship, intimacy. See LOVE in Index."

"Friend" found in the same thesaurus states: "A person whom one knows well, likes, and trusts: amigo, brother, chum, confidant, confidante, familiar, intimate, mate, pal. *Informal:* bud, buddy. *Slang:* sidekick. See LOVE in Index."

Eve: Homey!

Mattie: Homey should be in there!

Eve: It should be!

Mattie: Now the definition is: "Someone whom one knows and likes; a supporter or patron of a cause or group. **Friend**: a member of the Society of Friends; Quaker." So naturally, I looked up Quaker. And the definition of Quaker is: "A member of the Society of Friends."

Eve: It's interesting how it says "See LOVE."

Mattie: I noticed that as well; that's why I wrote it down in my notes. So, I went online to look up "friends" and there's many different websites you can go on to find out what a friend can be.

Eve: Did you just Google friendship?

Mattie: I did!

Eve: You know we should get some stock in Google.

Mattie: So Aristotle says: "What is a friend? A single soul in two bodies." I thought that was cool!

Eve: MMMM that's very cool! The only thing I could find from Albert Einstein that was close: "Only a life lived for others is a life worthwhile." Well that leaves us with a couple of really nice thoughts. I've got a book here from someone who is an amazing writer—Frederick Buechner. He has a daily meditations book called *Listening to Your Life* and this is just gorgeous. Here's a portion:

> *Friends are people you make part of your life just because you feel like it. There are lots of other ways people get to be part of each other's lives like being related to each other, living near each other, sharing some special passion with each other like P.G. Wodehouse or jogging or lepidopterology, and so on, but though all or any of those may be involved in a friendship, they are secondary to it.*

> *Basically your friends are not your friends for any particular reason. They are your friends for no particular reason. The job you do, the family you have, the way you vote, the major achievements and blunders of your life, your religious convictions or lack of them, are all somehow set off to one side when the two of you get together. If you are old friends, you know all those things about each other and a lot more besides, but they are beside the point. Even if you talk about them, they are beside the point. Stripped, humanly speaking, to the bare essentials, you are yourselves the point. The usual distinctions of older-younger, richer-poorer, smarter-dumber, male-female even cease to matter. You meet with a clean slate every time, and you meet on equal terms. Anything may come of it or nothing may. That doesn't matter either. Only the meeting matters.*

> *"The Lord used to speak to Moses face to face, as a man speaks to his friend," the Book of Exodus says (Exodus 33:11). In the*

Book of Isaiah it is God himself who says the same thing of Abraham. "Abraham, my friend," he calls him (Isaiah 41:8). It is a staggering thought.

The love of God. The mercy of God. The judgment of God. You take the shoes off your feet and stand as you would before a mountain or at the edge of the sea. But the friendship of God?

It is not something God does. It is something Abraham and God, or Moses and God, do together. Not even God can be a friend all by himself apparently. You see Abraham not standing at all but sitting down, loosening his prayer shawl, trimming the end off his cigar. He is not being Creature for the moment, and God is not being Creator. There is no agenda. They are simply being together, the two of them, and being themselves.

Is it a privilege only for patriarchs? Not as far as Jesus is concerned at least. "You are my friends," he says, "if you do what I command you." The command, of course, is "to love one another," as he puts it. To be his friends, that is to say, we have to be each other's friends, conceivably even lay down our lives for each other. You never know (John 15:12-15). It is a high price to pay and Jesus does not pretend otherwise, but the implication is that it's worth every cent.

Okay, I'm crying!

Mattie: (Mattie grabs the Kleenex box.) That's beautiful!

Eve: Isn't that amazing? He is such a good writer!

Mattie: I just learned something from that. Cars go to gas stations and people go to friends. Because you can't go without gas and you've got to have gas stations in your life. You've got to have a place to fuel up. You and I are married to our husbands and we each married a gas station. A big one! We all are such complicated individuals; there are so many facets to us that no one human can fulfill.

Eve: I love that bit about being someone's friend just because. There are reasons why we become friends but those reasons don't matter. I don't think about those reasons when I pick up the phone to call you. You don't think about those reasons when you call me; you just know there's going to be complete acceptance on the other end of the line. If you're calling with good news or you're calling with bad news, you are going to get support, which is why I think we're doing this.

Mattie: I've thought about the roots of my friendships. The very first friend I remember was when I was six years old and she lived down the block from my house. I really don't remember much about what we did, it's not like we went shopping and did things like we do today.

Eve: You didn't have play dates?

Mattie: We didn't have play dates or play groups or anything like that. She just lived down the street and my mom would let me go to her house. Something I would never let my kids do now, like walk down the street alone. I would just go over to her house to visit her, knock on her door and we would play. I remember really enjoying it. When I think about her I remember just how good she made me feel. She was a friend and she was fun and it was somebody's house I could go to.

Eve: It was simple, you didn't think about it.

Mattie: I didn't think about it at all and it was cool because it was somebody who wasn't in my family, somebody who was my age, somebody who lived down my block, somebody I could anticipate running down the street and going to play with in her house. It was great until one day Mom said, "You know the Laurensons are moving." Her name was Linda Laurenson by the way, and if you're reading this book, would you please call me?

Eve: What is your maiden name?

Mattie: Figueroa, that's my maiden name. I lived down the block from her. So my mom says, "You know, the Laurenson family is moving" and I said, "Oh, okay," I didn't know what moving meant because...

Eve: Right! When you're six...

Mattie: When you're six nothing ever seems to change. You don't think much of the possibility of anyone moving. Generally most of the friends that I knew still have their home in Yuma. Or, their parents still live there or somebody still owns it from that family.

Eve: Still a small town feeling.

Mattie: People lived in their homes for years and years and I didn't know what "moving" really was. So one day I ran down to Linda's house because I wanted to play and the curtains were open. She had a beautiful window in the front of the house and a really nice wood floor. And I run up to her house and I'm looking through the window to find the house was empty! No one was home and the sunlight from the back yard was shining through the back window and shining down on the wooden floor and she was gone! No more. That was really, really sad because she wasn't there anymore. Never said goodbye, never ran into her at school. She just moved away. But, I'll never forget her. So when you think about friends who really touched your life, I can hardly remember her face, but I remember how I felt!

Eve: Okay, Mattie's crying. Here's a tissue!

Mattie: That was Linda.

Eve: It's so funny because my first friend, just to show you a complete other side, my first friend was in kindergarten. Her name was Isabelle and she was my friend because I loved her name and I loved to say, "Isabelle, Isabelle!" And that's all I remember! I remember we were dear friends and we saw each other at school. School was a little different than knowing somebody on your block. But talk about a superficial reason to have someone as your friend. I loved to say her name, "Isabelle," and she was pretty. You have this beautiful story of this deep bonding friendship of playing, even though you're six. How deep and bonding can six be? But at that point in your life it was the deepest, the most bonding you ever knew from somebody outside your family. And mine was because her name was Isabelle!

Mattie: And what happened?

Eve: I attended first grade at one school and she attended first grade at another. We just stopped being friends because we went to different schools. Isn't that funny? Thinking about it, until I was more mature, a lot of the reasons I chose friends were just very...well, like my friend Kathryn Schorr whom I've known my entire life since first grade. We became friends because we were the most popular girls in the class and everybody wanted to be our friends. We used to tease each other by saying, "I'm more popular than you are." Then Kathyrn would say, "Oh no you're not, watch this!" Then she would walk across the playground and all her friends would follow her like little chickens. I'd stand there watching then I'd say, "Oh yeah? Well watch this!" Then I'd go grab a couple of girls and say, "Hey girls, come over here!" And that's what we would do just to see who was more popular! And that's the reason we were friends. As we grew up we became very good friends. Although we've fallen out of touch, she's a wonderful person and she can always make me laugh!

So now we grow up and we make choices and we have friends that stay in and move out of our lives and then, you and I meet.

Mattie: I guess we have friends along the way; for example, Kathryn. You can call her and really not miss a beat.

My next best friend after Linda was Elizabeth Delaney. She also lived down the block, but on the other side of the street. We were "blood sisters" and "spit sisters." She came from a family of seven kids and her family was very cool, very artsy and her mom smoked a pipe from time to time. Elizabeth and I would run outside on rainy days and yell down the street to each other (she was about two blocks away from me) "The sky is falling!" She would usually go first and I would try to listen for her faint voice in the distance. We would get so excited because we could hear each other's voice! She is now forty-six and a grandmother and I know that I could call her anytime and be connected with home through her. When you think about the good solid friends you've made along the way, you know those are the ones you can call at anytime without missing a beat.

Eve: You know it's funny you mentioned smoking. Kathryn and I tried smoking for the first time in the fourth grade. We didn't have any cigarettes.

Mattie: What did you have?

Eve: Paper! We rolled up a piece of paper, lit it with matches, smoked, inhaled and burned the back of our throats, which might be why I sing with a little bit of a rasp to this day. Yep, we got in trouble, a lot of trouble. Don't play with matches and don't smoke paper!

Mattie: I'm going to make a note of that.

Eve: I remember exactly when I realized in grade school how important "true" friendships were. My life was, (singing) "doot do doot 'n doo! I got a lot of friends, I'm cool, and everything is great!" Then one day in eighth grade we were playing volleyball and we were rotating players. Everybody is lined up on the side waiting for their turn. I had already done one whole pass and was in line waiting for my turn when I heard these two girls talking about me. One of them said, "She thinks she's so cool!" This was the first time I had heard dissension in the ranks! I just thought everyone liked me because I was likeable. There was no thought put into it. It was just, "Oh, I'm popular!" It hit me like a ton of bricks that other people had feelings, other people wanted friends. It wasn't all about me! I think it was more like the sixth grade when that happened because I remember being just totally humbled realizing I was taking it all for granted. That was when I started being nicer and caring more about other people. I started making comments like, "Your hair looks nice, I like your shoes..." We *did* go to Catholic school so you couldn't really talk about the outfit because we all had the same uniform! I just tried to say something nice to someone every day to make them feel good about themselves. I realized the importance of that and that's when choosing friends, dear friends mattered.

I realized what a dear friend Kathryn was, even though we came together under those superficial "just cuz" reasons. All of a sudden I realized how important she was. I became friends with Julianne Geraci because she moved in from New York and had a bit of an accent and that developed into a dear friendship. Then there's my friend Lori Rosolino. One of the reasons we became friends was because she was Italian! She had a huge Italian family like my huge Catholic Irish family. We bonded and spent time together. The most important thing I remember about friendship was something my mom said, which is probably a recurring theme of what our mothers and our parents said to us. "Consider yourself lucky if you have one good friend in life." "Consider yourself lucky!" Now I think I have just one, two, maybe three people I will call close friends. I still consider Kathyrn a friend; I still consider Julianne a friend and Lori, although we don't talk often. But I do consider them a "friend", just not the person I call for support every day. Then, there's you and me.

Mattie: It's a good thing I didn't know you in grade school...

Eve: You would have hated me!

Mattie: I would have been so scared of you! The fear of God was put into me in all different directions. We both went to Catholic school in different towns so we had the similar upbringing. I really fell for that fear of God thing pretty hard. To this day I still have bouts with being a "recovering

Catholic." If I feel something might not be exactly right, I usually end up saying "You know the Catholic girl in me just doesn't want to go there!"

Eve: For fear and the guilt!

Mattie: It worked!

Eve: You and I grew up differently. I came from a large family and you grew up in a small town. There are different things about us and yet we're really the same person. I mean, we're so different, but so many times it's just been, "Wow!" You went through it, I went through it. Even with our singing, often times in the recording studio we would listen to the play back and ask, "Who is that? Is that me or is that you?" It's so interesting. Did we find each other? Did we gravitate towards each other because we were mirrors of each other?

Mattie: You know I believe it was a "Divine placement." You ended up joining the band and it was great having new energy and it was great to have a new person to work with. As time moved on it seemed our lives were moving in parallel motion.

Eve: To quote Buechner, we were "bonded by circumstances" when we joined a band together. There were meetings and rehearsals and when I joined the band there were five to six gigs a week! Gee, when we were younnnnnger! Back in our twenties and thirties when we could do that! Goodness! But the underlying theme when you look at "friendship" and the definition you read, what kept us friends was LOVE.

Mattie: I believe that!

Eve: "See LOVE." I think that's such a cool thing! "See LOVE."

Mattie: I believe our friendship is deeply rooted. I believe there are degrees of friendship. There's the acquaintance-once-in-awhile friendship, everything is on the up and up and you don't really want to get into what's going on with your life because it might get too deep, too complicated and you just don't want to drag anyone in. So you keep it on the up and up level and it's somebody to hang out with and that's it. Probably for that reason I don't have that many friends. As a matter of fact this morning my husband was leaving for work and he asked, "What are you doing today?" I said, "Well, Eve's coming over and we're writing a chapter on friendship." And his response was, "Hmm, are you going to be okay with that?" I said, "Yeah." "Did you do any research?" I answered, "Yes, I did some!" Then he said, "Huh, well okay, good luck. I'm going to have to write me a chapter on music sometime."

He teases me because I don't have friends calling me all the time. I don't have that comradeship like he does. He's "Mister Friend"; he has many friends. At times I'm a little cynical because I can't believe that a person can have so many close friends. Or is it because he's a guy? But then there are other women out there reading this book saying, "That's not true. I've got tons of friends!" Again, this is just who Eve and I are and I'm just trying to say that I'm a pretty private cat.

Eve: I keep going back to this "See LOVE." To me love is simple. It's not something you have to think about. We've both had friends in our lives who have been, shall we say "negative pull, energy suckers" we've put time and effort into. It's not that you're friends with someone to get something back, but they do fill you up like you said—a gas station. If they keep draining your emotional bank account after awhile you have to cut the cord and say, "This isn't working for me anymore!" I think we're just a little more choosey and maybe our definition of friendship comes down to more than "chummy" and "mate" and, "Hey how are you doing, good to see you" in the hallway type friend. It's the person we can call up and say, "And then you'll never guess what happened" and go on and on and on and that person will still stay on the line. There's not enough time in the day with as much stuff as we have to do to have more than one or two or three "friends." We see enough acquaintances through our work through singing, who are completely happy and joyous to say, "How are you doing, great to see you, I'm so glad you're well!" But it is, like you said, it's just the surface.

Mattie: I have friends who are friendly, but they don't really know me. My sisters are my dearest friends. Both my sisters are. We talk on the phone every day. I think I start with my family and myself and really strive to make a friendship with them. If you have siblings, keep close to them. They should always be there for support. Of course we grow up and move in our own directions. But we came from the same place, the same mother or family group. I think it's important to keep in contact with family members in that sense. And then you have your friends who've been with you in the past and went through certain changes and transitions in your life and your roads parted. But still you know for sure, without a doubt, you could call them up and it would be like picking up where you left off.

Eve: I agree with you about sisters being friends. I have four sisters and we are all close as well. I love the bond we share especially when our family gets together for a special event or holiday. It's nice to catch up and feel that sense of home with my sisters. Then there are those friends who are supportive in your mission. Whatever it is, if it's motherhood, or music, in my case. I have a wonderful friend I've known since the 80s, Phoebe Shaffer, who's seen me grow and change through the years. I met her when I was singing pop music in a group called Notice To Appear. She was into heavy metal bands at the time and she showed up to the club I was playing at dressed in black lace and chains hanging everywhere. I knew I needed to meet this girl. We became fast friends and she came out to the club to see me often. As the years went on our friendship deepened and we became very close. We both sang at each other's weddings and were present for our sons' births. She is in the medical profession and I call her for any and all maladies that afflict my family or me.

Then there's my friend Anita. She is tried and true, the most loyal person to the end. She will stand up and salute you, help you and give you her last dime. And yet our lives only intertwine through music. As we've gotten to know each other more and more we'll send each other cards through e-mail or call each other up on holidays, and when tragedy happens we're there for each other and we are supportive. Music is our anchor.

I'm wondering. Here we are writing this book and we're thinking about being forty and being friends. What happens? In your twenties your friends are saying, "Hey, meet me at the bar!" Party, party! And in your thirties friends are saying, "Hey, meet me at the playground with the kids." And now we're forty. What does it mean when we are forty? It's definitely a transition; it's a different place with friendship. It's almost like a whittler, whittling down those friends that still matter and that still stay in contact.

Mattie: Most of our friends will be with us till the day we die. We transition, we change, and so do our friends. You were mentioning friends we have in our lives who don't make us feel good because we've tried and we've worked really hard to help them through and it's almost as if they didn't hear a thing you said to help them and it becomes more work than friendship. It's a lot of labor. I've learned at this point in my life to love those people away from me. Always, keep tabs on them, but I just don't have time for them anymore.

Eve: That's a very cool way of saying it, "To love those people away from me" because you have to love yourself first and if it's not working for you for whatever reasons you've got to move on.

Mattie: When you're younger, you just cut it off. You might have said, "I don't like that person anymore, I hate them, I'm never calling them again!"

Eve: They're so "high school."

Mattie: Yes, that was the attitude, but you have to stop and think about those people being in your life for a reason. I believe that we attract likenesses. What we are projecting we are attracting most of the time without even knowing it. As we grow and mature so do our choices in friends and we end up growing together. I've had some interesting friends in my life, some of whom I'm glad I've moved on from. I think about them from time to time, but I'm really happy I'm not there anymore because I've learned whatever it was I needed to learn from them and moved along. I believe we're all on assignment in each other's lives.

Eve: Like my friend Kim from Nashville who I met five years ago. She is like a blood sister or we were parted at birth or something. It's not like we're that similar, but we're bonded by our music. The fact that her music touches my heart so deeply and my singing touches her heart so deeply bonded us. Music is so much a part of who we are. You can't take that bond away; you are fused to that person. I think about her like I think about you, as family. Maybe that's what happens with friends in our forties. The friends that stayed and worked through life with us are now family. And that's how we have to think of them in order to keep them a part of our busy lives.

Maybe you say different things to your family, your blood family, than you would to your friends. But sometimes that crosses over and your friends actually become the persons you can say things to, sometimes brutal things and they'll love you no matter what. I'm trying to think of what we want to accomplish with this friendship chapter and who knows. Maybe somebody reading this book is somebody we haven't met yet who will enter our lives because they are going through the same thing we're going through. My friend Kim says, "There are no coincidences, there are CoinciGods!"

God really did send you into my life. I needed you. You pulled me under your wing because you could at that point. You didn't have as many children then and I needed your guidance. For whatever reason we were pulled together and then my strengths came to play and helped you when you needed help. So where does that leave us with our people?

Mattie: I think it leaves us realizing that we're in our forties and we need to get new friends all together!

Eve: Spring cleaning!

Mattie: Because we're now thinking about it. It's a really good time to take an inventory of your soul group of people. Who is in your life, who do you choose to keep in your life? Who's there that you are helping and who's there that's helping you and who makes you feel good? Who do you help feel good? Are you in check with all that? Are you happy with your group of friends? Do you want to have more friends?

Eve: Here's our *Forty Schmorty* test encompassing everything we just said, thanks to my dad, Dr. Robert Selis. He said this to me one time when I was involved in a difficult relationship, but it works perfectly with everything you just said: "You've got five friends, this group of five friends makes you feel great, you have a good time with them and every time you see their number on your phone you say 'yippie!' and it always fills you up, it's wonderful! Then you've got five friends who terrorize you, who torture you and make you feel horrible who, when you see their number on your phone you say, 'Oh I don't want to talk to them!' Now you have two seconds to choose which group you want to spend the rest of your life with, ready? Go!" It's that simple, and we make it so much harder. This works for any age. You don't have to be *Forty Schmorty* for it to work. It's taking an inventory and saying, "Hey, where am I going to be forty years from now and who do I want to be there with?" Keep it simple.

Mattie: Exactly, and LOVE each other. Start making time for each other. You know the thing that really disappoints me in people is when they say they want to get together and be friends, but they're too dang busy! I know in their heart they want to get together and I know when they say it they mean it at the time. I'm guilty as well, but to stop and make the time to follow through is so important.

I have a new girlfriend, Kathleen, who came up to me one Sunday at church and asked me what I was doing afterwards. I thought quickly about my routine. I'm going to get into my car, go home, do the laundry, and cook dinner...Then she said, "Do you think you have a couple of hours where we can just leave after church and do something?" Well, our two-hour get together turned into four or five hours. We ended up going to the park, walking and talking, eating lunch and getting to know each other. At times we were cautious about our conversations and prefaced our subject with: "I don't really mean to sound like this but..." I think Kathleen was just trying to get to know me. I'm pretty much open to accepting anything I hear and I think she was trying to be careful with her words. Actually, she ended up being very honest and open.

I think in your forties you need to stop planning and start being more spontaneous. If you know you have an extra hour or so, seize the moment. Some of the best encounters I've had with friends are spur-of-the-moment. Every time we would end up saying, "Had we planned this, it would have never happened!"

Eve: Is that because it was not important enough? Or because it's just a way of thinking?

Mattie: In my situation with the four kids, a husband, and everyday life that tends to get involved and unexpectedly eventful, I'll have plans with a mom friend and something comes up with them or myself. I always understand because I'm in the same boat at other times. It seems if I plan something there's always this hidden possibility that will keep us from getting together. Getting together with friends nowadays for me is to seize the moment when you can seize the moment!

Eve: Well do you think that your friendship with Kathleen might just end up being a friendship where it only happens when you do something spontaneous like that? Because of exactly what you just said, I am nothing without my stupid planner! If I don't write it down, it's out of my mind, it's gone because there are just too many other things that I need to do or think about. Does it really matter that the carpet's been vacuumed or the dishes have been put away? Does it really matter? Because I love what you're saying about seizing the moment, it's so true, it's so relevant in this day and age. I'm asking you, Mattie, because I want to know. Our deep friendship was cast at a time when we had more time and now that's why we're here.

I know you Mattie. You are a clean freak and that is important to you and your house is gorgeous and spotless and you have to make the time to make that happen. That takes up a certain amount of your day so you only have a little bit of time left to do other things. If we didn't make an appointment to sit down together and write this, it wouldn't happen. And it got pushed back today because I had to do some business and I was supposed to be here an hour ago and you called and said, "Is it not going to happen?" and I said, "Yes, I'm in the car, I'm coming!" Now your baby is asleep and we worked it out so we could get together because writing this book is a priority. It's important to make this happen because we want it to. Why? What are we doing here? We're trying to talk about friendship in our forties. Sometimes you just have to take chances.

Mattie: Take chances, change your priorities.

Eve: I have to tell you that lately I have been having dreams of the reality of death. I'm not dreaming that anyone is dying and I'm not dreaming of my own death, but the reality of what death means. We all live in denial because that's how we get through every day; we don't think about it. A couple of times I've gotten that gasp for air feeling and it's over. This could be because an acquaintance of mine just died, Buddy Blue. He woke up one day, took the time to be with his family, played with his kids. He didn't feel well, went to the bedroom to lie down and died. How would his last moments have been if he had said, "No, I've got to go mow the lawn?" and his last moments were, "The lawn looked good when I died."

I was talking to my husband and I asked, "What if I die tomorrow, what about all the crap that's on the floor and all my books that aren't put away and all the laundry?" and he said, "Eve, do you really think I would care and be thinking about any of that? That you left me with all this crap on the floor? Or do you think it would be *you* I would think about?" So, is friendship about finding the time to give "you"? I mean really, your time is who you are! Your time is, "I'm cleaning my house now. I'm feeding my baby now. I'm picking up my kids now!" That's who you are and that's who I am. But who am I really? I'm a little girl six years old walking down the street to play with my friend. That's who we really are. That's the friend we want to be.

Mattie: When I was getting my notes together for today I was thinking about going back to our first friendships. Maybe that person is not in your life anymore, maybe they are, but especially if they're not, what was the thing that really drew you into that friendship? It's as if the child inside of you is saying, "Gosh, I really wish I could go back there one more time to feel that giddy feeling and laugh at silly stuff and be free with a friend like that." There's so much seriousness around us. It's nice to escape with a friend and experience those feelings again. Today it's not as easy. Now we have husbands and they are our best friends who see us day in and day out. But I can't go shopping with Troy. There are some things that can only be discussed with girlfriends and I really couldn't sit and talk about the football draft with him. I just don't get it.

Eve: Maybe our friends are our friends because of what they give to us? My friendship with you, for example, I felt like you took me under your wing. I looked up to you. I wanted to be more like you. And I think a good friend makes you want to be a better person. They challenge you by example. I talk about you as my hero because of all that you do.

I know you love my family. I don't get to see much of your family because they're in Arizona, but I hear how you talk about them and I know what they mean to you. Family is important to me so there's another reason we're friends. I look at my friend Kim and I see her relationship with God. She is someone who has a deep connection with her faith. My faith is a little bit more hidden, maybe a bit more shy. Her example of living her faith every day is something I look up to and yearn for in my life. Her strong faith has enriched our friendship. I've come a long way from growing up with Catholic guilt and stoic nuns.

Mattie: That was the sign of the times when we were growing up, that's really how it was and I know it's different today. But growing up back then you had a true fear. Especially the way the nuns dressed in their habits, everything was covered up. All you could see was about five inches of their face from forehead to chin to cheek to cheek. That's it!

Eve: I remember my fifth grade teacher, who was a nun, asking this question one day. It was a sign of the times because the Cold War was still going on with Russia. She said, "Okay, we've just been invaded and Russian soldiers have arrived on campus with guns and into our classroom and forced everyone out to the playground. They tell us they are going to kill anyone who believes in God and we must choose between our faith and our lives. What would you do?" I'm thinking, "I'm only in the fifth grade. I don't want to die. I don't know what to choose!" I was terrified that I couldn't say, "I believe in God." I didn't stand up and say it. It was brutal!

Mattie: Was that like a fire drill? Did they take you outside?

Eve: No, they didn't actually do that, they just asked us the question. "Is your faith strong enough for that?" And I'm thinking "No, my faith is not strong enough. I want to go home to my family and I want to live!" That was terrifying! How can we do that to our kids? How could you do that to me? That's probably the reason why I didn't want to raise my daughter that way. I'm sure it's a lot different nowadays. It has to be! Our faith has to grow and change, just the way our friendship has to in order to survive.

Why has our friendship survived? Because there was a time we didn't talk as much. And there was a time, I don't want to say that we hated each other, but we didn't have as positive thoughts about each other. Jealously and insecurities and thinking, "I know what's better for you, why aren't you listening to me?" "You know what's best for me, why can't I hear you?"

Mattie: It's human nature. We try to fix our friends; we try to fix the ones we love.

Eve: Now, we can choose. Why couldn't we do that when we were younger? Maybe we needed the experience of *how to love*, because in school when they were drilling it into our heads, it was just words. It wasn't that fabric of love. It's like what you said earlier about loving someone away from you. With that same concept, you love them near you.

Mattie: When you're that young you don't know much and you haven't experienced life enough to know what's going on. You have to live it through.

When I think back about the hard times of our friendship I can honestly say that it never was *you*, it was always about where I was coming from. I was so depressed with my first marriage I stopped caring about myself. I felt like I was dying a slow death. I didn't know what to do or who to talk to. Everybody I did speak with knew exactly what I needed to do, but I couldn't do it myself. Everyone tried to step in and help and I felt defeated because I was really trying to make my marriage last. I came to the conclusion it was meant for me to live that way and I deserved everything I was going through. I ended up believing that was the direction I had to go for the sake of the family. I know that really upset you and I remember one night after a gig we ended up yelling and screaming at each other.

Eve: I was on the outside looking in and seeing you in such a different light not understanding how you were looking and seeing your own self! I'm thinking to myself, "You're worth it! You're worthy, you're worth so much more, you're strong, you're beautiful, and you have everything. Why are you taking this?"

Mattie: That night I wasn't mad at you. I was mad at my choice in life at the time.

Eve: You were doing the right thing for the wrong reasons.

Mattie: Exactly!

Eve: Which is why my first marriage didn't work out! Interesting? See, we were doing the same thing again!

Mattie: So now we've made this choice to come back to each other's lives. We've had our time working together as friends, you moved on to pursue your solo career and we didn't stay in contact with each other as much, but always remained friends. You had your life and I had mine. So here we are again.

Eve: When I left the band I felt like I needed to reinvent myself and have my own memories with music and you had to pick up and guide and build your memories from where you were as well. We needed to have that time apart in order to appreciate what we had together.

Mattie: I had so many people say to me after you left, "It's never been the same since Eve left the band. You two were really magic together!" So yes, I had to make good with my work situation without you and it has worked out beautifully.

So what would be your conclusion on being forty today with friends?

Eve: I'm just happy to be here. You end up reevaluating *what* you have learned up to this point in your life and you have to be grateful you have close friends. Then you think about *where* you are at this time in your life? And up pops some of the reasons we did get together to write this book: to share our thoughts on friendship, to share the journey of our personal friendship, and to look back and see what we can give and what we can pass on with this book.

So right now, you the reader should stop what you're doing and make a list of your friends. Think about your first friendships and how they have evolved in your lives. Take a moment to really appreciate what you have in your life and who you are because of it. You met your friends for a reason and you are at this point for a reason. Look around you and realize that the friends you have in your life right now are going to help you get through the next forty years.

So what can *we* do? I'm hoping we're going to build our community of *Forty Schmortys* who realize, "We're in this together, and we're going through the same things right now. Let's help each other!" Let's send each other words of encouragement through e-mails, phone calls, even snail mail. My sister Jeanne says to me, "Eve, I love getting cards in the mail." You even mentioned that, Mattie. With our busy schedules we don't do that anymore. We don't sit down, pull out a card and write a note. So buy a card for your closest, dearest friends and say, "Hey guess what? I was at the grocery store, I saw this card, I was thinking about you and I love you. You mean a lot to me!" Then send it!

I think we want this book to change our way of thinking when it comes to our friends. Mattie mentioned how important it is to be spontaneous and grab a moment with a friend. I don't think about things like that, but I'm inspired to do so more often!

Mattie: You hit the nail on the head when you talked about being grateful! We all need to be more in gratitude. At this point in our life we should be seasoned, we should all be done with childish behavior and immature thinking.

There are people our age running major corporations, people who are making decisions changing our children's lives. Here we are in the kitchen trying to change our little bit of the world. It seems so small, but like you said, it's that "drop in the water" that creates ripples of deep thought and gratitude going out to everyone reading this book. We are at a very important and pivotal age where we need to realize we've grown up and this is what it's all about. We have a lot more wisdom and we should try to be more "God like" and more "peaceful" and the spontaneous behavior of calling someone up on the phone and telling them you love them is something we all need to do more.

Let me tell you a little story. I was taking a nap on my daughter's bed and I had a memory flash of a girl I used to travel with in Up with People. At the time there was a cast nurse named Ann Liechty. I thought she was very smart, pretty, a great dancer, and a very caring individual. I really looked up to her. She helped me through a very difficult time in my life, being away from home for the first time. She's always had a special place in my heart. After my travels in Up with People, I found out she later got married, left nursing and went back to school and became an attorney. She was a high achiever. Ironically, she showed up at a gig I was playing at in San Diego. I think you were in the band at the time. She was in town with some convention and she walked up to the stage and said, "Mattie, it's me, Ann!" I remember looking down and being so surprised to see her because it had been so many years since we had traveled together. It was bizarre how she was back in my life again for that brief moment. We hugged, made the connection, I got her address and I think we ended up sending each other Christmas cards the following year. Then we fell out of touch with each other. She had a natural birth son and adopted two other beautiful children.

So fast-forward to today. I'm taking a nap and she crosses my mind. I'm thinking, "I wonder how Ann's doing?" So I get up, go to the computer and Google her name. Up comes the Ann Liechty Pro Bono Child Custody Award. I'm thinking, "Oh wow, how cool!" Then I continue reading only to find out that this award was named in memory of Ann who was "a dedicated child law advocate." She had died of cancer in

1999. I sat there in shock. I couldn't believe I was getting the word of her death so late and in this way. She was totally on my mind and in my heart that afternoon. I had no idea I was going to find what I found. She has been gone for seven years. She left her mark in this world by providing pro bono services to those in need of child custody assistance and adoptions. She did honorable deeds for those in need.

I was so sad that whole weekend. I cried and I couldn't believe she was gone. I found myself sitting in my garage thinking about Ann and the year we traveled together and another friend, David, came to mind. We traveled that same year in the same cast. I've kept in closer contact with him throughout the years and decided to call him. We talked about Ann for awhile and I was comforted by his words. I had a very strong need to remind him that what we went through the year we all traveled together was life changing and made such a wonderful impact on all of our lives. I was grateful that we were still in contact with each other and told him, "The bottom line here David is that I love you and I want you to know that." I told him I was shocked we had lost our friend and I didn't get the chance to tell her I loved her. I wanted him to know I felt the same way about him. Our friendships started about thirty years ago. David has a wonderful life in Los Angeles, married, couple of children, great career, and I had to take a moment to tell him I loved him. In my life, he too was someone who touched my heart and made a big difference to me. I needed to let him know what he meant to me and that he will always be someone special.

It's really important to think about those people who have touched our lives and our hearts. Are you able to get back in contact with them? Can you find them on the Internet? Are they dead or alive? It matters if you give them a call today and just say, "Hey, you know what, I know I haven't talked to you in thirty years, but you made a difference in my life and I want to thank you for being there and I want you to know I love you. It's because of you being in my life that I'm a much better person."

I think this is a great assignment for all of our readers!

Eve: Yeah, because imagine, at this point our readers putting this book down and calling someone from their past. Think of it, a million phone calls going out and all of a sudden the light switch turns on and the world gets a little brighter. What was accomplished? You were able to give LOVE and somebody felt it. Maybe you won't be able to talk to your friend David for another ten years, but the sentiment and feelings are there along with the memories. And likewise, when you come into their mind they'll think about your call and they might do the same and it will go on and on and on.

Mattie: One thing I want to tap on is how your sister Jeanne loves to gets cards. I think it's great! We need to be writing old-fashioned letters to each other. Receiving friendship mail is a wonderful thing. My daughter Gabby and one of her best friends write letters to each other all the time. They send each other candy, packets of flower seeds, and write beautiful short letters of encouragement. This girl only lives four miles away from our house! I'm learning from my fourteen-year-old daughter that writing a letter to someone you care about and saying, "I care. How are you doing?" or sending a little card or trinket means so much to the person receiving it. I hope letter writing never goes away.

I have a pen pal and we send each other Christmas cards every year. She's been my pen pal for thirty-eight years! I've watched her handwriting go from wobbly to mature and now it's like a mature wobble. It's funny to see how her handwriting has changed. I met her once in my life and we are two completely different people. I'm from the desert and she's from Wisconsin. She goes ice fishing and I used to walk barefooted on the hot concrete in 110-degree weather. Our lives couldn't be more opposite of each other. She's only had two addresses in her entire life. I can't even begin to count my past addresses. Her life is so different from mine, but yet she's touched my life. She has children and a job and looks forward to buying canoes and snowmobiles. I can't even imagine what that's like. I don't even own a bike!

So, we need to get back in touch with things that make us feel good with our friends like letter writing and card sending. We need to realize the friends we have in our lives and their importance to us. We need to keep our friends close to us and make time for new friends as well. We need not be afraid of becoming more spontaneous with our friends and be at peace. We're old enough now, we're grown-ups. Most important, we need to be in gratitude!

FORTY Schmorty!
...life keeps happening

2
PARENTS

Eve: Since we're starting off with inspirational quotes, I found a Chinese proverb: "To understand your parents' love, you must raise children yourself." Isn't that awesome?

Mattie: Ah! That's perfect!

Eve: And that's our whole chapter, thank you, we'll see you next time! Good night, tip your bartenders!

Mattie: Well, the quote I found is taken from Heraclites, and it reads:

> *The soul is dyed the color of its thoughts. Think only on those things that are in line with your principles and can bear the full light of day. The content of your character is your choice. Day by day, what you choose, what you think, and what you do is who you become. Your integrity is your destiny; it is the light that guides your way.*

Eve: I was also looking through my Albert Einstein quotes and I thought this one fit: "Only a life lived for others is a life worthwhile." And another Einstein quote I found was: "People do not grow old no matter how long we live; we never cease to stand like curious children before the great mystery into which we were born."

Mattie: Eve and I chose this chapter about parents not as professional experts, but as friends "shooting straight from the hip" with our life experiences. I have seen and listened to people who have written books about parents and parenting and some of them are wonderful! We likewise feel the need to share what we know about our lives up to this point and hope most of you reading will find comfort in the words written on these pages.

I lost my mother when I was twenty years old. She had a very rough battle with cancer. I was born when my mom was forty-one years old and I find it very sad that I can't seem to remember very much about her. (*The phone rings.*)

Eve: And the phone rings!

Mattie: I'm not going to get that. My dad is still alive and he remarried about six years after my mom passed away. Now thinking about it, he just celebrated his twentieth wedding anniversary. Had my mother still been alive they would be heading into their fifty-ninth year of marriage! That's two whole lifetimes for my dad! I'm very proud of him for moving on with his life after my mom's death. There he was with three kids, his wife dies and his life has to move on. I've learned from my dad never to give up. You just keep going. You've got to have love in your life and you have to keep replenishing, renewing and refreshing your loves.

Eve: Don't you think your mom would have wanted your dad to do that too, because he was still a young man. He had to be in his forties. I mean that's how old we are and we're very young!

Mattie: Absolutely! And you know, ironically for my mother, she was married before my dad. She had married the love of her life. He was shot down in World War II six months after their marriage. I am named after her first mother-in-law. Mattie was her name and she was from Louisville, Kentucky. I think for my dad to accept the fact that their third child, the surprise, that's me, was going to be named after my mom's first husband's mother was very loving and understanding of him to allow that. That example of being a loving parent was a very important lesson for me. We learn from example. We watch and learn from our parents.

Eve: That's where I think the root of a lot of problems in the world come from, parents not being ready to be parents. When I think about prejudice, we learn that from our parents. If our parents have prejudices we have prejudices. When you see kids of all nationalities, races, and religions in a room playing together they don't have any agenda. They just want to play and have fun, smile and laugh, and sure maybe there'll be pushing and shoving at some point, but it's not about anything else. We learn that from our parents. I often think you should have to get a license to be a parent. You know? There should be something you have to pass in order to have the privilege because it really is a privilege.

My parents met when my dad had appendicitis and my mom was the nurse's aide at the hospital!

Mattie: That was a great day to have appendicitis!

Eve: Yeah! He started flirting with her right away. He captured her heart coming out of anesthesia! Back in the day, when our parents wanted to be seriously involved in a relationship they got married. That's just what you did. It was a short courtship; I think they got married in 1958. Still doesn't seem like that long ago, but it was over forty years. They went to Disneyland for their honeymoon. It had just been opened for a year or two. It was such a huge thing that they went to California to Disneyland for their honeymoon! Then along came all eight of us kids!

As a child in a family of eight you grow up learning to share. You grow up sharing everything from food to rooms to hand-me-down clothes. But you really can't appreciate what being a parent is about until you have your own! I remember the first thought that came into my head when I had my child: "I need to apologize to my parents for every rotten thing I ever said or did!" I remember it so clearly, "Oh my God I'm sorry mom and dad!" And secondly was just pray, pray, pray. I just started praying, "Please God, watch over my child!" You just feel so helpless because anything can happen to your child. And if something happens to your child you know your life is over! "Put me in the looney bin; I won't last!" How some parents go through tragedy with a child and get through it is another chapter I suppose. My parents were so young when they got together and my mom had eight children and twelve pregnancies. She had four miscarriages before she was thirty!

I look at it this way: You have toddlers now, Mattie, and when Nate is doing something he shouldn't be doing you try to discipline him, but you're also giggling at the same time because he's so cute! That's how I see God looking at us, because I feel we are all children of God. Even though I'm forty He's still pointing the finger at me and saying, "Now Eve..." but He's also giggling because you know He can't believe how cute I am! And that's how I want to exist with my children because I believe that's how God is with me.

Your dad's a bit older than my dad; my dad just turned seventy and your dad is eight-five.

Mattie: Well, he's eighty-six and his health is very fragile. He suffers from many things but yet he can walk and take care of himself to a certain extent. These are delicate years for aging parents when they are in their eighties. I'm not at home in Arizona to take care of Dad and his wife. They both live on their own in their own place. I do have a sister who is there to pick up Dad from his house and take him to his work. Dad has his own business, which my sister has now taken over. He goes to the office and sits at his desk, reads the newspaper and falls asleep in his chair. He just wants to be there!

Eve: It's probably keeping him going!

Mattie: It does keep him going. He doesn't want to stop. Some days my sister Kay can take him out to measure property and other days he wants to be home just to sleep. I get very frustrated when I think about the things he could be doing. Why doesn't Dad get into yoga? Why doesn't he stand outside his front yard and try some Tai Chi? Isn't there anyone out there who can help him stay active? When I stop and think about that, I ask myself, "Am I going to be eighty and doing that same thing? Am I just going to stay asleep in bed because there's nothing else to do and all the kids are gone and I might not have a husband?"

Eve: I find that so hard to believe. Mattie is Superwoman, I swear. She'll still be flying with that red cape at eighty-five!

Mattie: And a bottle of 409 in the other hand! I think about how it's going to be when we as parents get older and what we will expect out of our family. I've got one sister taking care of my dad and there are three of us, but I have my family and responsibilities here in California and my older sister has her responsibilities in a different city in Arizona. My sister in Yuma is at home taking care of my dad and his wife and their daily needs, which is awesome. It's a scary thought but we should think about how we are going to live our lives later in our years. Didn't someone just tell us the other day that our life expectancy could be...

Eve: One hundred and fifty!

Mattie: One hundred and fifty years old!

Eve: Did you know there are new drugs being developed for people who were born in 1960 and beyond that may extend their life expectancy to one hundred and fifty years?

Mattie: No, I hadn't heard that! That reminds me of a movie I recently saw called *Bicentennial Man* with Robin Williams.

Eve: Missed it. Okay, tell me.

Mattie: I think that was the name of the movie…It was about a man who lived over two hundred years watching the circle of life repeat itself over and over. I got tired watching him live so long that I wanted him to die already!

Eve: Well, it's interesting because it's also a way of thinking: that older way of thinking. Sometimes in certain instances that old way of thinking needs to evolve or die so that the new way of thinking can come in to our lives. Take communism for example. Those people were raised their entire lives believing in it and that's all they knew. They didn't have the understanding to grasp the idea of democracy or anything close. That way of thinking needed to die off so the next generation could survive.

Mattie: Most definitely! As I reflect about being a parent now, it's so important to be on top of their health, safety, discipline and love. It's also important to give them as much space as we can; watching them discover how to gain independence but learning where to go for safety. It's all about balance. Now when you're giving your children their space to grow, do you ever reflect on your parents and how they raised us?

Eve: It's hard for me to remember when I was a teenager.

Mattie: Actually it's hard for me too, but I know I had a lot of fun.

Eve: I did too and in my twenties as well! I'm thinking about what you just said, that your dad is eighty-five and slowing down. If you cut our lives in half to our twenties, do you remember all the late nights staying out having fun, partying with our friends then getting up early and working all day long and then going out and doing it again? Have we slowed down a bit since then?

Mattie: Yeah, we have!

Eve: Back then we had all that energy. Our life was an open book and we were just living it.

Mattie: So much fun!

Eve: We weren't really planning ahead, we were just having fun. I see that now with my stepdaughter Megan. She's almost nineteen and as a parent I want to say, "Oh, make good choices and be careful and don't drink and drive." I want to say all the things my parents said to me just to make sure she's safe. But I have to let her go and make all her own mistakes like we made when we were younger. It really is amazing that any of us...

Mattie: Survived! I am surprised we survived. I'm sure there were a few times you and I were close to losing our lives and not even realizing it, whatever silly things they were!

Eve: Then you're standing in line going to heaven and you're asked, "So how did you get here?" "Oh, well, there was this accident that had something to do with electricity and drinking and..." OH!

Mattie: A butter knife and a toaster!

Eve: Exactly, the butter knife and the toaster, OH!

Mattie: I grew up with a hyper-vigilant father; so today I'm a very hyper-vigilant individual. Let's say we would go on an out of town trip. We pack up the car and get in the car, leave, and about forty-five minutes out of town Dad would ask Mother, "Did you turn off the coffee? Did you unplug the toaster?"

Eve: Classic!

Mattie: Then there would be this worry in the car about...

Eve: Oh no, the house is going to burn to the ground!

Mattie: There were a lot of things my dad warned me about. Usually it was him who put that "fear of God" in me about being careful about things and keeping my eyes open and "Lock the front door." But I have to thank my dad for that because in today's world you have to do that!

Eve: Or you can live in L.A. for a couple of years and it stays with you no matter where you are! "Lock all your doors! Turn your lights out!"

Mattie: Yeah, shut your blinds! I remember the day my dad said, "We're going to have to start locking the front door, people are starting to break into other people's homes, always lock the front door from here on out!" There was a time where we left the front door unlocked, the car was unlocked, there was no key to security, there wasn't anything locked up, it was just wide open!

Eve: It's so interesting you mentioned that because I want to share something with you. This is a book I gave to my mom for Mother's Day one year (shows Mattie). It says, *Mother's Memories for My Daughter*, but being the space cadet that I was I didn't see that it said *For My Daughter*! I just saw *Mother's Memories* and thought, "Oh wouldn't that be neat if Mom wrote this all down and we could have this as a memory?" Well this book said "For My Daughter" so she gave it back to me that year for Christmas! So classic! "Here mom, here's a gift for me! Get to work, love ya!" So it says: "To Eve Marie with love, mom." Isn't that sweet? She wrote something in here that reminded me of what you just talked about. It says:

> *Diane and I had a friend with a very big dog who was sort of scary looking and there was this café on the corner, no one ever locked their cars and we would wait till they had gone into the restaurant and then sneak the dog in the backseat and wait for the fun. They would get in and start the car and start to back out and suddenly stop and everyone would jump out of the car! They never caught us!*

Oh my mom was so sneaky!

Mattie: I wish I had a book like this. You have one of the best gifts you could have ever given your mom and yourself. This is something to treasure for the rest of your life and you can pass it on to your daughter, Sarah!

Eve: I highly recommend it as something we as adults should start for our kids! My mom has a great memory when it comes to sharing stories about her childhood and growing up. She even describes the way things smelled. She writes about those one-piece swimming suits and how they had to wear those...

Mattie: Latex swimming caps! I remember having to wear those!

Eve: I do too! We had to wear them at camp! I remember the unforgettable smell of chlorine and latex! I want to read what my mom wrote here under the heading, "What I've Learned and Would Like to Tell You!"

> *Childhood is wonderful and should be made happy for our children. Teenagers are just children trying to grow up, keep your sense of humor! Love is the most important part of our lives and the people we love. Always tell your children every day you love them and thank God for them always! They are our greatest treasure!*

Mattie: That is so beautiful.

Eve: I know, isn't that sweet? So, so sweet. There are little stories in this book from her life complete with pictures. And some of the dresses she's wearing she made, you know back when people sewed their own clothes. I was telling Mattie the other day that we just bought a sewing machine, my very first sewing machine ever at forty-two years old! My daughter sewed a shirt inspired by a show on television called *Project Runway*. Now my kids want to be clothing designers. So we found a pattern and altered it a little. Sarah had great ideas and it was so much fun. Then I was calling my mom: "Mom, we went through steps one, two and three. Can you come over and help with the zipper?" And even Mattie learned something about zippers...

Mattie: You need a special foot for your sewing machine to sew zippers on your dresses or whatever item of clothing.

Eve: Mattie has always done zippers with the regular foot!

Mattie: Regular foot, not good. Very difficult to do that! So you called your mom to come over and she helped you and Sarah. What a cool time you all spent together!

Eve: And a memory that we'll always cherish! "Remember when we made that first top, Mom? Look how far we've come." Or, "Remember the last time we took the sewing machine out?" Whichever the future holds!

Mattie: It's very important, I believe, to be consciously aware of your parenting. Children grow very fast; you hear this all the time. Stop, slow down and cherish the moments you have with your kids. Don't be so anxious to jump up and do things that don't include them or put them aside because you've got to take care of other things. Being a parent is the ultimate sacrifice in your life, giving up certain things in order to learn a new level of love, understanding, giving and sacrifice. I know there are a lot of parents out there or moms especially who seem to be so exhausted with all their responsibilities with their children. Yes, it's a lot of hard work and it's okay to feel that way, but don't drag that feeling out everyday. You have to learn to enjoy what you've got no matter how hard it can be.

This book could be a wonderful tool; while you're reading it you should find a journal of some sort and write down what you're going through or what you've been through in your life and where it is now that you might want to pass on to your child or children. I have nothing like that from my mom. I don't know very much about her life, just a few bits and pieces from my cousins, some of whom are in their seventies. These are her nieces and nephews I'm talking about. I was born so late in my mother's years.

Eve: Did your mom have brothers and sisters?

Mattie: My mom came from a family of four, three girls and one boy. How ironic that today I have three girls and one boy!

Eve: And you are now older than your mom was when she passed, correct?

Mattie: My mom was fifty-nine.

Eve: Oh, your mom was fifty-nine. I thought she was forty-one!

Mattie: She was fifty-nine when she died.

Eve: Oh, so she was forty-one when she had you.

Mattie: I heard a sermon one time regarding the importance of leaving behind for your children your "legacy" and not your "lunacy" (thank you, Jack). There are things of importance in life you teach your children and they become your legacy. And there are lunacies, like short tempers, or our neuroses of what we do or how we handle situations poorly. Our children are watching and they take this information and carry it on with them for the rest of their lives. It's so important to be aware of the legacy you leave for them.

Eve: Which brings me back to what we said in our "Friends" chapter about writing letters. Marc and I just got back from a writing trip to Nashville where we wrote a song. Right now we don't know what the name of it is going to be, but the chorus is "Love letters from the past, tell our stories from the start. More than just a photograph, I hold the thoughts of your heart." This was inspired by a story Marc had read about a guy who was married for fifty years and had tons of photographs of his wife and video, but no love letters. He didn't have her thoughts written down that he could read and hold in his hands.

I have two letters I saved from my childhood, one from each of my parents that I cherish and keep in a special place because I know they reveal how my mom and dad felt about me at that time. They were both very supportive letters. My parents sent me these letters because for some reason or another we had a misunderstanding. I can't even remember what it was about, but they both felt the need to write their feelings and send them to me. Both letters were written around the same time. I still hold on to those letters because my parents expressed so much love and support and what they hoped for me. I would like to think that when I go, my children will know how I feel about them, because I tell them every day how much I love them. You know, you learn a lot from your parents and how they parented and there were times you probably said, "I'm never going to be like my parents!" But there are some things you will want to do that your parents did.

On the last page of the book I gave my mom, there is a heading that says: *What I Wish for You.* I'd like to share what my mom wrote:

> *When you are my age Eve, I want you to be happy with your past—no regrets. Our lives won't always be a fairytale with 'Happily Ever After' endings, but most of the time they will be happy if we always follow our conscience and try to do what is right. Then maybe we can say we have fought the good fight and run a good race and deserve the reward.* [And my mom is talking about heaven of course.] *Even knowing how my life has turned out* [my parents divorced after nineteen years of marriage and eight kids] *I would still do everything the same because I wouldn't want to miss you or your brothers and sisters. Besides, the story isn't over. Who knows what may happen next? Love, Mom.*

Mattie: That is just a beautiful and incredible gift!

Eve: Do you have a baby book that maybe your mom started?

Mattie: There's a baby book at home somewhere. Almost

all of my baby pictures are there. As far as letters I have kept, they were all written after I graduated from high school and traveled with the international musical group Up with People for three years.

Eve: Isn't it interesting how our lives dictated how we communicated because there were no computers then, so e-mails were non-existent?

Mattie: I traveled everywhere. I traveled across the country; Europe, Mexico, Canada, and we depended on letters. We waited for the big mailbag to arrive every two weeks! Those letters from my mom and dad are the ones I still have in a box in my garage. My dad was mostly the letter writer and my mom was mostly the quiet one, very observant and always wanted me to call. She taught me to always keep my mouth shut! "Listen," she would say, "You need to listen to people and be one of few words because you'll learn more and become wiser. Don't ever speak without thinking about what you are going to say." When my mother spoke she had a lot of wisdom. It's so hard to remember everything because it's all so blurry. I can't ever remember having a deep "heart to heart" with her and if I did, it was a conversation with very few words.

Eve: I remember asking you once when we were working together if you ever dreamt about her and if she ever visited you in your dreams.

Mattie: From time to time she did. I could feel her with me when I was pregnant with my oldest daughter, Gia. I totally felt her with me. I think after Gia was born that feeling and presence of her near me went away, it was gone.

Eve: That must have been such a comfort to you. That whole feeling of being pregnant and all the questions you must have had when you're having your first child. Were you able to go to your sister Margie for advice?

Mattie: Yes, she's the one that has children in my family. I was depending on her a lot and I think I was a little sad at times because I didn't have my mother there to talk to or ask her questions about what it was like when she was pregnant with me. I wish I could have heard those stories but I didn't have that opportunity. So, I was pretty much on my own.

Eve: My mother also wrote about her pregnancy in this book. She talks about getting sick and the first days finding out about being pregnant with me. For me with my Sarah, I tell her stories about my pregnancy and how she kicked me in the ribs during that last push out! We have a video of the birth and I jumped on that kick! I tell Sarah what it was like being pregnant with her and what it was like having her and how I just seemed to glow! She never gets tired of hearing those stories. "Tell me Mom, tell me again how I kicked you!" Then we go through the whole story. It's so sweet.

Mattie: My two oldest girls have both asked me what it was like. It's funny, when you have more than one child the second child gets less pictures, there's less information documented about their first everything. So quite frankly you remember a lot less and it's nothing personal!

Eve: I can't imagine my mom with eight children!

Mattie: I don't know how she did that.

Eve: I don't either! I have two beautiful stepchildren that I obviously didn't have from birth, but I did have them before they were teenagers. So, it's a lot different, as we all know. But how do you do it, Mattie? I can barely do it with one, how do you do it with four? How did my mother do it with eight and not kill any of us? We were brats! All my brothers and sisters will agree.

Mattie: But she didn't work right?

Eve: Growing up my mother was a full-time homemaker and took care of all of us. My father is a dentist, but even on a dentist salary with eight kids you're still struggling. But she was able to stay home and create beautiful memories for us. Like on rainy days I always knew I could come home and expect freshly made bread and homemade chicken soup. I loved it when it rained, I still do. I'll always have that memory.

I finally got around to suggesting to Sarah one day, "Hey, let's make some bread!" We've done it a half a dozen times and we love it! Did you ever do that with Gia and Gabby? I mean don't you have those special things that you did? I know your life was harder when they were younger. I don't know; didn't you have seven jobs?

Mattie: I divorced when they were five and seven. The marriage was very turbulent so my focus was on my children. I wanted their environment to be peaceful and I wanted them to have the freedom to be able to do whatever they wanted because I didn't have that freedom to just be me and to express myself and the list goes on and on. I didn't insist on any stern rules that were idiotic like, "You can't listen to music!" I wanted to make sure there was nothing controlling their lives. So when I divorced and we were left on our own I told my girls, "Listen, if we're going to make it, you have to get along! We have to all love each other, there cannot be any arguing or you guys can pack your bags and move out." That was intense for a poor five-year-old! "We have to love each other—that's the rule! We have to get along! You two as sisters need to take care of each other, we need to take care of each other! Take care of Mom, Mom takes care of you and everything will be fine!"

You know that rule, that tough rule, really stuck with us. The girls ended up having a very wonderful childhood regardless of the fact that their dad wasn't there. It was a blessing he wasn't there. I think he would agree even today. As a single parent, I couldn't have been more blessed at a more horrible time with the people who came into my life.

Eve: It's such a testament to you too as a parent because knowing your children now, it's very evident how much they love each other and they are very close in age. Girls can be extremely competitive and they both have very similar interests and they are so supportive and loving towards each other and it's so tangible! It's such a testimony of wanting this for your children and actually having it happen.

Mattie: My wish is for them to have that love and support the rest of their lives. I think they will and they can pass it on to their children and I know they will.

Eve: (Sidebar from Eve to Mattie's daughters) "Many years from this book, girls!"

Mattie: So I remarried and had two more children (that wasn't the plan by the way). When Nathan was born I wanted the girls to be in the delivery room. As a parent I felt it was important (even though they were ten and twelve years old) that they saw what childbirth was all about. Of course back when I was born there was never a consideration of anyone being in the delivery room. The doctor was covered from head to toe with scrubs and the dads weren't even allowed in the delivery room. It was a very sterile environment and now it's so wonderful how the whole birthing experience takes place. I wanted to share this with my daughters and it was the best sex education they could ever have. I believe it has helped them make better choices with their lives. I do know they don't want to have children for a long while. And just to drive home that thought I went and had one more child and brought them back into the delivery room with me and Troy and Auntie Lu!

My mom and dad never talked to me about the birds and the bees. I really didn't know very much about that stuff when I was younger. I learned about it in Catholic school. It was a slide presentation illustrated in a cartoon form. Sister Aleena had a big pointer stick and guided us through what we needed to know from the slides.

Eve: I remember one time when I walked right up to my mom and said, "Mom, tell me the truth, are you the Tooth Fairy?" She answered, "Do I look like the Tooth Fairy?" Classic parent answer! That was how it went with sex education for me. I was able to come back and ask my mom and she was very good about explaining everything. Remember when we had the *World Book Encyclopedia*? Since there wasn't an Internet everything we needed to know was in the *World Book Encyclopedia*. She'd get the books out and together we looked up the reproduction system. When she was finished explaining it to me I said, "Eeeww, gross, I'm never doing that!"

I was a professional aunt for many years. I adore my nieces and nephews, but that love is different from the love I have for my children. That love for my nieces and nephews is huge. So you can imagine how much I love my children and as a parent, you know that kind of love, there's no way to explain it. When you had your second child were you worried that you wouldn't be able to love her as much as the first?

Mattie: I was worried about that at first. After Gabby was born I felt so much love for her right away. I can't even imagine loving any of my children less than the other. It's such a ridiculous thought!

Eve: I think about how much I love my children and I wonder, "Does God love me even more than I love my own children?" This is really mind blowing! Such a comfort! My oldest sister lost her first baby at thirteen months. She was born very, very ill. I don't know how you ever move on through something like that, except that we are all just on loan here. We all think we own our children. I think that's why it's hard for parents to let go of them as they get older and more independent because we think we own them. The problem with an ownership mentality is that if you try to control someone, what are they going to do? The only recourse for them is to violently break out and fight to get their freedom instead of us easily helping them up and on their way. Gently guiding them like when they were toddlers.

Mattie: There's a quote from Hodding Carter that I love, and it goes like this: "There are two lasting bequests we can hope to give our children. One of these is roots, the other, wings." In the "root" years you are guiding them and making sure they are safe and are learning to make the right choices. When they are getting ready to get those "wings" as I am experiencing right now as a parent, I'm very excited for my oldest to experience life more. I see her grasping a ton of wisdom every day. Our conversations with each other are great. We can get very deep, or laugh and really come to terms with a good understanding of what we're talking about. It's very exciting for me to see her developing wisdom. I'm really proud of the legacy I have given my oldest because I know she will thrive in this world and make a difference. I know Gabby will do the same. She's just starting to grasp the concept of the "wings." She's a couple of years younger than Gia and I see her following in Gia's footsteps. Soon it will be Gabby's turn.

But to think about eighteen more years from now when Morgan (the baby) finally gets her wings is going to be interesting. It saddens me to think about it because she *is* the baby. I know this is where a lot of parents experience the "empty nest" syndrome. But I planned it perfectly because just as my nest is about empty, I expect Gia to come back with her children so I'll start all over again. So, I think I've got it covered!

Eve: You planned ahead!

Mattie: I planned ahead so I wouldn't have a sad heart but a happy heart because I receive the richness of my children and their children. So I'm hoping that it will be a wonderful experience.

Eve: You had a rule you laid down with your girls about loving each other and getting along. But were there any other things you imparted to your kids that maybe you can hear your parents' words coming out of your mouth? And you think to yourself, "I never thought I'd say that!"

Mattie: So many times I see myself reflected in my children! It's as if my parents jumped into my body and the very same words they said to me are coming out of my mouth! At that moment I feel like I just became one of my parents. I believe we all need to raise a more loving, conscience and peaceful generation with a sprinkling of our parents' wisdom.

Eve: I appreciate what you just said about seeing yourself in your children. Children are a part of us and they can be just like us, and if there are things about us that we don't like then we need to make sure they don't make the same mistakes we did. It's so difficult with the life we all lead right now, everything is so filled with, "Go, go, go, fast, fast, instant gratification!" It's hard to stop and ask if you are really doing a good job raising your child. Doesn't it feel like we're on a tightrope sometimes trying to juggle all this stuff?

Mattie: Yes it does, and another thing that comes to mind is how we communicate with our children. Some parents can be so condescending with their kids. Talking down to them or starting off sentences with phrases like, "Don't you know the difference? How come you're always...? What is the matter with you?" To me these types of approaches hurt. I often think about when I was a child and how much I hated disappointing my parents or teachers. I always wanted to do the best job I could do; I didn't like making someone feel bad. I think our angry words can really kill a childhood sometimes. I'm so aware of these things with my children. We don't use the words stupid, idiot or dumb. We never say, "You're such an idiot" or "You're so stupid."

Sometimes I'll hear one of my kids say out loud, "Oh my gosh, I'm so stupid!" I tell them, "No you're not. Don't say that, take that back!" I believe words really can "create" your state of mind and eventually dictate your life. We should try to be more edifying with our children. If they do something wrong, I approach them with a sentence like, "That probably wasn't the best choice was it?" It gives the child an opportunity to stop and think about their actions. I want my children to know I think they are smart and they are loved and are beautiful human beings without having them go through the destructive lines like, "What's the matter with you?" "How come you did that?" "Aren't you thinking?" To this day when I hear those phrases I shudder a little. So when dealing with my own children I have to stop and take a deep breath and think before I speak so I can get my point across clearly. As a result I receive respect and understanding in return. They understand that what they did was maybe not the right choice because I gave them more space to reflect on their mistake, on their own, instead of me pointing my finger at them. I held up a mirror for them to see what they did and at that point they understand.

This is challenging because children will misbehave at times when you are the most tired or you don't have time or are at your weakest. It's normal to snap with a reaction like, "Don't do that!" Or bark out something. When children are younger it's easy to do this. But as they get old enough to understand you with a "heart to heart" conversation, that's when they've got your number and know the rules you've laid down for them. When my girls were old enough to understand what I was talking about there were times when we needed to "have a talk" about something. I would make sure it was quiet in the house and we could all look at each other face to face. Then I would ask, "Is that the best choice you could have made?"

Eve: You hit it; the perfect tie in; it's all about respect. If you think about your relationship with your own parents, the respect was there. Children didn't challenge their parents back when we were kids like they do now. But it's that old rule, if you want somebody to respect you, then you have to respect him or her. I try to teach that to my children all the time. "If you want me to listen to your words then you need to listen to my words!" We need to try to understand each other and hear each other. It's what you were just saying about your girls and how you want things to come out in a positive way. You were talking about something that didn't work and said, "Okay, let's change the prism a little bit and look at this a different way." It teaches your children how to do this with every aspect of their life. It's such a valuable and rewarding gift to give to your child, "This isn't working for you, let me show you why."

If I have a misunderstanding or an argument with someone and I walk away from it thinking, "They were right and I was wr, wr, wr, not right!" I need to acknowledge I was wrong. It's the only way I can grow. I think this is rampant in the world today. Nobody is taking responsibility for his or her actions and saying, "Oh my gosh, I made a mistake. How do I fix this?" There always seems to be a way around the situation by passing the blame.

Mattie: There are children out there who are rebellious even if mom and dad "say so." But you have to stop and look at yourself and ask, "How am I living my life? What examples am I leaving for my children?" From time to time I hear a story about a troubled student at school and I'll ask my girls, "What's going on with their situation at home?" Usually I'll get a response like, "Well, the dad smokes pot and the mom is always gone and is never around..." It's always a story about how something has gone wrong at home.

Eve: I have a perfect quote from someone unknown: "Children are natural mimics who act like their parents despite every effort to teach them good manners."

Mattie: So it comes from us! We're it! We learned from our parents, they were it! You take everything you like about the way they raised you as a child and everything you didn't like about it and add everything you want to add to that part of your life and that's what makes the recipe of the parent you are today. We only have the elements of what we learned mostly from our parents to build the foundation for the kind of parents we are today. I knew I was raised with a lot of love from my family and that is the main element I knew I was going to pass on to my children. On the downside, I didn't like being "barked" at when my parents had tempers. Today as a parent when I'm challenged by my children I take a deep breath, then try my hardest to handle the given situation with a much calmer approach.

There were a few things I wish my parents could have purchased for me when I was a child like a Barbie car and the game Operation! My Barbies had to drive around in a high heel shoe (single seat) for all my childhood! Just as soon as I got my "ticket" to parenthood I purchased that Barbie car and the game Operation! I've really had a lot of fun being a parent!

If I were ever bored around the house when I was a kid my mom would say, "Go play outside!"

Eve: Ah, the "Go play outside" ploy. Today we can't even let our kids play outside, not without watching them like a hawk! It's a parent's worst nightmare, somebody stole your kid, or your kid ran out in the middle of the street and got hit by a car! There are so many different kinds of dangers for our kids than we had. We left at 10:00 or 11:00 in the morning and didn't come back till 6:00 in the evening! My mom wasn't worried. She checked up on us every once in a while during the day by calling a neighbor and asking, "Do you have one of my eight kids there?" That's just the way we lived.

Mattie: In the summertime I was gone all day till the sun went down and if my dad wanted me home he'd go outside in the backyard and yell at the top of his lungs, "Yahoo!" And I was supposed to answer, "Mountain Dew!" Do you remember that Mountain Dew commercial with a hillbilly wearing a straw hat and a pair of jeans with a big ol' hole in the knee and was barefoot yelling, "Yahoo, Mountain Dew?" So my dad would use that as his signal for me to get home. I'd leave my girlfriend's house out the back gate, cross the alley and crawl through the trash container holder that lead right into my back yard!

Eve: That's just not our reality today. That is a little piece of the past that will never be again. Until we transcend into that *Star Trek* new planet world where there is no war, we all wear white and it's Utopia!

Mattie: So we all make our own safety areas for our children. If they are going outside I'm going to be with them; if they're going to the park I'm going with them. Even now when my older girls want to walk to the store I never let them walk alone. They have to have at least a couple of friends with them. Or I offer to drive them where they can meet up with their friends.

Eve: If you ask my Sarah what the number one rule is she'll answer, "Don't run ahead. Stay with the group." She knows.

Mattie: So we do have to be "hyper-vigilant" these days. There's a new park in Carlsbad (California) called the Passive Park. It has no sports fields, just a huge playground area for the kids, and there's no sand for health and safety reasons.

Eve: This brings it all back around. When you think about people who try to harm our children I always stop and wonder about those same people being babies once who were loved and innocent. You don't raise your child to be an axe murderer or a bank robber, you just don't. I think every parent wants their child to have a better life than they did. That's got to be the golden rule about being a parent, don't you think? "My child will have a better life than I did!" I think about my childhood and until my parents divorced when I fourteen years old, I was Cinderella. I remember swimming all summer, putting Crisco Oil on my skin to bake in the sun because we didn't know any better about skin cancer. Ignorance was bliss! I had a fun, wonderful childhood until the reality of the world stepped in and my parents got divorced. So the one thing I was not going to do was get divorced. I wasn't going to do that to my kid. What did I do? I got divorced!

Mattie: I thought the same thing with my first marriage. No matter how difficult my marriage was, the day I drove to the attorney to get the divorce process started, I was praying to God: "Dear God, if you don't want this to happen, if I'm not hearing you, please let my car break down, delay me, send me a sign!" But I was really going through a horrible time and was very guilt ridden that I had to let the marriage go. So my car didn't break down as you know, nothing did happen. I think I had a whole stream of green lights on the way to the attorney's office so that was a huge sign! But I'm grateful today as time has gone on and the healing has happened it has worked out okay. Everything happens for a reason and this was a huge "supposed to be" kind of thing. God had His hands on that whole path for you and for me.

Eve: That's the kind of thing I try to tell all three of my kids,

"Everything happens for a reason" and you don't understand why it's happening until later. You had no idea that Troy was there and little Nate and Morgan were waiting to come into your life. But now you know the reason, this is the reason. I'm fortunate I had a very reasonable divorce, although I still felt like a loser and didn't want to go through with it. I tried as hard as I could, even went to counseling and it still took me two years to be able to commit to leaving. Even though we split up we still have a relationship because of our daughter and that relationship is forever. I know you don't really have much of a relationship with your ex-husband because that was his choice. My ex-husband is a great father and extremely involved in Sarah's life. So as long as we were able to focus on our parenting and what was best for our child, we were able to overcome any of that ugly stuff that comes with divorce. Mattie, you had to make your choices; you became the parent you are today because of life's circumstances and because of what your parents gave you. They gave you the strength to get through and to know what's right and wrong and to do the right thing.

I remember one time I wanted to go somewhere and my mom didn't feel comfortable letting me go. She was trying to explain to me why it was not okay for her to say, "Yes" when "All the other kids were going!" She told me, "Eve, when I die and I stand in front of God and He asks me, 'Did you do everything you could to keep Eve safe, did you try everything you could, did you give her a good foundation and wings to fly? I want to be able to say 'Yes!'" At the time I thought, "This is just an excuse!" But now I think about what a beautiful thing she did for me because I'm a parent myself now and I want to do the right thing.

I think one of the most important jobs you will ever have is being a parent. I want to wrap this up with a segment from a book by Frederick Buechner titled *Listening to Your Life*. The following segment is called "The Child Within Us":

> *We weren't born yesterday. We are from Missouri. But we are also from somewhere else. We are from Oz, Looking-*

Glass Land, from Narnia, and from Middle Earth. If with part of ourselves we are men and women of the world and share the sad un-beliefs of the world, with a deeper part still, the part where our best dreams come from, it is as if we were indeed born yesterday, or almost yesterday, because we are also all of us children still. No matter how forgotten and neglected, there is a child in all of us who is not just willing to believe in the possibility that maybe fairy tales are true after all, but who is to some degree in touch with that truth.

Mattie: Mine is a prayer written by Marianne Williamson from her book *Illuminata*.

Dear God,
Please bless my parents.
Thank you; thank them for the life they gave me.
For the ways they helped me and made me strong, I give thanks.
For the ways they stumbled and held me back, please help me to forgive them and receive Your compensation.
May their spirits be blessed, their roads forward made easy.
Please release them, and release me, from my childhood now gone by.
Release us also from any bitterness I still hold.
They paved the way, in all that they did, for where I have been has led me here.
I surrender my parents to the arms of God.
Thank you, dear ones, for your service to me.
Bless your souls.
May your spirits fly free.
May we enter into the relationship God wills for us.
Thank You, Lord, for I am free now.
Glory, hallelujah.
Amen.

FORTY Schmorty!
...life keeps happening

3
CHILDREN

Eve: So, Mattie and I are both aching and tired and crabby this morning. I'm crabby because my eighteen-year-old child came home late last night and woke me up and then I couldn't get back to sleep.

Mattie: I'm crabby and achy because I totally slept wrong last night and I was in a deep, deep, deep, deep, deep sleep and Gabby came into the room this morning about 6:45 a.m. and asked me if I could take her to school because her sister was not waking up. We have an agreement that if her sister oversleeps I would take her to school so she wouldn't be late. So holding to that agreement, once I realized I was awake, the first move I made every bone in my body was hurting. All I could do was moan. I felt like my mattress beat me up all night long. All I was doing was trying to lie down and sleep and the mattress just beat up my shoulders and my neck.

So Eve and I have had a very hard evening of sleeping, but we're here talking about children as we see it—our lives and how we've lived our lives with our children. We'll try not to go off on tangents here. We're only talking about what we know and the world as we see it with our children. And up to this point, my fifth load of laundry.

Eve: I beat you! I did eleven loads of laundry in forty-eight hours.

Mattie: Did you really? I would like a little counter in my laundry room where I could slide over the beads that would keep track of how many loads of laundry I do a day just for my own satisfaction. So I could see how many loads are coming and going!

Eve: Oh perfect. See look what I did! Well don't you always feel though (we just said we weren't going to get on a tangent!) like you really get something accomplished when you get the darks, the whites and the colors of one person in your family's laundry completed?

Mattie: Yes, absolutely!

Eve: Folded and put away. It really feels like you did something.

Mattie: Absolutely! And I try to tell my kids, "Don't sneeze on your clothes and throw them in the laundry room." I've made this horrible discovery; if you don't wash their clothes and they sit there for a while they grow these colonies of bacteria spores that actually smell really bad. It's beyond sticking a sheet of *Bounce* in the drawer to make it better. You just have to wash the clothes.

Eve: And try to tell your kids they can wear their jeans more than once in a week, that they can wear their jeans two-to-three and sometimes up to five days a week.

Mattie: I think I have my whole family beat on this one. I'll wear my jeans three days in a row. And sometimes I'm so tired I even go to bed in them. But the joy of it is that I wake up the next morning and I'm dressed. I'm ready for the day! And nobody saw me the day before, except my family and it's okay because I still have a great set of clothes on.

Eve: So there are advantages. You gotta take every one you can get.

Mattie: We love our children and we chose to speak about where we're coming from raising them and how we are guiding them from the day they were born, to leaving home, to moving on to other things. So I chose a quote this morning, actually within the last hour, from Ann Landers. She says, "In the final analysis, it is not what you do for your children but what you have taught them to do for themselves that will make them successful human beings." Very important!

Eve: Mmm…that's so good. And just because we are such good friends, I chose one very similar from Eda Leshan. It reads:

> *Becoming responsible adults is no longer a matter of whether children hang up their pajamas, or put dirty towels in the hamper, but whether they care about themselves and others. And whether they see everyday chores as related to how we treat this planet.*

It's amazing how it really is the little things that add up, what you say to your children and what you repeat fifty or a hundred times. But what are the most important things? Ann Landers, boy that was really good.

Mattie: Yeah, raising your kids. I have four children—two are from my first marriage. One is sixteen at this time; the other is fourteen, soon to be fifteen. And from my current marriage I have two children. I have a boy who's four and a little girl who is fourteen months. And so, I am now looking at the dynamic of what it's like watching an older child getting ready to leave home and rearing a young child again sixteen years later, sort of starting over again.

Eve: And you understand the saying, "God has a sense of humor!"

Mattie: Yes, He sure does! But you know, I was thinking about it this morning and last night and I truly believe our children are an assignment from God. No matter where they come from. Whether they're adopted or they're our stepchildren or they're our own children. We have a serious assignment. And I truly believe this is God's work. He chose us to become parents and watches how we handle and deal with the situations of our children's lives.

Eve: Oh so true.

Mattie: "What are you gonna do with this, Mattie? What are you going to do with these children I've given you?"

Eve: I've often said to my daughter, who is twelve years old right now, "Thank you for choosing me to be your Mommy." Because I really believe what my friend Kim always says, that it's a "CoinciGod." There are no coincidences, we choose. I've told my daughter the story about why we have this little indentation right above our lips, because we know everything before we're born as spirits. And right before we are born the angels put their fingers on our lips and say, "Shhh, don't tell." And that's how we get that little indentation above our lips. I love that story.

Mattie: That's great!

Eve: Isn't that a great story? I tell my daughter, "You knew everything about Mommy before you chose me and you picked me, so thank you!"

Mattie: Great! My favorite thing to say to my children is, "Oh, wait a second. Wait. Did I tell you? Did I tell you today that I, I love you?" It really grabs their attention and they stop for the moment and they're waiting to hear that I might have forgotten something really important to tell them pertaining to the day or what we're doing. And I just stop and out of the blue say, "Wait, did I tell you that I love you today? Well I do!" It's just amazing and I know you've known this, that the more love you give your children the more love you tend to get back, and how rewarding and loving and incredible that is.

Eve: My daughter and I used to play a game when she was little where I'd say, "Mommy loves you so much. Not this much, not this much, not this much…" And as I'm saying it my hands are going out and out and further out, "But THIS MUCH!!!!!" And my arms would be stretched out as wide as I could get them. And she would just giggle and giggle. It really is something you can't say enough. I don't think the phrase "I love you" ever loses its effect on your children. Sometimes people can say things and they're just saying words, they don't really mean them; there's no emotion or thought behind them. But when you're saying it to your child, I think the deep feeling and the meaning behind what you are saying never fades. Even when you want to kill them for throwing the towel on the floor for the 500th time! You still mean it just as much. Mattie, you said it so well, you can never say I love you enough!

Mattie: Never. Didn't our lives shift when we had our children? All of a sudden our priorities shifted.

Eve: Your whole world shifts and you realize, "Oh! The world DOESN'T revolve around me!"

Mattie: Yeah.

Eve: It revolves around our children and we lose our selfishness.

Mattie: Again, this is Eve and I talking about how we feel. Sometimes it's so easy to be so giving and so caring that you can forget about yourself. But it's very important not to lose sight of that because children learn from you. They watch you. They mirror how you handle situations. If you over react to an emergency, they're going to over react to an emergency. If you are calm about a stressful situation, they are going to follow suit. They watch you and they learn. And I'm proud of all my children for that; as I watch them grow and as I spend my days now as a stay-at-home mom, I am so grateful for that.

Eve: Well, you didn't have that the first time around.

Mattie: No. Actually, when I was first married and had my children I was holding down a daytime job and singing with the band at night. And I would take any other jobs I could find in between, studio work mostly.

Eve: And singing in church.

Mattie: Oh yeah! I would sing in church once in a while back then. It was all I could do to support my family and make ends meet.

Eve: A time in your life when you couldn't say "No" to any job.

Mattie: Yeah, that's when I started forming a really bad habit because I couldn't afford to say "No." That's one thing I've learned to do in my forties.

Eve: The beauty of saying "No." "Just say no!"

Mattie: You finally have to stop and not make yourself so crazy with activities or jobs or things that you want to take on because you just can't do enough to make ends meet. But you are only as good as the last bit of energy you have. And if you give in and say "Yes" all the time, everything suffers!

Eve: And it's not fair to your kids, because they are the ones who suffer the most. Mommy has to go to work again. "Mommy, don't go!" My first marriage was the same with my daughter. Mattie and I joke about this, it felt like we had thirteen jobs between us. Not at first, and not always, but probably the majority of our first marriages we were bringing in most of the money. And when you have to be responsible for someone's welfare as well as your own and pay the bills and buy the food, you do whatever you can.

My second marriage afforded me the opportunity to be a stay-at-home mom along with a new dimension to my life, being a stepmother. I think it's a challenge being a stepmother because there are so many unspoken rules and boundaries. I have two really great step kids, a stepdaughter who is almost nineteen and a stepson who is fourteen. Sometimes the realty of the situation will bring up the ol', "Well you're not my mom!" which is spoken and unspoken. You want to be their friend, but you also need to be a parent and you need to be a responsible role model. It's a fine line to obtain the respect afforded of being the mother of a household and trying to do things your way, but also being respectful of the fact they have other roots and their loyalties lie there. And it's an interesting lesson I learned because *I* have a stepmother, whom I did not like at all in the beginning because in my childhood she was one of the reasons my parents split up. You don't realize when you are young how hard it is to be in relationships and how hard it is to make things work and that your parents didn't marry you, they married each other. What an ironic twist that I ended up being a stepmom. I now look at my stepmom in a different light and think, "Wow, I see how hard it is." And I realize there are so many factors and I'm one of eight kids so jeez, everybody has their own personality and their own way of dealing with divorce and all that. But being a stepchild and then being a stepmother, what a lesson!

Mattie: What has enlightened you about being a stepparent? What have you learned if you could sum it up?

Eve: One of the many reasons I fell in love with my husband was how much he loved his kids and how much he wanted to be a part of their lives. And it opened the door to seeing them through his eyes. I was able to love them because I loved him so much. And there was a lot of push-me, pull-you going on. He was divorced for over six years before we got involved, yet we had issues of us getting together and joining our two families. And I always hated having to say this is my daughter and this is my stepdaughter and my stepson. It was difficult for me to say because I didn't feel like I was the evil stepmother, but I also didn't want to tread on their mother's toes. So you just get to a point where you say these are my kids. And these are my two daughters and son. And as people get to know me then they learn they're my step kids, even though my stepson looks a lot like me and people think that we're all one family. I'm very proud of that and very honored because my step kids are beautiful.

Mattie: So it all worked out.

Eve: It all worked out and it's been a wonderful, eye opening experience. Wait a minute...I'm not sure if I answered your question.

Mattie: No, you have. It's been an eye opening experience.

Eve: Ah yes, the blending of two families.

Mattie: Yes, I have that too. Troy and I got married six years ago this July. And when he met me, he'd never been married before and here I was with two children, six and eight years old. And my children came first. I was divorced for five years working very hard for our family to stay together. We shared, we loved and prayed together, we did everything together.

Troy had been a bachelor all his life and it was very difficult for me to even accept the fact that I had a man looking at me. When he asked me out on our first date, I lied and said that I wasn't available to go out with him. The truth was that I was too scared to leave the girls and get out of the house. I was enmeshed in my life with my children. But then there came a point where I felt bad that I kept turning him down and he was so persistent I decided to go out with him. And I remember he was twenty minutes late for our first date. I was looking out the girls' bedroom window between the blinds just looking at the parking lot. My oldest tugged on my shirt and whispered, "Mom, I don't think you should go. He's not here." My heart sank and I felt terrible I was going out with some guy I barely knew that had just been asking me and asking me to go out. And I'm feeling guilty for leaving my kids. But he showed up at the door and he was so happy and so excited and so sweet with the girls and it turned out that our babysitter knew his mother! And our world just got really small. It was a CoinciGod, Eve.

Eve: Yes it was!

Mattie: We ended up going out to dinner that night. I didn't eat because my stomach was so upset. I watched him have dinner.

Eve: Guilt, guilt, guilt, guilt!

Mattie: I actually had a beer!

Eve: Woo-hoo! That probably helped things a little bit.

Mattie: It helped me to want to go home even faster. No, it did. It was really hard. It was a pleasant evening and I tried to enjoy it as much as I could. But the next time he asked me out I said, "Look, I'm not in the dating market right now. I have a family to take care of. My daughters have homework I need to help them with every night along with making dinner. If you want to go out, then it would be great if you could just come over and help my girls with their homework and I'll make dinner for all of us. But my family comes first." My girls come first and they always have. I committed my life to raising them and to make sure that if they couldn't have both of their parents, they were going to have me there as much as possible. So Troy started coming over almost every night.

Eve: And it all worked out. We know how it ended because he obviously won you and the girls over. And that's what he chose to do.

Mattie: I tell Troy that he was on a mission from God. I wasn't looking, but I knew I did not want to be single the rest of my life. I knew I had a God given duty to raise my children and I didn't want to miss a minute of their childhood. So when Troy proposed to me, he also proposed to the girls. And he got down on his knee and had rings for both of them and said, "I want to know if you'll let me be part of your family." I remember Gabby (my youngest) started crying she was so happy. And Gia (my oldest) was in shock. And they both thought it was really cool. Then the reality set in. They thought it was great, except...

Eve: "Hey, wait a minute, Mom...You mean he's going to be here all the time now?"

Mattie: And then they said, "Wait, this means we can't sleep with you anymore." And I said, "We don't sleep together anyway. You guys are too big and there are two of you!" But that really helped me direct the focus of creating a family unit. Because then there was, all of a sudden, a father figure in our family. And it meant a lot to make sure we had dinners together as much as possible. We even found a favorite show to watch on Thursday nights, *Survivor*. We would pull the table out to the middle of the living room floor and I would serve dinner and we'd watch the show. That was creating memories for the girls. Troy really worked so hard to fit into the family. He really was meant to be there.

Eve: And it seems like it all was a CoinciGod. And because your priorities were focused on your children when he met you, you were being true to your circumstance. And he wanted to be a part of your lives so much that he chose to say, "Okay ready-made family. I'm jumping in and the water's warm and I'm swimming here." The fact that you kept it focused on the kids made your truth happen. And if it wasn't going to happen it would have been very apparent right away. And, obviously, he's a pretty special person to make your children his focus too and then along came two more. People, Mattie has beautiful children. She does not know how to have an ugly child. And these kids know that they are loved. You can see it right away.

Mattie: They are so loved, with every bit of my life, with every part of my being. I had Gia when I was thirty. I had Gabby when I was thirty-two. I had Nate when I was forty-one and Morgan when I was forty-five! Notice how slowly I'm saying this, because I can't seem to remember exactly. But here I am in my forties and I'm having children. And my childhood best friend is a grandmother.

I want to say something to moms out there who are so hurried and tired and complain so much. It seems there are many moms out there who find it easy to complain about what they're doing. Even though I know they love being moms, I think, "Sure you are tired and sure, we all have our household duties, our grocery shopping and an endless list of errands to do along with the kids we need to take care of." I just feel so bad for their kids when their moms complain about everything they do because that's what their God given assignment is. Love it, don't complain about it. Share it with another mom and talk about how many loads of laundry you did that day. Laugh about it! Enjoy the honorable, reasonable service you are doing for your family. These are the things your children observe. Are you going to be complaining until they leave home? Or are you going to turn it around and say, "Boy that was a lot of satisfying work" and feel better about it?

It seems to really dampen a mother's spirit when she is so harried and can't say no. There are birthday parties, carpooling, rehearsals, sports events and so many other activities that these moms honestly don't have time for themselves, let alone their husbands because they are wasted tired. Take a moment. I ask all these moms to just stop and breathe. Take a deep breath and love this time. I'm seeing both ends of the spectrum right now. I've got a daughter talking about college, for which I'm so grateful, and another who is just barely starting to walk. And I understand that cliché: *Love your children because the time goes by really fast.* It does!

Love what you have and do it without anger or bad feelings because they depend on you. Your children depend on you to be there for them. As moms, you are the stars of your show. Your home is your Broadway. It's your big stage and they come home from school and they look for those things, like that freshly baked bread on that rainy day. Those memories are *created*. I think that's the kind of stuff you have to be aware of every day. Because when they do get older and they go to high school, whatever activities they get themselves involved with you don't see them as much. And you don't know who's coming home for dinner. I find myself trying to take a count, "Okay, who's going to be here tonight because I've got dinner. And I need somebody to call me to let me know." All of a sudden I'm taking roll call for dinner. But when we can all be here, it's awesome.

Eve: I have a quote here from Jacqueline Kennedy Onassis, which says, "If you bungle raising your children, I don't think whatever else you do well matters very much." And that's exactly what you have just said. So who cares if you are a really great accountant? Who cares? How's that going to matter, in the grand scheme of history and the world, if you spent an extra hour doing your job at work well, if your child needed you and you let them down? It's not fair to put that kind of pressure on everything. Sometimes we do have to work extra because of our responsibilities to support our families. But it's like you said, the time goes so fast. I remember the very first time I met Gia. You were pregnant with Gabby and we had that gig in Mission Valley, at the Red Lion Inn. And there was this big huge blow up plastic gorilla (I think it was a fundraiser for the zoo) and there's little Gia running around at two years old. And now she's drop dead gorgeous, sixteen and driving. Where did the time go? It was a blink!

Mattie: Keep in mind, I was working full-time and did not have the opportunity of being a stay-at-home mom. Every morning I would get the girls dressed and ready, take them to school and then I would go to work. At the end of the day I would pick them up from after school daycare, get home and make dinner. This is of course, if I didn't have to work at my other job that evening! Sometimes we would eat dinner at Nona's house (Grandma), which was a huge blessing for all of us.

When your schedule is as hectic as mine was, it's easy to be fatigued and worn out all the time. I feel this is when you are the most challenged as a parent. My girls would love for me to read to them bedtime stories. I can remember falling asleep mid-sentence only to wake up with one of my girls patting me on the face saying, "Mommy, please finish the story. Open your eyes." I did the best job I could do as a single mom trying to make ends meet. Today I feel like I have a new lease on life as a mother. I now have the freedom to spend every day with my little ones and truly enjoy being a stay-at-home mom.

Eve: Do you have your little rituals? Are there things you do every day with your kids? For instance, bedtime. Sarah and I do the same thing every night. "Get your pajamas on, brush your teeth." I've got to bring the water. And then we lay down in bed and we talk about the day, and she says her prayers and then she grabs her bears and turns on her side and says, "Mommy, scratch my back." So I sit there and I tickle and scratch her back. But some nights I'm so tired I scratch for two seconds and say, "Okay, that's enough, Mommy's too tired." And I'm sitting here thinking about what you just said. What would another minute matter? What would thirty more seconds matter? Sometimes when you have a headache or you're sick to your stomach and you just need to lie down, you can't help it. We're only human, although I have my suspicions about Mattie! Because I do think she's Superwoman. I've seen the costume in the closet.

Our kids will remember the rituals and those memories are the things you want them to have always. I want my Sarah to say, "Oh Mom, I remember when we used to do this..." (Some special thing we always did together). I want her to have that because I didn't really have it when I was a kid with my mom. I was one of eight kids and there were so many of us, there wasn't much alone time with her. You can't have alone time very often when there are eight kids, you just can't. And so I don't have a lot of those special, Mommy and me memories. Except for the time when my mom and I went to a Girl Scout horseback riding activity. I wanted the spunkiest horse because I was a spunky kid, but the horse wasn't having any of it. He was hungry so he turned around and galloped back to the stable to eat. I would have missed out on the ride if my mom hadn't jumped on the horse with me. We tried again, but now the horse was really mad, and took off bucking and jumping trying to dump us. I was so scared I wanted off, so I pulled us both off. We got hurt and I thought I killed my mom because she had the wind knocked out of her and couldn't speak. She couldn't catch her breath! Now I have this scar on my chin and she has this huge scar down her arm from when we fell off of the horse into the cow manure. Yeah, good memories Mom! Good times.

Mattie: Cow manure?

Eve: Cow manure!

Mattie: Oh my God!

Eve: It was bad, bad news. So a special memory I have with my mom is when we both got hurt. I'm one of five girls and every morning before we went to school we stood in line to get our hair done. NEXT! NEXT! Consequently, I have a very strong scalp. You can do anything to it and it doesn't hurt because of standing in line while my mom brushed, parted and braided my hair. Then I had my Sarah and I was able to focus on only her, one child. And I often say it, I say it to you, I say it to my mom, "How did you ever do it? I can barely do it with one. How do you do it with four, Mattie? How did my mom do it with eight?" And then I got my step kids, but they were older. I met Jake when he was six and Megan when she was eleven. But they didn't start living with us until they were ten and fifteen. So they were already kind of independent, and Megan definitely wanted to spend time with her friends. You're almost embarrassed to have a family when you are fifteen. "Drop me off on the corner. I don't want people to see I actually have a mother, or a stepmother!"

Mattie: I truly believe moms are what make or break our families. We have a need to keep it all together with ourselves in order to help our children. Teaching our kids how to work through problems, to work through the challenges they will have to face in life every day.

Eve: I want to throw in a quote here because you mentioned something about this in our last chapter. This is from Jane Nelson:

> *Where do we ever get the crazy idea that in order to make children do better, first we have to make them feel worse? Think of the last time you felt humiliated or were treated unfairly. Did you feel like cooperating or doing better?*

That really hit me because we were talking about not saying idiot and stupid, you know those kinds of things to our children. And yet in the moment of frustration things just come out of your mouth that you wish you could…you can just see the words and you wish you could grab them back in. We should try to make our children flourish instead of putting them down and making them feel bad about who they are. It doesn't really make sense does it?

Mattie: No, not at all. Our words really can make or break our child. And even if you did slip that one time, it's amazing how that would be the one time they would remember you blew it!

Eve: That's human nature. We always remember the bad one. What about those thousands of good things I said?

Mattie: "There's that one thing you said about twelve years ago Mom…"

Eve: Oh, kids have memories like elephants. You have to be careful what you say and what you promise—all those empty promises. "We'll go to the park later" or "We'll go to the zoo" and they'll remember, "You said we could do this." There have been many times when I've really felt bad I wasn't able to come through with some promises. I'm sure I had every intention of making them happen. But did it really matter that all those loads of laundry got finished? Or could we have just let it go for another time? I think in my forties that's what I'm learning most. As opposed to trying to do it all when I was in my twenties and thirties and trying to portray myself as the perfect wife or mother. Does it really make a difference? Is that what people are going to remember? "Yeah, her kids are great but boy, she couldn't do laundry!"

Mattie: It's so important to be careful with your choice of words, of what you promise your children. That's a big one. I have seen and witnessed and even done it myself a couple of times where you make a promise to your kids and something comes up. Something will happen and it falls through. Make a point to explain *why* to your child. It's okay to teach them about life's interruptions. It's imperative that you follow through with your words or they may grow up to be a person that makes empty promises. They'll want to make people feel better but they won't follow through with what they say.

Eve: Remember that song by Harry Chapin: "Cats in the cradle and the silver spoon, little boy blue and the man in the moon. When you comin' home son? I don't know when but we'll get together then." That song, boy does that ring true. I mean, our kids might not listen to us when we say, "Pick up the towel!" It took me two years to break Jake of the habit of throwing his towel on the floor after his shower. Two years!!! And we joke about it now. But now he hangs his towel up and we've moved on to putting his dirty clothes into the hamper. Our kids might not listen to us all the time, but they sure imitate things we say and the way we say it. And when you hear them say it back, it's kind of a slap in the face. I'm thinking, "Is that how I'm talking to them? The way they just talked back to me? I don't like that." And that leads back to what I was saying before, "This isn't working for us. We need to change this because it's not working for me. Is it working for you?" When kids are older you can talk to them that way. When they're younger they are like little sponges. It's like the movie *Meet the Fockers* when Ben Stiller's character says a cuss word and that's the very first word the baby learns.

Mattie: Isn't that the truth! I taught my older girls precautions and warnings. There were so many things to look out for and things to be careful of when they were younger. Now they play back in their heads what I've said. It's kind of nice and in a way it's sort of funny to hear them talk about it because they say, "Mom, I can't stand it because I can hear you saying, 'Be careful when you...'" But that tells me whatever I said, worked.

Eve: And it was all for their safety and well-being. Regardless of how many times you had to ingrain it into their heads. When they're little like that they get it.

Mattie: They get it. They totally get it. Right now I'm teaching Nathan that every time we go to the store doesn't mean we're going to come home with a toy. Remember that one?

Eve: That's a hard one too, especially now that we're in our forties we have a little more expendable money than we did in our twenties. We are so fortunate, both you and I have husbands who work really hard and that allows us to stay home with our children during the day and that is a gift. I tell my husband, "Thank you for working so hard for US." It's not like I don't work hard or you don't work hard for your family. But the opportunity not to have a nine-to-five job allows us to have the time we need with our kids. So in our forties we do have better incomes and we can afford to get our kids something every time we go shopping. The world we live in right now is all about keeping up with the latest technology and what everybody else has. Our kids want iPods and computers, things we didn't have and certainly would have wanted if they had been around when we were kids too. However, giving your kids everything they want turns them into brats!

Mattie: Yes, that's the recipe for BRAT. If you prep your child before you go into the store it helps. That's what I do. I park the car and while we are still in our seats with the seat belts on I say, "We're going into the store. Mommy has to get paper towels and shampoo," whatever I have to get. "And I'm not going to get Nathan anything because we are buying things for the house. Today is not a day to buy things for Nathan. You can look around and if you see something you like please show me. But I'm not going to buy it. We can enjoy looking at it in the store together." Then I top it off by saying, "And when we leave you are not going to cry. You are not going to fall down on the ground. And you're not going to make me drag you out of the store." I tell him exactly how he's going to behave for me. And most of the time it works. Because I look him straight in the eye and I finish it off by saying, "Is that understood? Do you understand what I'm saying? Nathan is not going to cry when I say it's time to leave the store." And I'm looking at him straight in the eye and he's looking at me looking at him and I make sure he says, "Yes." When that mission is successfully accomplished, I make sure that before I put him into the car I give him a big hug and a kiss. And I tell him, "You are the best buddy in the entire world." And I love him up with my words and I love him up with my hugs and love him up as much as I can. There's a great satisfaction on both ends. Even though he didn't get his train or whatever toy he really liked, we save it for another time. Or we save it for maybe a birthday present or a Christmas present. It's been a really important lesson I've learned with my younger kids.

Eve: Did you ever say things like, "Money doesn't grow on trees?" We heard that in our childhood. Or, "Mom's not made of money."

Mattie: I usually ask if "he" has money. "Will you check your pockets to see if there is any money in there?" And he'll feel and he'll say, "No." "Well, Mommy doesn't have that money either. So let's see what else we can do." This comes from experience from my first two children.

Eve: I think a book for parents to help them get through situations like this would be great. Mattie could write that book, a companion book to *Forty Schmorty: What I Learned From My First Two That's Helping My Second Two.*

Mattie: Absolutely! Just love your children. Love them. Tell them you love them. And follow through with your words. Don't just say the words, give them action. Even today with teens, it's very common for them to come home from school and take naps. They're just exhausted. It's so funny because now they've become the best nap takers in the world. They come right through the door and say, "Hi Mom, we're so hungry, but we're gonna go take a nap." And boom they're in their rooms, doors are shut. And it can continue for the rest of the evening until they surface for dinner and then they have to go back upstairs for homework. Every once in a while I take a moment to knock on their door and go inside their room and just hang out; it's usually a lot of fun. I'll lie on their bed and they'll find that moment to share a story with me or something that's happened at school or perhaps something they completely forgot to tell me about. And it tightens the bond. I leave one bedroom and I go to the next bedroom and I'll talk to my other daughter. Sometimes we'll all meet in one room and then the guitars come out...

Eve: And you start singing hymns!

Mattie: Yeah! Kumbayah! They'll start playing some songs. They'll play for their little brother or sister and we'll all clap. And then someone says, "I've got to finish my homework." And when that happens we just leave the room and go about our business. But it's just stopping by and visiting your children when that door is shut. You have to learn not to take it so personally. You have to stop and think where it's coming from. That door of their bedroom is shut because they're doing their homework or they might need some privacy. It's not because they don't want to talk with you. Knock on that door! Say, "Is everything okay? Do you want some tea? I'm going to go to bed. Can I please have a kiss goodnight?" I always make sure I get a kiss goodnight. Do you say goodnight to your children? Do you hug them in the morning? Do you tell them to have a good day? Are you in check with all those things, because those things make a big difference?

Eve: Reinforcing that you like to hang out with your kids is so important. Sometimes you have to go do errands, and it's not fun. And our kids would rather sit home and watch TV or just veg on the computer. But I say to them, "I really like hanging out with you. You are a cool person and I like you. There are not that many people on this planet I'd like to spend this much time with. Will you come hang out with me?" And it's interesting because that's how you talk to your older kids as opposed to your younger kids who don't want to leave you. And they cry and scream when you have to go. It's such an interesting juxtaposition that Mattie has going on in her house all the time.

Mattie: That's one thing I don't ever remember my mom saying to me. I don't remember my parents saying, "I like hanging out with you."

Eve: It was definitely a different time. When I was growing up we were not allowed in the living room. It was the one room in our house my mom wanted to keep clean and looking nice. With eight kids you can imagine how trashed it could be. We were not allowed in there, especially when it was adult time. Probably the only way they kept their sanity was to have a place they could go that the kids were forbidden to enter. How else do you find time alone with eight kids?

I don't know. If my husband and I don't have date night, we don't have time alone. There is just too much going on because you really do focus on the kids and what they need. And you see how much the younger ones need you, and the older ones still need you too, but they also need their independence. You are teaching them how to fly. Giving them their wings and saying,

"All right baby, jump out of that tree and let me see you fly. Because I need to make sure, I need to know you're going to be okay. It's for my sanity, it's for my heart and it's for my soul to know you're going to be okay because Mommy might not be here tomorrow."

Mattie: I've learned a lot of lessons in my later years. As soon as I learned them I passed them on to the girls. I try to make sure they know the importance of each lesson that I've learned. I'm not the know-it-all of wisdom. I'm gaining insight every day. And as soon as I get it, I pass it on. And it helps them because they can certainly relate. My children tell me they observe adults acting like high school students, like eighth graders. And I have to explain to them it's not too far from the truth. When they grow up and become adults they'll find people their age that are still acting like they are in eighth grade. But it's up to them to utilize their knowledge and wisdom and to learn about the boundaries they must set for themselves.

Eve: Talk to your kids. It's so important. How else are you going to find out what's going on in their lives? How else are you going to find out what they think? Mattie, do you remember the first time Gia said, "Mom, I think..." It shocked me when Sarah said it. Oh my goodness, she has cognitive thought. It was no longer, "You are going to do this, you're going to do that, and this is what you have to do." All of a sudden they have their own opinion. And they have their ideas. It is so-o important as a parent to let your kids work through those thoughts, especially since we basically tell our children how to think. They learn how to think from us and from their teachers and their school and their friends. But as they grow older, I don't know if you've noticed this with your teenagers, they start holding on to what they think is true. And they start letting go of what doesn't work for them anymore. And it's okay that it might be different than what you think, because that's how they've got to do it. It's so hard to understand until you learn by your own mistakes. How can you learn lessons in life if your parents are always saving you? If your parents are always the safety net! Sometimes that tough love comes in and we have to stand back and say, "Okay, I'm going to let you crash and burn, with love, because I really want you to get it. The way you're doing things isn't working. You'll only get it if you really feel it, instead of the softer version where you'll make the same mistake again."

Mattie: Here's a quote from Goethe: "Too many parents make life hard for their children by trying to zealously make it easier for them." If you make life too easy for them it's actually going to be harder on them later in life. Our lives today are so much more complicated, so much more convoluted with horribly bad things in this world. We are fighting to try and bring out the good in our children so they can go out and be in this big troubled world. But at least they know their truth. At least they are grounded with faith. And at least they know they've got the inner strength of hope and faith and knowing what they've learned from home. We can hope what we've taught our child allows them to go out there and try to make the world a better place. We grew up in a different time, of course. But it wasn't anywhere near like it is today. I remember every Friday night looking forward to watching *The Brady Bunch*. I loved happy shows, especially old reruns of the *I Love Lucy* show. My life was really simple.

Eve: *Popeye*! I used to watch *Popeye* every day, even in high school. Just come home and veg out in front of *Popeye*, a cartoon, and why not?

Mattie: I don't know how much time there is for them today to come home and watch TV after school. In kindergarten they're already bombarded with homework. I'm ashamed to say that I look back on my high school education and I think it might be equivalent to a sixth grade education with what they are teaching kids now.

Eve: Our kids are so much smarter now then we were at their age. They just are.

Mattie: I loved my high school, but at that time there wasn't the kind of advanced learning there is today. Our kids are learning a lot more and they have a lot more pressure on them to learn, to do and excel and be better than the rest. I have concerns for those children who are being raised that way, who are being tutored so they can exceed over an "A," better than a 4.0. Where are they going to learn how to practice the real nitty-gritty when it comes to soul searching? They have all the technicalities of what it takes to figure out a very difficult math problem or to come up with some cure in science. What about their souls? What about their faith? What about social skills and interaction with everyday human beings?

Eve: I'm waiting for the teenager to write the book titled, *"Everything I Learned About Life I Learned on Myspace.com!"* Because everything *is* so different and you are right, pushing your kids will only make them rebel more. If you just try to be supportive of everything they do and give them structure they can make it. How horrible does Nate act out if he doesn't have his nap or his normal routine? He is out of whack and your life is crazy because of it. I remember coming over to your house when your girls were younger and you were cleaning with Gabby in a backpack on your back. You had things to do and clean and they wouldn't get done if you didn't do them.

Maybe that's the difference about *Forty Schmorty*. We want to make our lives easier. So how do we make our lives easier for our children? By being supportive, by listening, by caring about the things they care about. By not saying those negative words that kill their creativeness and ambition. Okay, so we need to be perfect! I mean I am so far from perfect it's not even funny. I hear some things come out of my mouth and I stop and say to myself, "Why did you say that? You didn't need to say that!" But I'm crabby or I'm overly tired or it's the 1000th time I've had to repeat myself...

Mattie: Don't you think this far along in the game we know why we do what we do? We totally know why we react, why we went off the way we went off. We've known ourselves for forty years or so. We know how we're wired. And we know the cause and effect of our action or what our words can cause. We have control over that. I encourage all the *Schmorties* out there to challenge themselves to make their lives and their environment and their family atmosphere more peaceful, more of a sanctuary for them to be in. For our children, this is the beginning of what they are going to go out and show the world. This is where it started. Is your house dwelling in peace or is it dwelling in chaos? Is it because of you or is it because of what you don't have control of? Do you project your inner angers about others on your family or are you trying to encourage and edify and lift up and help your family to be better? We are in a serious state. And we have a very important job with our children. And that's to love them and give them a solid foundation to start with. It's up to us.

Eve: It's the most important job we will ever have. I ask a few questions when I meet a new mom-to-be. "How do you feel? How far along are you? How much weight have you gained?" But the most important thing I always say is "Your life is going to change forever." You have no idea until you are holding that new life in your hands. And you can't remember what your life was like before. There's the before and after in all the major events in your life. Before we had children our life was "Woo-hoo party, let's have fun, me, me, me, it's all about me!" And then after children it's, "Oh My God! Please keep my baby safe. Help me be a good parent!" It truly is the best thing you'll ever do. And some people who've never had children or expecting their first child don't get it until it happens. Some people are that way with their pets and pets are their kids, which is beautiful because there are so many animals needing love. It's a great choice to share your life that way, but it does not compare to having your own child.

Mattie: Not at all. Human beings are going to go out there and change the world. However, our friend Anita says, "My dog Zoey gives me unconditional love, she doesn't talk back, I don't have to put her through college or buy her an iPod. The older she gets the more she adores me. She is the apple of my eye, the center of my universe and I tell her she is 'Mommy's little lump of gold.'"

Eve: That's so sweet. Pets do a lot of pooping, you know? But they're still cute!

Mattie: Still very cute!

Eve: Everybody poops.

Mattie: I've got that book.

Eve: I do too. I love that book! Why do people get so embarrassed talking about poop?

Mattie: We never had that book when I was a kid, *Everybody Poops*. It was like there's the toilet, you go poop in there. Done! And now there are movies and picture books and DVDs and sing-a-long CDs and stickers to put on your toilet seat. And videos on the Internet—Wow!

Eve: There is a perfect Chinese proverb to go with what you just said: "One generation plants the trees. Another gets the shade." Our kids are in the shade right now, but they're going to have to plant trees for their kids to be in the shade. And you and I will be centenarians. Is that what they call hundred-year-olds?

Mattie: Centenarians, yes.

Eve: Over a hundred years old and we'll say, "Remember when we wrote that book called *Forty Schmorty*? Boy, we were so stupid. We didn't know nuthin'."

Mattie: Will we be writing a book called *Hundred-Schmundred*?

Eve: I hope so. I'll still have my teeth. How'bout you?

Mattie: I hope so.

Eve: Remember, ignore your teeth and they'll go away!

Mattie: That's probably a really good quote for you out there that have children who don't want to brush their teeth. Just say what Dr. Selis told Eve, "If you ignore your teeth, they'll go away."

Eve: That's my dad!

STOP THE SHOW!

Eve: Okay, today is a very important day, May 18, 2006.

Mattie: Mother's Day has just passed and on that day I found a lump in my right breast and suddenly I'm faced with the question, "Is this cancer?" I was concerned when I first found it, but when I woke up the next morning I was horrified. The panic of wanting to know right away if this is cancer or not took over my whole being. That's all I could think about. Is this cancer? Am I going to die? I have so many questions about what is going to happen in my life.

Monday morning I woke up in a panic. I called my doctor and explained to him what I found and he said, "Come on in, I'll take you in right away and we'll try to see exactly what it is." I thought to myself, "Great, I'll get the kids off to school and I'll drive to his office and have him check me out." I had that all taken care of and right when I was going to leave, I received a phone call from my oldest daughter who was at school. She explained to me she thought her toe was broken because it was difficult to walk around the campus and she was coming home in hopes we could go get an x-ray.

The agony I was experiencing at the moment knowing she needed attention immediately and I would have to wait for the x-ray and the result, then drive her back home just about killed me.

She came home, we drove to the doctor's and every second seemed like forever. Here I am with my sixteen-year-old daughter whom I'm trying to take care of, my four-year-old son and one-year-old daughter in tow. We arrived at the emergency care facility, checked in and took our seats in the waiting room. We wait. Finally they call us in to see the doctor. All four of us walk in. They check my daughter's toe then ask us to walk over to the x-ray department. We walk over to the x-ray department, check-in, and we sit and we wait again. Gia finally goes in for the x-ray. I continue to wait while my heart is pounding with fear for my own life. My daughter comes back out and we wait again for the x-ray to be developed so we can take it over to the first doctor so he could tell us her toe was *not* broken. Great news! I was so relieved Gia did not have a broken toe, but at the same time I wanted to fall apart with stress and fear. I just wanted to scream.

As a mother I want to take care of everybody else first. Aha! Therein lies a problem. I take time to take care of everyone in my household including my house and every nook and cranny in the home and what about me? What about taking care of myself? Now don't get me wrong, it was important to take care of Gia's situation and I did. It's just that the timing of everything that day wasn't exactly how I would have scheduled it. I couldn't help but feel God's total control over all of this delay. Two hours of delay seemed like an eternity, but deep in my core I knew this was all happening the way it was supposed to. We finally got back to the house and I asked Gia to help me out with Nathan and Morgan. She was so awesome; understanding my own immediate concerns, that as soon as I pulled into the driveway she got the kids out of the car and took them into the house so I could get to the doctor's.

On my way to the doctor's office I called Eve and broke the news to her about the lump I found in my breast. Everything was going so well with writing this book. We had all our chapters outlined, we would get together every week and sit here at my kitchen table with a box of tissue, two tape recorders, coffee, tea, lots of notes, books, a Bible and everything's going great and this comes up! A situation where life steps into our perfect flow of creativity and changes our direction with the book—quite a bit—a diversion to say the least.

It's amazing what the possibility of having breast cancer has done to me thus far, and it's only been a couple of days. Everything means so much more. I'm grasping life as I face a brush with death and I tremble with fear not knowing what lies ahead. Yet at the same time, I know God has complete control of the journey I'm about to take. Eve, I am so grateful you have come back into my life. Because of you, I am learning how to be a better friend. I'm learning to accept that a friend can love and care for you honestly, and sincerely want to be in your life. It was time for me to understand the importance of having a girlfriend and to be open and accepting to friends who want to be there for me.

The meeting with my doctor was quick and to the point. He immediately gave me the name of a surgeon and filled out a form for me to have a mammogram. So today was the day for my mammogram. I was so nervous and filled with anticipation wondering the fate of this lump. So of course, what was basically a twenty-minute drive to the radiology clinic turned out to be an hour and a half because of an accident on the freeway involving a semi-truck. I couldn't get there fast enough! Finally I arrived at the clinic and got my mammogram.

Eve: This, by the way, hurts really, really bad.

Mattie: You're watching your breast get squeezed in a vice and there's always that little moment after they take the picture where you're wondering if the vice is going to release or stay stuck.

Eve: Yes, we've all done it, one of the joys of turning forty! Well, as a matter of fact, if you're in your twenties and thirties and you're reading this book, this is what you have to look forward to!

Mattie: Every year, you need to get a mammogram. Make it an annual habit. As a matter of fact, if breast cancer runs in your family it's best to get a mammogram before you turn forty.

I thought it would be appropriate to write about this little detour in my life. Where would you be without your support system? I want to get the word out everywhere. I'm asking people to pray. We all know life is too short, we hear that all the time. Now I'm hearing it loud and clear. By the way, the results of the mammogram were negative. There was even a marker placed on top of the area where the lump was located and nothing showed up on the film! So now my next step is to see the surgeon in about three weeks and I'll get a better idea of what needs to take place.

Eve: When I got the phone call from you my stomach dropped. The only thing I could think of was "I gotta call my people." I have to call all those people who have the direct connect with prayer and put them on the job because we just have to beat this thing, we just have to. You feel so helpless when something like this happens. It happened to my sister, now it's happening to you.

Everything turned out fine with my sister. With you right now we still don't know for sure, but we are in a much better place because nothing showed up on the mammogram. We're in this place where we have a little bit of relief, but there's still panic. The only thing I know that gets rid of that panic is prayer. Even if you're just saying over and over, "I'm going to be okay, I'm going to be okay." Repeating that affirmation and knowing that God loves me, I'm worthy, it's okay, I'm going to get through this, there's a reason, everything happens for a reason. There are all these things you can say, and you can hug someone and rub their shoulder and say, "I'm here, I'm here." The power of prayer is huge. It's gets even bigger when you get a community of people focused on praying for one thing. It's how I feel about this *Forty Schmorty* attitude. If we got one hundred women in a room to pray for one thing we could probably lift the room off the ground with that strength and power! I'm not going to sit here and say prayer "fixed" things, but I think if enough people put a positive attitude out there what was already going to be revealed would be revealed. Turn the prism a little bit and say, "Okay, we want it to come out this way!" If we could have a choice, we want this one. We are going to choose and then we're going to pray for it.

Mattie: I placed my order! Yesterday I sent you an e-mail.

Eve: Yep.

Mattie: Eve came over to the house on Tuesday (we meet every Tuesday to write this book) and God bless her, she came over with a love quilt that's on loan to me, DVDs of Betty Davis movies and what else did you have?

Eve: I had books. I had my stuff for writing this book just in case. I didn't know what we were going to do and it just didn't feel right to continue as if nothing happened. Our next chapter was career and I said, "Mattie, I don't know, it sounds trite to be sitting down and talking about 'Well this is what *I* wanted to do!'" It feels like life or death right now. It's as if a black hole is opening up and it's going to suck us in and we just needed to talk.

Mattie: And we did, we talked for two hours. And we cried and I think I cried more than I ever have in a long time. I think it was a good cry that I needed to have. Probably we both needed to have.

Eve: Our cry was very cleansing.

Mattie: Yeah, it was. It was a cleansing morning. And I gave Eve a little gift about a week ago or actually before Mother's

Day. It was a bracelet that says *Listen to Your Soul* and I think she's wearing it today. I have mine upstairs because I was giving the kids a bath. It was interesting because one day I was shopping before I even knew I was going to find this thing on my body. I saw these bracelets and one bracelet read *Follow Your Passion* and I thought, "Gosh, that's a great inspirational gift I want to give to Eve because that's exactly what we're doing." We've found this passion we're following through with and we're going to do this. Ironically there was only one bracelet and I wanted to have that bracelet as well so we could wear them together. But there was only one. The clerk told me of another shop in Del Mar so I went there a day later and found more of the same bracelets. In the collection of bracelets I found again only one *Follow Your Passion*. After a brief moment of disappointment, the clerk lifted up a bracelet and said, "Well here's one that reads *Listen to Your Soul*." I instantly realized that's the one we need! I asked, "Do you have two of those?" She did and I bought them both!

Eve: CoinciGod!

Mattie: "Wrap this bracelet up and I'll put this one on!" I said. There's a lesson I'm learning this time together with you and that's to listen to my soul. Listen to God, listen to Him speak, listen, just listen, just be quiet for a moment, be still and hear Him speak. I think I've heard God more than I ever have before on this book venture. There have been more serendipitous situations occur in this time than I have ever noticed before in my life. I think it's because I'm more silent and more wanting to hear God "out there" talk to me because He's got something to say and He's pushing us through this whole project and I feel it. I know that anybody reading this book, those who believe in God, who have faith, you've got to know what we're talking about because it's real and it's time to give the world the message that this is what drives us, this is what moves us, and this is what keeps us alive. You've got to have faith!

Eve: It really is sad to me to think about people who don't have any kind of faith or don't have that belief system and that knowledge that you're going to be okay. How do they get out of bed in the morning? How does fear not rule their entire life? Imagine you've lived forty odd years with the kind of fear you've had in the last four days? It would kill you!

Mattie: It'll kill us somehow with some kind of disease. Something would go wrong physically. That's what happens to people; we "scare ourselves" to sickness and to disease.

Eve: There's so much beauty and love and wonderful things in the world that get shrouded by the darkness. There's a book called *The Screwtape Letters* by C.S. Lewis where the devils are talking to their underlings about how they could "trick" people with everyday temptations in order to obtain more souls. It's every day, it's something that gets by you on the television that you don't like and you think, "Wait a minute, I don't want my kids to hear that!" Or it's something you see in a magazine or in a paper or you hear on the radio. I don't know, there are so many things that get by us and we have to be more diligent against them and say, "No, that's not acceptable, that's not okay!" There is beauty in this world. There are great people out there; there are amazing people doing wonderful things to make life better for all of us. We need to focus on them. It makes you want to turn things over and say, "No, no I want the good things to come back!" Maybe it's just a matter of stopping and listening and inviting it in and saying, "Okay, I'm ready, I'm ready for the good things to come now." I'm ready for the peace to come. I think that's what you get from faith.

Mattie: Yeah.

Eve: It's a sense of peace.

Mattie: You have got to be in gratitude and thank God for everything. Thanking God for everything like this detour we've taken in the last few days with my situation, because our regular Tuesday for writing this book was taken up by a lot of emotional "shedding of our souls."

Eve: Yeah, release!

Mattie: Emotional release.

Eve: And a bit of psychology and a little couch session.

Mattie: It held us up a day trying to write this book.

Eve: And then we had to go sing a jingle, remember?

Mattie: That's right.

Eve: We cried for two and a half hours and then realized we had to go sing on a commercial.

Mattie: We had to go sing in the studio. We finished up here at my house and went to the recording studio. We showed up with puffy eyes, no make-up and my fourteen-month-old baby girl, Morgan. There we met with our very loving and understanding producer and dear friend Stan. He was there with open arms and...

Eve: We sang some theme park music of which, by the way, made us feel a lot better and really cheered up Morgan. She loved the music!

Mattie: Morgan was in the studio with us standing there holding on to my legs or in my arms or grabbing the music on the music stand or reaching for the microphone and she finally ended up falling asleep in Stan's arms. This is what we do!

Eve: It's so true isn't it? That's the strangest part I think, the humanity of it all. Life goes on and here you've got this heart stopping, gut wrenching reality check: "Guess what, you're mortal, we're all going to die someday and you might be going sooner than the rest of 'em!" That's a scary feeling and then there's a phone call, "Oh, could you be down to the studio because I need you to sing!" It was a wonderful diversion. Mattie and I sang and then I ended up having to go sing another jingle and had a great conversation with friends at the other studio and asked them to pray for Mattie. I'm asking everybody to pray! Later Mattie and I spoke that night and I'm sure you were more tired than me because the whole thing was on your shoulders. We were exhausted. I haven't been that tired since I had babies in the house.

Mattie: What is today, Wednesday?

Eve: Wednesday? No, today's Thursday.

Mattie: Today's Thursday, we've been at this since Monday. Monday, right?

Eve: Yeah, and Tuesday was...it feels like a century has gone by.

Mattie: This has been an entirely emotional week, emotional drainage on both our parts. You know. No sleep, a lot of emotional distraught.

Eve: Weird dreams.

Mattie: Weird dreams.

Eve: Even when I laid down to take a nap on Monday, I don't think I told you this. After you told me what you heard from the doctor, I was so tired from the knowledge of it and calling everybody I knew to pray for you, I thought to myself, "Okay, I only have forty-five minutes before I have to get the kids from school. I'm lying down, I'm exhausted." Then I woke up with a start forty minutes later; I had dreamt I had cancer.

Mattie: Oh God!

Eve: It was that whole adrenaline thing that gets into you and you wake with a start yelling, "Neahhhhh!" You're trying to wipe it off your hands and it's just a blanket of fear. So I asked God to send me peace. Whenever I thought about Mattie all week long I'd pray for God to "send angels to surround her and enfold her in their arms and protect her and send healing positive vibes her way." I asked that you'd feel a little breeze go by your face and somehow you would know that was an angel. I wanted you to know that someone was thinking about you and praying for you.

Mattie: I totally felt it. I might have mentioned this, but it was Wednesday morning. I sent you this e-mail and I said, "Eve, I am cancer free and so are you. I'm not going out this way. I've already placed my order with God. Please take me in my sleep, make it quick. I don't want anybody scraping me up from anywhere. I don't want anybody hanging over me waiting for me to die, just make it fast please!" For the convenience of those I love, I would like to go in my sleep. I think people who die in their sleep are blessed in a way. It wasn't a tragic accident, it's tragic news but hey, they didn't have tubes and IVs hooked up to them and they didn't have people hanging out waiting for them to go. It was in an instant. I think God really graces those people and family members around them, those who can go quickly. That's what I want. Make it quick! But we've got the rest of our lives to live here and the rest of this book to finish.

Eve: Actually, when I was thirteen, this nation was celebrating the Bicentennial and I decided I wanted to live to see the Tricentennial. That would make me 113! It could happen. Then when I die in my sleep people won't be sad. Who could be sad about somebody dying at 113 years old? It's almost more of a celebration. Wow! You cheated death and lived to be over one hundred. Of course you're sad for the loss, you'll miss seeing them every day, but the fact is they lived a long life. And you hope it was a great life.

I already told Mattie, "There's no way. Cancer ain't gettin' me!" I don't think cancer is a state of mind, but I do think we cause things to happen to us physically. It's been proven that stress can give you a heart attack, so cut out the stress and maybe you'll live longer. Maybe you'll still have a heart attack, but maybe you'll live longer, who knows? None of us will ever know when it's our time to go. But as for cancer,

"No, sorry! Don't have time for you."

Mattie: Not doing it!

Eve: We got great news today, *great* news. But we're not out of the woods yet; we don't have definitive news. Mattie still needs a biopsy.

Mattie: And I'm completely hopeful that the results will be fine. I just know it's going to be fine. I feel it in my heart. Yesterday morning I woke up and said, "I can't drag around this sadness and fear anymore. I have to move on!"

If you're reading this and you've got something like cancer threatening your life, pull in your support system. They are there for you; they *want* to be there for you, God has put them there for you. See what happens, see what kind of miracles you can get though the power of prayer. Make note of it because all you have to do is ask.

Eve: *Ask and you shall receive. Seek and you shall find. Knock and the door will be opened.* It's resting in the Lord, resting in your beliefs, resting in your faith. No matter what, somebody loves you more than you can possibly love anybody else on earth. That knowledge gives you a sense of peace and knowing there is nothing you can do to fall out of that person's grace. That to me is the most peace of all.

People want to be needed, people need to be needed and it makes them feel better that you feel strongly enough about them that you're willing to surrender a little bit and ask for help. I know it always makes me feel better when someone needs me or needs my help, and I'm more than willing to be there. It's a different situation right now for you and me. We've become such good friends; we've become so close.

I told you I was almost more upset about your phone call than I was when my own sister called to tell me she had breast cancer! I knew somehow she was going to be okay. However, knowing what she went through, I knew it might be a tough road ahead for you, and that scared me.

Mattie: There was urgency in my life immediately. I looked at all my kids. I looked at my situation and I couldn't believe something like this could happen to me. As I've been saying in these last few months, "If God brought me to it, He's going to bring me through it." He truly has. How amazing is it that potentially tragic news can wake people up to their own mortality? I can see that the news of my possible breast cancer has moved many in my circle of friends closer to God.

Eve: God is using this situation to bring people together. You never know how situations affect your support circle and something like this can be a wake-up call for them to pray more. Then all of a sudden things start changing in their lives and it becomes a ripple effect. We're all here as perfect pieces of puzzles from every walk of life. We all fit into each other's lives and it's amazing how you never know whom you are going to affect.

I jumped into fundraising for breast cancer when it affected my family and me. It was my way of saying, "All right cancer, you're not going to take over! I don't know what's happening right now, I'm scared right now and all I can do is fight. If I can raise one dollar to fight you down I'm going to raise one dollar, I'm going to raise ten dollars, whatever!" I was then able to go to my group of supporting fans and friends through music and say, "This is what happened to my sister, I need help!" It's going to make me feel better, it's going to help her, and it's going to make other people feel better, so let's all do something together. So that group of people came in to do something. What does that do to their group of friends? The help goes on and on and on. When it's positive it's going to be this tidal wave of beauty, and power and wonderment of things changing and the world evolving and growing and the vines reaching out farther and farther and farther!

Mattie: It's the positive feeding the positive, getting the word out there. It's so important to have faith, it's so important to have that in your life. I'm going to read a passage from the book *Listening To Your Life, Daily Meditations With Frederick Buechner*. The day is January 1st and its titled *Life Itself Is Grace*. It reads:

> *Listen to your life. All moments are key moments. I discovered that if you really keep your eye peeled to it and your ears open, if you really pay attention to it, even such a limited and limiting life as the one I was living on Rupert Mountain opened up onto extraordinary vistas. Taking your children to school and kissing your wife goodbye. Eating lunch with a friend. Trying to do a decent day's work. Hearing the rain patter against the window. There is no event so commonplace but that God is present within it, always hidden, always leaving you room to recognize him or not to recognize him, but all the more fascinatingly because of that, all the more compellingly and hauntingly...If I were called upon to state in a few words the essence of everything I was trying to say both as a novelist and as a preacher, it would be something like this: Listen to your life. See it for the fathomless mystery that it is. In the boredom and pain of it no less than in the excitement and gladness, touch, taste, smell your way to the holy and hidden heart of it because in the last analysis all moments are key moments, and life itself is grace.*

And what we're saying today is that all moments are key moments and everything you do...

Eve: Matters!

Mattie: Everything you do, everything you say, everything you think, matters.

Eve: Frederick really says it all! We hear it from our kids when school lets out for the summer, "Mom I'm bored!" There are ways we get into this rhythm of our lives and we stop thinking and we go on automatic. It takes something like this cancer scare to shock you, almost like when you watch those emergency room television shows and they're putting those zapper things on the patient's chest. It shocks your whole life!

We were starving after Mattie's mammogram so we went to The Original Pancake House. This is such a yummy place and we had Dutch Babies, which is a smaller version of a German pancake. I told Mattie these pancakes would never taste the same to me again because they are always going to taste a little sweeter, a little better now. It was our celebration lunch after hearing such great positive news that the results of the mammogram were clear. Mattie and I joked about laundry earlier and even in laundry you can find grace and you can find God there helping you, talking to you, whispering to you while you're folding your whites!

Mattie: Today I opened the door to my laundry room and found a pile of laundry up to my neck. I'm about five foot six on a good day. And this is no joke. All the laundry was piled up to my neck! I have to find the humor in that horrible picture because I know I am the only one who is going to attack that laundry and I'm going to do it with grace and I'm going to do it with joy because I can.

Here's another thing that comes to mind. Whenever anything bad happens in your life, approach it with an attitude of faith and an attitude of gratefulness and an attitude of knowing that you know God's got his hands on it. If you approach your situation with a faith driven heart, silently with inner strength you'll pull through. I know that I have to approach the next challenge God brings my way in gratitude. Whatever it is I'm just going to have to know there's a reason for it, there's a reason why these situations come into our lives. To challenge you, to frustrate you, to make you angry, to move you into something else, and there's a purpose for it. But go into it gracefully. Don't go into it kicking and screaming, but instead turn it around and be in gratitude for the challenge. Be in gratitude for the pain, be in gratitude for what you are about to face and pray your way through it because you will get through it. Those people around you who are watching you and supporting you will also feel the grace. They'll either learn from you or they'll learn from the grace you have shown by example. I think this world needs to work on attitude, everyone all together. There are so many high emotions out there, a lot of drama. I say it's time to cut the drama out of your life, make things less dramatic and shoot straight from the hip. Go in with your truth, speak it, feel it, know it, say it, and leave all the rest of the junk behind. We've wasted so much time lingering on drama.

Eve: Exactly! When you release, you are released, when you control, you are controlled. And what is the alternative to what you just said? You hit on it before, if you don't have that attitude and you don't have that faith and you don't have that knowledge deep in your soul that you are going to be okay because God's watching after you, what's the alternative? Kick and scream and yell and fight and be mad and cry and then where are you?

Mattie: Exhausted, emotionally exhausted. You haven't accomplished anything.

Eve: At least when you pray you've done something, you've said, "Lord, deliver me from this, help me get through this, send somebody to help me." Whatever it is you have to pray to get through it. "Show me a sign Lord, tell me through an angel, tell me through a friend, or tell me through a commercial from McDonald's." Okay, I'm just kidding. Sometimes I hear something and I know it was God actually talking to me speaking through another person and telling me exactly what I needed to hear right when I needed to hear it. That is the ultimate CounciGod!

Mattie: I can guarantee every reader knows this. Everyone in this world has been through something challenging. Listen to your soul; listen to what God is saying to you. How are you dealing with challenging situations in your life? Are you handling them with lots of drama? Well, stop it because it doesn't need to be like that. You don't need to cause pain with everyone else and drag everyone else down with you. We're better than that now. We're in our forties and we're a bit more refined.

Eve: You're not a two-year-old.

Mattie: You're that fine wine ready to be corked. You know what I'm saying? You're that great cheese ready to be smelled by the great cheese master. I don't know!

Eve: It ain't easy being cheesy, but someone's got to do it. I think you should lift your expectations, expect more from yourself. It's funny right now in my forties there are certain things that will come up and I think, "Wow, I feel so grown up." In my mind I have always looked at myself as a young kid. I think that's why they say forty is the new twenty because we're all still in our twenties in our minds. It's the realization of what you are saying, "Yeah, I guess I really am grown up now!" Well yeah! Hello! You're grown up and guess what? You have an opportunity to make a difference and you *need* to make a difference. You have to step up to the challenge.

Mattie: We are at an age where we can make a difference. We are a large demographic. There are presently more women in this age group than any other age group. It's up to us to make a difference and I know we can do it. We can change the world for the better. I know that's a bold statement, but Eve and I are holding up a big mirror to you right now and we encourage you to look at yourself in this mirror. You are powerful, you are beautiful, you are strong, and you are capable of helping others through difficult times. You are capable of being gracious and you are very capable of being in gratitude every day of your life, and you are capable of being an example to others. Life doesn't have to be so chaotic. It can be peaceful and it can be full of promises and faith and strength.

We are the generation that has to do this. That's why we feel so strongly about getting the word out. We are the decade of women needing to go out there and make a difference in the world; a difference that women younger than us and older than us will feel in their lives. Handle your challenges with more faith.

Eve: Here are a few lyrics from one of our first *Forty Schmorty* songs I wrote in Nashville with Kim McLean and Marc Intravaia called "I'm Still a Dreamer." The chorus is:

> *Look through the looking glass*
> *See how much time has passed*
> *Everything moves so fast*
> *And nothing moves at all*
> *Hey watch me*
> *I'm not flying*
> *Just to fall*
> *I'm still a dreamer.*

When you were talking it was as if the light went on in my head with a "Ding!" "Hey I can say what she just said in four words; I'm still a dreamer!" Keep that dreamer attitude. I've always been told I'm a dreamer and I've always been told I'm not realistic. I look at things in a "magical, mystical" way. But it's gotten me this far in my life and along with my faith it's going to get me through my next forty years.

It seems like the first forty years are really selfish years. It's all about me and then it's about my family and then it's about my career and my life and me, me, me, me. The next forty years will still have the "me" factor because you're no good to anyone if you don't take care of you. But from now on we can say, "It's about my family *and* your family." It's about my thoughts *and* your thoughts. It's about what I can do to help me feel better about myself and I'm going to share it with you. That's where I hope the next forty years are going to go for us. We want to help people feel better and inspire them to do more for others: building their communities, trying to make a change, getting women together and focusing on the positive.

Mattie: And it all starts with me and you and the person reading these words.

Eve: We can get through anything together. We can't do it alone. What we just went through these past four days, I see some grey hairs and I found a few extra lines on my face, "Thank you very much Mattie!" But my mother has said it so many times, "What doesn't kill you makes you stronger." It's so true; it's forging the glass in the heat until you bring it out and it's that perfectly shaped figurine. We're being molded and melded through all this together. We'll get back to you with the next results, but I do feel like a big weight has been lifted.

Mattie: Anything could happen at any time. This happened to us and we want you to know that we are real people sharing real stories. We really want to get the point across about what we think is important and what drives our souls and what drives us to do what we have to do. Hopefully we can encourage you to do the same.

Eve: Amen.

Mattie: Amen.

FAITH

Eve: Before we started this chapter Mattie and I decided to begin with a prayer. We wanted to set the tone because the subject is so important. It's a topic that really matters to both of us, one that has always mattered in our lives.

My mom used to tell us we were lucky to be born into a family where we were given the gift of faith. Looking at it from her perspective it's almost as if faith chose us because that's what our parents believed and they passed it on to us. Well, I love that! I have thought about what my life would be like if I was raised without a spiritual religious denomination or belief and then found faith. Does it make a difference? She really did make me believe I was the lucky one and that it was given to me. I didn't have to earn it or find it or discover it.

Mattie: It *was* a gift given to us. Having faith in our forties is such an essential part of our lives. I pray every day and my most favorite place to pray and the only time I can get a good solid prayer in is in my car.

Eve: The place where you spend eighty to ninety percent of your time?

Mattie: I make business phone calls in my car, I listen to music, I learn songs in my car, I have deep heartfelt conversations with my children and I talk to God. Thank God for my car because that's one of the most peaceful places I can speak to God.

When I was in my late twenties I felt my relationship with God grow. It became more of a relationship than it did a "practice" to say the prayers you and I in particular learned in Catholic school like *Hail Mary* and *Our Father*. There's nothing wrong with that at all by the way, I think they're beautiful in their own right.

Eve: They're guides to help you learn how to pray.

Mattie: Exactly. Every once in a while I will say a *Hail Mary* or an *Our Father* and sometimes I forget a word or two but I get through it. I feel God really touched my life in my late twenties. I started praying more, but I was praying for *things*. I used to pray for things to happen and things I needed and sometimes I felt like a nagging child. Then I realized I should start praying for help. Through the years I've watched my praying mature. I think now I know how to pray—for my life and for others. I've learned there's a way to pray where you can cover all the ground. It's not so much asking all the time but also being in gratitude and thanking God for everything. In my forties I feel I've come full circle knowing exactly how to pray. Prayer is a big and important part of my life. When I can, I'll hold my four-year-old son's hand and we'll pray before he eats and this morning we prayed before he went to school. I said, "Hey wait, give me your hand and let's pray." I prayed for God to watch over him and to bless his teachers with compassion, love and understanding, and keep the children safe at school and to keep my son safe at school and allow him to have a great day. Whenever we finish praying he always wants to finish with song.

Eve: Wonder who he gets that from?

Mattie: We sing to the tune of Frére Jacques, "God our Father, God our Father, we thank You, we thank You, for our many blessings, for our many blessings, Amen, Amen!" He learned that from his sisters.

Eve: What a beautiful gift you've given him to incorporate into his life. So it's a natural thing. There are a lot of people who have never had that or haven't prayed from a young age. It's awkward and they may stumble through or feel stupid or not know what to say. It's such a great gift to give him because he'll have that ability all his life and he'll only get better at it. When you first start doing something like writing a book, the first few chapters might be tough, but as you get going you develop a natural flow.

My faith also came to me when I was in my twenties. I was raised Catholic. I went to Catholic school from kindergarten to twelfth grade. I had religion surrounding me from the day I was born. Back then, there was more of an attitude where you were always told you have to do this and you have to do that. It was very strict and very stoic and there was not a lot of breathing room to be human. My religion always felt heavy and very guilt oriented. I realized I didn't have a lot of the basis I needed in order to build faith, which is knowledge. So I started attending a Bible study. That was a shock to me in my late twenties. If you had said to me a few years before, "What would you think if I told you that in three years you would be in a Bible study?" I would have replied, "You're crazy! I'm too cool for that!"

Well I started going to Bible study and it just filled me up! It was what I needed; it was what I was missing, that empty space. I had no idea about the close relationship I could have with God and the Holy Spirit. I gained the fulfillment of knowing it's all going to be okay and letting go and letting God. Maybe faith was a better fit in my thirties, a time when most people get married, have success and something to show for what they've accomplished up to that point in their lives. But I didn't have those things so I searched for something else and faith was what I found.

Mattie mentioned praying with her son and I think it's a wonderful gift to give your children. My daughter Sarah and I have a routine we do together every night before we go to bed. We talk about her day and then we say our prayers. It always starts off the way I learned to pray from my mom with "Dear Jesus." Her prayers began the same every night: "Dear Jesus, please take care of Mommy and Daddy and me and everybody in the whole wide world" and then we add names of certain people we are praying for, for whatever they are going through. We add the names and the list gets longer and longer and when she gets tired of naming names she'll say, "And all those people who are on the list because I'm too tired to say all their names!"

As she's gotten older she says, "Mom, we need to thank God for something that happened today." Or, "It was a great day, isn't that worth thanking Him for?" I think for most kids it's a foreign concept to pray in gratitude. We need to teach our children to be grateful every time they pray.

Mattie: These are things I've learned within the last decade, praying in gratitude. I've been singing worship every Sunday at church for the last four years. Worship, by the way, is when the congregation is lead by the "worship team" consisting of a band and singers who sing songs that are played before the actual sermon takes place. It's like a warm-up before the preacher speaks.

Eve: And the lyrics are put up on a screen so everybody can sing the words if they don't know the song.

Mattie: Exactly. Singing worship has become such a part of my life that I can't wait for Sunday to come. I get up very early on Sunday to drive about twenty miles across town to sing worship, but I don't want to miss it! I don't want to miss what the message is going to be because I get fed. I listen to Pastor Jack speak and he relates scripture from the Bible to everyday life. Sometimes it's very ironic when I leave church thinking, "How did he know I was going through that?"

Eve: Right.

Mattie: I am always amazed when a subject is covered in church that I was experiencing the week before. I realize most of these people are going to church for the same reason I am, they believe in the Good Lord and want to receive His message. It's community counseling according to God. Hey, it's free, there's coffee and donuts, you hear great music, and connect with friends. It's been a wonderful change in my life. I realize many of us are in the same boat and we have similar life experiences. One of the biggest problems we have is that we are human and sometimes it gets in the way of our spirituality.

Eve: I was the youngest participant in the Bible study. I went with my mom so they were all my mom's friends, twenty-five to thirty years older than me. I was the kid and I'm in my early thirties! The woman who ran the Bible study would always say, "It's the living Bible!" I loved that phrase. You think about something written over two thousand years ago; how does any of that pertain to our lives today, especially because the world has changed so dramatically since then? How can these words relate to me; they were written before I was even thought of? But that's the whole lesson about the Bible. It's the grace of the Bible that provides everyday sustenance. You have to see it to believe it. And interestingly, that's not what faith is. Faith believes without seeing and yet a lot of us are the "Doubting Thomas" type. When you're living it and you're saying to yourself, "Okay, God's really talking to me, I feel it and I get it. Oh wow!" It's a great feeling and should inspire anyone to read a Bible verse and see how it relates to his or her everyday life.

Mattie: Everything's in there!

Eve: It's better than a soap opera.

Mattie: It's all there. For example, it talks about how you look, the clothes you wear, giving, receiving, marriage, friends, truth, faith, disaster, discouragement, encouragement, getting drunk, drinking, earth, sex. Everything is covered. Think about it; it was written long ago; it's a blueprint for our lives. I have learned to face the storms in my life with a lot more tranquility than I could before. Life is always bringing you surprises and unexpected events. I'm still practicing this because I haven't perfected it yet, but I now know that in the face of difficulty I have to stop and realize that what's going down at that moment has got to be for a reason. I know God has His hands on it. I ask God every day to please watch over me and my entire day and my children: "Please have your hands on this Lord because I can't do this alone." So when I am faced with troubles or great sadness or whatever might attack my heart, there's always a moment where I stop and say, "Okay, God's got to have this because I've already asked Him to watch me." So whose lives are going to be affected? I know it's not just about me, it can't be just about me; it has to be about my family unit or my friends around me who will be affected in some way or another. I'll look back at this and get a realization of God's plan: "Oh, I get it!"

Eve: That's what faith in our forties has brought us. The ability to finally let go, finally be okay with, "Okay, I've lived enough years on this earth to have God show me and prove to me He is there with me and prove to me He always comes through and there's always a reason." Why do I keep doubting? Because it's human nature! Why am I still living at times in fear? Human nature! That's why He's here. That's the gift of faith and when all else fails, get down on your knees and start praying.

Years ago, my brother Pete had appendicitis and was rushed to the hospital. They performed an emergency laparoscopic surgery. Unfortunately, towards the end of the surgery the doctor nicked one of his arteries and my brother started bleeding internally. They didn't catch it until later and they had to go back in, open him up and stop the bleeding. It was bad; my brother almost died many times during that three weeks, it was touch and go.

I went to visit him in the hospital and he literally lost forty pounds in a couple of weeks. He looked like he was dying; he was a skeleton. My brother's a big huge burly guy who's always been in great shape and this was a big slap in the face for me. "Oh my God, my brother could die!" I got down on my knees in the hospital and I said, "God you can have anything I have, you can take it all away from me as long as he can live." I prayed my most desperate, desperate prayer. I didn't need to do that because what was going to happen was God's will. He'll take us back when it's our time but it was the only thing I could think of to do. It was the first time I felt that feeling of, "Oh my gosh, this is real, this is what life is all about!" All I could do was give it up to God.

Of course my brother lived and he is now a dad with three children and his life is great. It's amazing how human nature comes in and fear takes over. It seems as though faith is always there, but we as humans try to take matters into our own hands. You have to give it to God and let God handle it. Instead, we grab it back and say, "No, I'm in control; I'm going to make this work."

People in our lives have died; we've had friends go though tragedies, we've had children die; there have been accidents and disasters we've all had to endure. Without my faith I wouldn't have been able to get through. How do you get through? My mom always says "I don't know how people get out of bed without faith." Would you just be afraid of everything? Mattie, I know you've had things happen to you. How did your faith come into play when your mom passed? You were younger.

Mattie: I was younger, in my twenties, and my whole family knew she was going to go. She had been sick for about a year. I was traveling at that time with Up with People and my relationship with the Lord hadn't really grown yet. I prayed for her, but I wasn't as good at praying to God as I am now.

It wasn't until after her passing that I came to understand my relationship with the Lord through a friend I was traveling with in the same cast. Today he is pastor of a church on the West Coast and I remember so well what a wonderful, energetic person he was. Such zeal for God! I loved his childlike innocence; he was so joyful. He actually encouraged me to audition for the Oral Roberts Singers at Oral Roberts University. I had the opportunity to go to the University to meet the musical director only to find I was one week late for the audition. The timing was off, but I was grateful to get to that point in my life. Jude, my friend, taught me how to pray to God by simply speaking. I remember feeling somewhat uncomfortable and embarrassed talking normally to God without some sort of ritualistic prayer. I also remember watching Jude pray with me, holding my hand with his eyes shut tight and praying this on fire prayer as I'm taking quick peeks to see what he looked liked. I thought to myself, "What in the world is he going through?" Well, this was my introduction to the joy of Christianity.

Eve: So he was there when you were going through all of this with your mom and you had him to lean on. It's never easy to lose someone. People who have lost a family member to cancer know it gives them an opportunity to make amends and prepare for the loss. There are people we meet whose faith is so strong you can almost touch it.

Mattie: I had stopped going to Catholic Church every Sunday, basically because I was on the road for three years. But I remember my travels before my mom passed away. I had been to countries like Ireland, England, Belgium, Holland, wait not England, strike that. I was just on a bus in England.

Eve: In Italy, right?

Mattie: Yes, I was in Italy, that's right, that's right! I was at the Vatican. Geez!

Eve: That's a big one!

Mattie: I used to take time while visiting beautiful cities in Europe to find a church. The architecture is so beautiful and

I've always loved the smell of frankincense and myrrh and that musty smell of a great old church with the very high ceilings and the choir lofts. Not to mention the statues of saints and the candles. I love all of those things that make up a great church. To this day I can walk into a church like that and feel "God is right here!" Every once in a while I would light a candle and say a prayer. But it never was a part of my everyday life until my mother passed away and until Jude came into my life and introduced me to developing a relationship with Christ.

Christians are always curious and will often ask: "At what point in your life did you accept Christ?" I grew up with "the faith" and I went to Catholic school for nine years so I always knew God and Jesus and the Holy Spirit were present. I had my spiritual tool belt, which was good, but I didn't understand how I could have an actual relationship with the Lord and actually pray like I was talking to someone I love and trust. I didn't realize I could lay my problems out on the table and say with all my heart what I was feeling. I am forever grateful for my friend Jude. About two years ago Jude came to mind; I hadn't seen him in over twenty-eight years so I went on a computer search and found him.

Eve: Well, there's a CoinciGod! I'm sure you feel like God sent him to you.

Mattie: Absolutely! He was one of my dearest friends on the road. But when you're finished with your year you're really lucky if you stay in contact with the people you've traveled with because each cast was about one hundred people strong. There are less than a handful of people I keep in contact with on a regular basis.

Eve: Seeing someone years later brings back all of those memories.

Mattie: I am so proud of him today. As a pastor, I know he is inspiring people with that same enthusiasm and zest for life he had almost thirty years ago.

Eve: I have to chime in here because I have a friend I've mentioned several times in this book who came into my life through music. I met her the day after 9/11. She is a singer/songwriter, a producer and one of my dearest friends. I have told her many times I felt God definitely sent her to me because of her music and how it affects me and how her words touch people's hearts and lives. I believe He sent her to me because of her faith. Her faith is like your friend Jude. I swear I could cut it with a knife; it's that real and tangible. Her faith inspires me and I'm a bit envious of it, which might not be the best thing, but when you see someone with that kind of faith you think "I wish I had that, I wish I had that foundation." Since we met she has gone back to college at Trevecca Nazarene in Nashville, Tennessee, and graduated with honors with a degree in Bible. Now she can quote in Hebrew and tell you all sorts of things that are amazing. But that's not what makes her faith so true; it's that she gets it. She understands it so much that she lives it every day.

She wakes up every day and prays, "God, what do you want me to do today and how can you use me to help others and to change lives and to matter?" That's what I want in my forties and maybe that's what I need to focus on. It's so easy to be distracted by all of life's interferences. One week I purchased Lancôme makeup for the lines under my eyes. I then bought GloMinerals makeup with SPF along with products from three other different lines of makeup and spent all this money on my credit card. And I thought, "What am I doing?" My skin is okay "as is." Regardless, I was distracted by the sale and getting older. Fifty-nine-year-old Susan Sarandon was quoted in *More* magazine: "You have to start working on the inside because the outside is a losing battle!" Now that's good advice!

Mattie: How wonderful you would mention that because I have a quote from the Bible I want to read, 1 Peter 3:1-4: *What matters is not your outer appearance, the styling of your hair, the jewelry you wear, the cut of your clothes, but your inner disposition. Cultivate inner beauty, the gentle, gracious kind that God delights in.*

Eve: Okay, so that is part of the Bible and it speaks to us today. It makes sense and it totally fits into what we are talking about and it's something you can crochet into your day.

Mattie: Or you could say, "It becomes the thread in the tapestry of your life."

Eve: "Oh, I like that!" Here's another quote from the Bible, Hebrews 11:1: *Faith is the substance of things hoped for, the evidence of things not seen.* Wow! Faith is available to everyone. I don't care what religion you are you have to have faith. You have to believe there's something unseen going on. Mom used to say to me, "If you want evidence that God exists, if you have to have evidence, go out and look at a flower and see all the intricacies that it has in order to be that flower." Think about it, there are over two thousand different kinds of flowers on this planet, maybe even more. She would say, "A beautiful flower doesn't just 'bang' happen like that. Poof! Ta-dah! The planets smacked into each other to make that happen? I don't think so!" Speaking of beautiful flowers, we are so lucky to live in San Diego!

Mattie: Today the sun is shining, the birds are singing, the air is clear and the wind is mild.

Eve: The sky is perfect blue. There's a place by my house I see every day when I get on the freeway where the hills are a rich green color and the sky meets it just at the horizon. It's a perfect green and a perfect blue and I always pray, "Thank you God for a glorious day, you did a good one today!"

I want to share another quote I found on the Internet. It's by Major Nerys and it says it all: "That's the thing about faith, if you don't have it you can't understand it and if you do, no explanation is necessary!" We can spend weeks talking about how faith has affected our lives and it won't really mean anything to somebody who doesn't get it. If the Bible is too scary, go online and Google somebody you respect and get their quotes and find out what makes them tick. I love people who are afraid of science because science says, "No, there is no God." But there are lots of scientists who will tell you right off that science *is* God; that it's just the back-story of how things happened. Even someone with an analytical mind can accept and believe in faith. That's very inspiring.

Mattie: So you've known Kim...

Eve: It's been five years. Can you believe this year in September it will be five years since 9/11? Five years since our entire world changed. The rest of the world has dealt with war and terror and battles in their homelands, much more than our country. We've been so blessed, and we have so much. For that to happen on our own soil: "Hello, wake up, you're part of this earth! This is happening everywhere!" People ask me, "How do you feel about that? How could God make that happen?" God had nothing to do with that happening, people did! People screw things up, give them a chance they'll make a mess of it!

Mattie: Big time! That was a life-changing day, September 11th.

Eve: I'm sorry I interrupted you about Kim, that's when I met her.

Mattie: That's okay, because you met Kim the next day right?

Eve: The very next day we had a gig.

Mattie: Since meeting Kim back then, where do you stand now with your faith?

Eve: I would definitely say it has deepened and it has grown. We became die-hard fast friends and realized that in a way we are from the same family, separated at birth. We had different parents, but somehow we are similar in so many ways and our friendship grew.

I've watched her live by faith; what an example. It really is a gift and if you don't work at it you don't get any better. Like how your praying improved, for example. You feel you've gotten better and better. Having Kim as my friend and having the inspiration of somebody who lives by faith every day compels me to ask myself, "Okay, Eve, hello? What are you doing with your faith?" I feel I could have the same thing if I tried harder. Mattie, you mentioned your friend Jude and how the career he chose couldn't have been more perfect for him. But it's not for everyone; you really have to have that calling. Kim has that calling. She was invited recently to sing worship and speak to an audience of two hundred priests at a retreat. Even priests need to be rejuvenated. They were so inspired by her words and her music and her faith that she's been asked to come back again. She's a gem that's been found and that's her calling. That's not my calling, which is fine because we can't all be a "Kim" or a "Jude." Like with acting, we can't all be the playwrights; some of us have to be the players. That's okay!

Despite the fact that last week was an earth-shattering, time stopping week of dealing with the "C" word, yes cancer, we've gotten great news and we're at a much better place this week. Mattie had two gigs and a bunch of events this weekend and she still managed to get up early and go to church. I told her after my gig on Saturday I was exhausted and I didn't get to bed till after 2:30 a.m. and I'm thinking, "How's Mattie going to do this?" I remember taking my makeup off and thinking of you wondering, "How is she going to get up tomorrow morning and sing at church?" Not only have a voice to sing with that early, but do it willingly and happily.

Mattie: Would it be too sappy to say that I woke up with joy that Sunday morning? I often wake up with joy knowing I'm going to go to church and sing. At this time in my life I have found a beautiful connection with my church and I have witnessed people's lives touched by the sermons. I enjoy talking to people after the service and making a connection with them. I truly look forward to all of this.

Eve: It's simple. You do this because you want to do it and you give because honestly, you get so much more. I don't go to church like you do every Sunday, but I'm invited to sing at different churches once in a while. On those particular Sundays I get up at 6:00 a.m. and usually think to myself, "Why did I say yes? Why did I say I'd go sing at church? I'm so tired and my voice is scratchy. What am I going to do?" So I just pray about it and when I get to church, I start singing and have the opportunity to listen to the sermon. When the service finishes I say to myself, "Oh yeah, that's why I do this!"

Mattie: What you're doing is what I'm doing when I sing worship, leading in prayer with the worship songs. We are simply praising the Lord. It gives me comfort knowing we are all in this together. It's like a big vitamin that we are all taking to ensure the health of the upcoming week.

Eve: And I know you truly mean it. People feel it when you're singing. It's not just "lip service." People really feel it from you. It's a gift; it's the inspiration for somebody who's not feeling faith-full that day and they can look up at you and think, "Wow, Mattie's really feeling this, maybe there *is* something to all this?" Why would there be so many people feeling there's more out there? Is it human nature or are we just an inquisitive people who think there's got to be something more? How can God's story exist for all this time and never falter and never change? It has lasted because it's *true*. We know human nature and if you're not telling the truth you're going to get caught! It's going to come out somehow, especially if you bring twelve people together claiming, "Okay, here's our story..." Sooner or later someone is going to break and say, "You know what, it is not worth lying for these people. I'm giving up the bus!"

Mattie: People from all walks of life come to church. There are such a variety of likes and differences, but they all have faith and the belief that God is guiding us through our everyday lives. The song that comes to mind right now is the one with the chorus: "Your grace is enough for me." I love that because it brings me hope.

I think about people whose lives are full of stress. I was once caught up in that disease of stress where I didn't allow time for *anything* and I worried about *everything*. Stress has become such a huge factor in our society even elementary and high schools are teaching ways to cope with stress in health classes. Someone was asking my daughter the other day what she was taught in health class. She named a list of topics and finished by adding, "Oh yeah, and they teach us how not to live our life with a lot of stress and worry." I found that very interesting.

Eve: It's the sign of the times.

Mattie: Well I never learned that in my health class when I was going to school. There are wonderful stories and phrases in the Book of Matthew about not worrying: *Therefore do not worry about tomorrow for tomorrow will worry about itself. Each day has enough trouble of its own.* (Matthew 6:34) It's in the Bible for you to believe. I personally can't worry about tomorrow because for us tomorrow often doesn't happen the way we expect it. Be in the moment and take care of it prayerfully. Be in gratitude for what you are experiencing because it's only making you a better person, if you allow it to.

Eve: I know what you mean. When somebody comes and tells me exactly what was worrying me or exactly what I needed to hear, I acknowledge that God used this person as an angel to give me the message. And at that point I say, "Okay God, I hear you!" and I stop worrying. I honestly believe it. I've gotten to a point now where I'm so in tune with it I can say "thank you" to God and I can tell the person, "You just told me exactly what I needed to hear and I'm thanking you because God used you in my life." They'll look at me like I'm crazy, especially if it's a stranger. But who better? We'll listen to a perfect stranger but we won't listen to our own mother. It's human nature.

Mattie: Another cool thing to do when you're around other friends is to ask them how God has changed their lives or ask them about a miracle God has given them. Ask how their faith has changed them or how they are a better person today than they were before. I met a woman yesterday who was intrigued by my necklace with a cross. She was hesitant, but asked me about my faith: "Are you a believer?" I responded, "Oh yeah!" The band was on a break at the time, this was during a job I had.

Eve: Oh, the three-hour job that turned into eight hours?

Mattie: Ten.

Eve: Ten hours, and you were two hours away from home, took you four hours total round-trip?

Mattie: Good times.

Eve: That was after this weekend people! I'm telling you. That's a God thing right there. God kept you so busy so you wouldn't worry. You didn't have time to worry. You were exhausted!

Mattie: I haven't had time to worry about my situation since Wednesday of last week. I have been very busy; my cup has been very full this entire week.

Eve: That is not a coincidence; that is a CoinciGod!

Mattie: CoinciGod once again. I was singing in the studio the other day with a woman I'd never met before. During a break she was happy to share her story with me about God and where she is with her faith today. I ended up asking her how she found her faith and she told me things got to a point in her life where she was completely broken, her marriage and her children. She related how she got down on her knees and prayed, "God, I will do whatever it takes to have this marriage get back to where it was or even better. I need your help. I will give you anything you want!" She was very passionate about her story; I was blessed to have her share it with me. She continued to tell me about the little miracles that happened one after the other and how she would find herself worrying about something and pray her way through it. Our lives are parallel because she too sings in church and also does voiceover and jingle work.

Eve: A voiceover is when you are the voice for commercials. Mattie is the voice that says, "Come on down to la la la la la la!" and jingle work is singing a commercial. Just to let you know.

Mattie: Correct. We want you to understand this is a part of what we do for a living. It was nice to run into someone whose career is parallel, but she does all of this in Spanish. For the eight hours we spent together in the studio I felt a bond with her and I was at peace. She was so sweet. I really enjoyed being in her company. Thank you, Lela!

There are people like Lela everywhere around you. Someone has a story about something they have struggled with, something God has seen them through. They could have been sick then healed or their marriage could have fallen apart and been restored stronger than ever or it could be the case of inconsiderate teenagers turned into "mean-agers."

Eve: Good one!

Mattie: My niece said that to me yesterday. "My son is such a mean-ager!" Well, God will see you through it. All you have to do is ask.

Eve: And what is faith but belief. And what is so important that you would believe in it? Love! You can't see love. You might see the manifestation of it, but you can't see it; it's a feeling. Faith really is a feeling. My faith is so deeply rooted in me I sometimes take it for granted. This might not always be a good thing and maybe that's when God starts "rocking the boat" a little. Maybe it's because my mom explained it as a gift that was given to me and was woven into my life. But there are days when I wake up and I say, "What is this, come on! He loves me? He was on the cross dying for me? He thought of my sins? Riiiight!"

And that's what faith is, the ability to believe when you don't *know*. What makes it stronger is when you question it. You actually make your faith stronger when you doubt it. The first time I was ever allowed to doubt my faith (because I was raised Catholic remember) was in high school. I thought they were playing a trick on us and I'm thinking, "We're going to get in trouble, we're going to start saying things you're not supposed to say and not supposed to think." I was in class and they said, "Okay, we're putting all our cards on the table. Let's start asking the real questions, who really believes all this junk?" We were allowed the freedom to doubt faith, which in turn built it up and made it stronger. I loved that! It's when something bad happens to you like what happened with my brother and I prayed my desperate prayer and God spoke to me in my heart, He calmed me. I was desperate like anybody would be in that situation. It's just like Lela did when she got down on her knees and prayed, "I am at the end of my rope, and I tied a knot. I'm hanging on. God you have to help me!"

You're always going to get through because tomorrow is going to come and the next day is going to come. Whatever is going to happen, will happen. I choose to believe God has His hand in it and *He's* changing it, instead of "Hey, whatever!"

Mattie: God has His hands on everything, especially on what we're doing right now. Look where this has brought us. Eve and I hadn't kept in contact with each other; nothing personal, it's just that we have gone on with our individual lives and that's okay. But we came together because I had a jingle to sing and the producer wanted a rock and roll singer and Eve is the best rock and roll singer in this town and this side of the Mississippi and the other side, so I called her and said, "Let's go do it!" So we went together and...

Eve: We just started talking in the car on the way because it was a long drive.

Mattie: Our lives changed during that drive.

Eve: We asked each other, "How are you doing?" "Not so good, how are you doing?" "Eh, not so good either." We talked and realized we had arrived at the same place in our lives and we were going through the same emotions. Then on February 14th, Mattie left the Soft Scrub-inspired message on my cell phone saying, "We need to write a book!" Here we are talking about how faith has changed our lives and how it affects our lives in our forties. I'm sure in our fifties it's going to be even deeper and we'll continue paying attention to the important things we need to get right.

Mattie: The more I hear God, the more I'm able to look out and see other people who haven't quite made it there yet but you know God's working on them.

Eve: And who are we, Mattie and Eve, to write a book? We're not authors, this is not our expertise. What we're talking about today is what we know, what our truths are, what we've learned.

This is what I do with songwriting when Marc and I write songs together. You can only write what you know. We could sit down and say, "Okay, we have to write a hit and it has to be about balloons because balloons are hot and red is the new blue so it's a blue balloon song. Let's write it." That's just wrong! You don't believe it; you don't feel it; you don't want to know it. We've always had a way of weaving in spirituality to our songs because it's what we know. Christians will come up to me and ask: "Are you writing about God? Are you a Christian?" They get it, they hear it, and they recognize it right away. But somebody else might hear our music and think it's about them or their boyfriend or girlfriend, husband/wife and that's great too. Maybe that was my calling. I'm not going to be the preacher, but maybe my calling is to sing a song that is spiritually based, that will someday inspire someone to look for more. And then maybe they'll say, "I like her music. Oh she wrote a book? She wrote a book with her friend Mattie?

Well let's read it and see what the heck is in that crazy head of hers!"

Mattie: And "Bam!" there it is.

Eve: And "Bam!" Here we are together talking about faith and we are experts in what we know!

Mattie: Yeah, we have huge degrees in what we know!

Eve: We're in graduate school right now, getting our PhDs from the college of life.

Mattie: One of my favorite verses from the Bible is in the Book of Corinthians 13:4-7. This verse came to mind when my friend Lela inspired me. We know people get it because it's very simple. Check it out:

> *Love is patient, love is kind. It does not envy, it does not boast, it is not proud. It is not rude, it is not self-seeking. It is not easily angered. It keeps no record of wrongs. Love does not delight in evil but rejoices with the truth. It always protects, always trusts, always hopes, always perseveres.*

Eve: My friend Kim has written a great song called "Not So Far Away." Everybody calls it the faith, hope and love song. She wrote about each entity—faith, hope and love—as if they were each a living human thing. The entire concept of the song is about heaven not being so far away because if you stop and think about faith and hope and love being part of your everyday life, it's actually a glimpse into heaven. It's like looking into the window of heaven and seeing what it's always going to be like. I believe Kim's intention for the song is to get you to think: Isn't it interesting if you really stop and imagine that maybe heaven isn't so far away, that maybe it happens every day!

I was just thinking about someone who owes my band money and it's caused me a lot of anxiety. And as we've been talking about our faith this morning I'm realizing maybe I just need to let it go. I called before we got together this morning and left a poopy message. Now after everything we talked about, I feel I need to call back and say, "Its okay, pay me back whenever you can." You know? This has been weighing on my heart for a while. It's so easy to stand on my soapbox and speak my peace and then the reality of what's happening here with this situation makes me feel like a hypocrite. I guess I'm falling a little short here.

Mattie: Well you spoke your truth. You *are* owed money, you did make your phone call and you did plant the seed and I think your next step is prayer.

Eve: Yeah.

Mattie: I'll back you up on that!

Eve: Okay.

Mattie: I think this situation needs nothing more but prayer: good, solid, diligent, prayer.

Eve: We've been talking about our faith and that last Bible verse and its message rings true with something that is happening in my life right now, today, the living breathing word of the Bible.

Mattie: I'll tell you God doesn't want you to have a bad day today.

Eve: No, He doesn't and I'm not going to. You know, this is great! I feel like we could talk for hours and hours. I want to say something about the Bible that's filled me so much. When you take a Bible class, if you've never done it before, you take a chapter—for example, 1 Corinthians 13—and you start from the beginning of the chapter and go to the very end. Along the way, you study the chapter, talk about it and bring it into your everyday life.

The book that changed my life was the book of Romans. The

book of Romans is an incredibly hard book to read because it's a finger-pointing book. Before I understood it I couldn't really read it because it was saying to me, "You can't do this, you can't do that and if you do this you're this, this, this, and this!" That's what I understood at first, but then I realized what the book of Romans was actually telling me, that there's nothing you can do to change the nature of who you are. You are human and you will always fall from grace. You will always trip, you will always mess up, there's nothing you can do to change that. God knew this so he sent His Son because that was the only way any of us were ever going to get into heaven. When I finally understood this book it filled me with so much peace because I realized, "Wow, I don't have to try so hard, I'm already taken care of!" Because when God looks at me, His Son is standing right in front of me. I'm saying to God, "I'm sorry, I'm sorry, I did that thing I shouldn't have done; I know I shouldn't have done it. I did it anyway!" and God is questioning "What?" Because all He sees is His Son!

So it gave me peace and freedom because it helped me realize I don't have to worry about all these things. I don't have to be standing on this tiny tightrope trying to walk through life not making any mistakes and not choosing the wrong thing because it doesn't matter. I'm going to choose wrong and that's why God is there, to catch me. This really helped me. If you get the chance and you want to challenge yourself, read the book of Romans. Actually the first time we went through it I didn't like it at all. But once I understood it, it spoke to me.

Mattie: While you were just now speaking about the book of Romans, I flipped my Bible open to the book of Romans and found a message I wrote in pencil on the first page that reads, "Life makes no sense without God!" Then I turned the page to Romans 5:1-5 and found this on peace and joy:

> *Therefore, since we have been justified through faith, we have peace with God through our Lord Jesus Christ, through whom we have gained access by faith into this grace in which we now stand. And we rejoice in the hope*

of the glory of God. Not only so, but we also rejoice in our sufferings, because we know that suffering produces perseverance; perseverance, character; and character, hope. And hope does not disappoint us, because God has poured out His love into or hearts by the Holy Spirit, whom He has given us.

Eve: You know if you were reading that as a teenager, it would sound like Swahili. But here we are in our forties and it is a gift. It's crystal clear to me, wow! I feel we're pretty lucky to be forty! Honestly, I don't know how any of us made it out of our childhood? There are so many things that could go wrong and there are so many accidents that could happen and tragedies. It's angels watching over us who got us out of our childhood into our adulthood and then for God to give us the gift of getting to our forties!

Romans 5:18-19 says:

> *Consequently, just as the result of one trespass was condemnation for all men* [that would be Adam and Eve], *so also the result of one act of righteousness was justification that brings life for all men* [Jesus dying for our sins]. *For just as through the disobedience of the one man the many were made sinners, so also through the obedience of the one man the many will be made righteous.*

Now I'm skipping down to Romans 6:14: *For sin shall not be your master because you are not under law, but under grace.* The Bible is a pretty amazing book when you finally get through the whole thing and you realize how much freedom God gives us. When you know love you don't want to go out and kill, murder, rob and do wrong, you want to do right. You want to do right because it fills you up, because love is such a beautiful thing. That's why when Jesus came it was as if He said with regard to the Old Testament, "You don't need all those rules now, I'm here. And what I'm saying to you is love yourself so that you can love others and love God above all else." It's that simple.

Mattie: Simple rules for a complicated life. That's our faith. That's what Eve and I believe and will continue to believe for the rest of our lives.

Eve: I want to end with a quote from Rabindranath Tagore: "Faith is the bird that feels the light when the dawn is still dark." I know we're going to be okay. We're going to be okay, Mattie. The cancer scare we had last week with you, we're going to be okay. God's got His hand on it and we believe our faith is guiding us, even if they come back next week and say, "Yes Mattie, it is cancer." You're going to be okay. It happened to my sister, she is fine. In my heart of hearts I feel they are going to come back and say, "Mattie, it's a cyst, no big deal. What do you want to do?" And then you're going to go with my mother's advice: "It didn't come with the set; take it out!"

Mattie: Amen!

Same day, some hours later…

Eve: After Mattie and I wrote our Faith chapter, I took the kids to the beach and jotted down some more thoughts. Like Buechner said, "All moments are key moments." I'm sitting here at the beach in San Diego after an amazing morning writing session with Mattie. This time at the beach was not planned, but inspired by my daughter and her friends, a last minute attempt to enjoy God's perfect day. All the adults said "No." Even I did. After all, I had things to do today. Important things like laundry and cleaning and answering e-mail. But when I got in the car to go pick up my daughter and bring her back home, the day was so breathtakingly beautiful I changed my mind. And now I've got on sunscreen and my cowboy hat and jeans and a t-shirt and I'm sitting in a beach chair watching the girls jump over waves while writing on the only paper I had with me in the back of my planner.

I need to let you know what happened after I finished up at Mattie's house. I felt as if God spoke to me today. Right before

I arrived at Mattie's I had left a phone message with the person who owed my band money. I was very frustrated and believe me it came across on my voice mail. It was the wrong thing to do before embarking on our chapter about faith. It put me in a bad mood and the darkness was hanging over me. Even though Mattie prayed with me before we started, it took a while for me to let it go and concentrate on our writing. As we moved on with our subject and started quoting passages from the Bible, the feeling lifted completely and I was engrossed in our talking and listening. We mentioned how the Bible passages had meaning in our everyday lives, even though it was written over 2000 years ago. Then Mattie decided to read 1 Corinthians 13: *Love is patient, love is kind...* And when she got to the part about holding no grudges my words from this morning's phone message came back to slap me in the face—hard!

It was happening right on tape! God was using His words to speak directly to me. And it stung because I was speaking about listening to and living in faith and I was acting selfish and stubborn and angry. What a powerful lesson. Mattie suggested I pray about it. After our session I felt the need to leave another message. I said my goodbyes to Mattie, got in my car and called again. But this was a 180-degree different phone call from the first one. I apologized for my earlier words and said I was letting it go, that our relationship was worth more to me than the money owed to my band. "Pay it whenever you have it, or don't pay it at all." I was really able to let go of it and feel good about it. For the first time in weeks I felt the weight of all the negative energy dissipate. I was released and it felt great. It also felt right. What a powerful, liberating action letting go can be.

So I will take Mattie's advice and pray for my friend and pray for myself to continue to be able to leave it with God and not try to grab it back. I feel so much lighter and I feel God's love and words working in my heart and in my life. It's a beautiful moment, a key moment, a powerful, wonderful, magical moment.

"Coincidences are when God remains anonymous."

6

MARRIAGE

Mattie: Marriage.

Eve: "Marrwige. Wuv...twoo wuv!" (Eve quotes from the movie *Princess Bride*) We both just looked at our wedding albums and are in such good moods.

Mattie: Didn't it put you in a good mood?

Eve: You want to know one of the reasons why I'm in a good mood? My wedding is paid off, is yours?

Mattie: I'm pretty sure it is.

Eve: Okay!

Mattie & Eve: Yes!

Eve: Your wedding day should be the happiest day of your life.

Mattie: My wedding was absolutely a blast! We want to

encourage all married women in their forties to pull out their wedding album and or video and take a look at it.

Eve: Celebrate with a glass of wine or champagne and make it an event!

Mattie: With a glass of Dom Perignon! Taking out your wedding memorabilia brings you back to that one beautiful day. It's a significant time to remember for the rest of your life and it should represent how you will live your "twilight years" together.

Eve: We've been friends for a very long time and have become much closer in the past year. But we just realized that neither one of us has seen each other's wedding albums. So aside from sharing that moment with your husband, it's also nice to share it with your friends and talk about "Who is Uncle Joe?" And who's this and who's that? It really is worth sharing with people you love.

Mattie: Looking at my wedding album brought back all of the excitement of that day, and quite frankly, I can't wait to see Troy when he gets home!

Eve: Yeah!

Mattie: From Phoenix.

Eve: Your honey's out of town. This is a second marriage for both of us. When we look back on our lives, there's a reason it's our second marriage. The first ones didn't work out! We both have said, "This is it!" We're not doing this again. It was hard enough to go through the first experience along with the heartache. I'm not doing that again; even though there are no guarantees in life I'm really hopeful this is going to be it. I wanted this to be the wedding of my dreams and it truly was!

Mattie: It truly was for both of us. When this marriage came around for me, no sooner did Troy ask me and I was already thinking, "How soon can I get married?" The timing was right and we got married two months after he proposed.

Eve: But you and Troy were together for about two years before he proposed, so you knew.

Mattie: Yes, I knew and I was thinking, "Why wait?"

Eve: And this was his first time around so he knew. Even my first time around I was thinking, "Oh my gosh, what am I doing?" But I was ready to be married and I was also pregnant.

Mattie: I was too the first time around.

Eve: I wanted to do the right thing and there was no way I was going to be pregnant and not married. So we did the wrong thing for the right reason.

Mattie: And now this time, we've done the right thing for the right reason and we want to share it with you.

Eve: I found a wonderful quote from Nignon McLaughlin: "A successful marriage requires falling in love many times always with the same person." When I was looking at Mattie's wedding album I could feel the love from the pictures. I was thinking, "Isn't it amazing how you're looking at those pictures and thinking about how in love you were!" And here we are six years later and I'm more in love with my husband, aren't you? I am more in love with Tom and I never thought it was possible to love him more than the day I said, "I do!" in front of my family and friends.

Mattie: I had a beautiful wedding. Everything about it was beautiful. I remember saying to Troy that our wedding was for everyone who attended. Everyone there needed to be there. We wanted to share the day with all of them. Most of our guests knew the path I had gone down before this wedding and this was for all those people to see that love can win and it can work and you can make it happen. It was verification to all that you can be successful with love and you can have great new beginnings regardless of the past. Everyone who attended was deeply touched by the love of our union and our families and it was wonderful to feel the joy for us and for everyone present.

I can't even describe the energy, the feeling, the music, and the day. The sun was shining and later created a beautiful sunset. It was perfect. I think it's really important that when a commitment is made both individuals need to try to fall in love every day. Try to make it new every day because it is so easy to get comfortable and get familiar to the point where your relationship is sort of mundane. I think that's a challenge for a lot of married couples. You have to take the time to make time. I always hear people talk about the things you can do to rejuvenate your marriage. Well for me, getting together with Eve as often as we have been lately has made me take a second look at my marriage. For example, Eve and Tom have a date night. Every other person will tell you to take time out with your husband and go out on a date and get "reconnected" especially if you have children. Well this is true; I believe you have to do that. Troy and I have been married for six years and we have really not had a regular date night. We hit the ground running when we got married. I had my two daughters with me full time from my previous marriage and then I got pregnant during our first year of marriage and then again three years later.

Eve: No time for anything, much less sleep!

Mattie: Baby, baby, new home, a car, and then another car and one thing leading to another which led to pure exhaustion! It's so important to check in with your marriage. Ask yourself questions about your relationship. Are you getting too comfortable with your marriage? Is it becoming routine? Is there less of a relationship and more of a function? I have the comfort of knowing that when the day's over my husband is going to walk through the door and "A, B, C and D" are going to happen and then it's time to go to bed!

Eve: There are just so many hours in a day. It really is true and then you get up and do it again and then all of a sudden "boom!" it's the month of June and "boom!" it's Christmas! If you don't have a date night, I so recommend you make it happen. My situation with Tom is a little different than yours, there are no babies involved and our children were older even though my youngest was six when we got married. But both of our exes lived in the same town so we were able to work out our schedule by sending our kids to their other parents on the same night once a week. We actually got alone time, which is as precious as Fort Knox! You just don't get that when you've got young kids and then babies come. You can only take advantage of Grandma and Grandpa so many times.

We would have our date night every Thursday night and sometimes I was too tired to go out but I'd say, "All right, let's take a walk around the block and hold hands, let's go sit in the car and neck and let's have some silly alone time together or watch a movie and try not to fall asleep!" As long as we were doing something together! Sometimes I would have Tom read to me, he's a great speaker and he's so good with reading and books are his thing. Tom reading to me is so romantic. Buy your husband a book of poetry.

Mattie: That's wonderful! Troy has read to me, but I do have to admit I appreciate the stories he reads to me from *Sports Illustrated*. There are some very...

Eve: Romantic stories with deep meanings?

Mattie: I speak truthfully because the stories he did read were very heroic stories and stories about the agony of defeat...

Eve: Overcoming...

Mattie: Overcoming, yes those kinds of stories I really appreciate. They weren't exactly love stories, but he did read to me a couple of times.

Eve: And that brings up such an important factor in any marriage—a sense of humor.

Mattie: Yes, you have to have a sense of humor.

Eve: You *have* to have a sense of humor. I am now going to read to you a quote from Bill Cosby.

Mattie: Oh please, do!

Eve: "For two people in a marriage to live together day after day is unquestionably the one miracle the Vatican has overlooked!" Isn't that a crack up? Oh my goodness! It is a challenge to live with someone. I only lived alone for a very short time in my life and I lo-o-o-o-o-v-ed it! Luh, luh, loved it! And then I got pregnant, then I got married and then I got separated, divorced and then I met Tom and that was it! But we had to make sure this was going to work so we moved in together. He asked me to marry him before we moved in together. I wanted to know for sure; I didn't want to make the same mistake and go through divorce again. Regardless, living with someone is different than dating. When you take the time to get yourself all dolled up, wearing your cute little black dress and they come to the door you are on your best behavior, and so are they. Dating is different than waking up with morning breath and your hair looking like Bozo the Clown. If you can look at someone then and still say, "Oh my gosh, you are the most beautiful person I've ever seen," you know it's going to work!

Mattie: Troy and I had a very unique dating method because I had my two daughters who were six and eight years old at the time. I just didn't date. I really wouldn't date. I didn't want to take that time away from or leave my girls because it was very important for me to be with the girls as much as I could since I worked during the day. So when Troy came into our lives I had him come over more to our house and spend time with us, helping the girls with their homework or whatever they needed help with while I got the evening rolling with dinner. Then it was maybe a television show or a game and off to bed for the girls. That is if there wasn't a school project that needed to be completed and it kept us all up till about 2:00 a.m. in the morning. Like those last minute projects that needed to be videotaped for grade school.

Eve: Oh this is when you had the girls in private school where every penny you made went to their tuition and they had these insane projects. You couldn't believe how much homework they had.

Mattie: A *lot* of homework. So they really didn't have a set bedtime because there was so much homework. At that time it mattered more to me that they finished their work rather than to have an incomplete project and get a bad grade. I wanted them to finish their homework and they would stay up pretty late. This was a habit Troy didn't really appreciate because it didn't give us time.

Eve: Sure.

Mattie: We didn't get much together time because the girls weren't in bed by 9:30 p.m. or 10:00 p.m. They were in bed by 12:00 a.m.

Eve: That is a tough one because I am a "stickler" about bedtime at my house. It's the only time in the entire day I get some alone time with my husband. I adore my kids but when it's bedtime I say, "Go brush your teeth and let's get to bed!" My husband is a bit more lax about it because he's usually finishing up work or a project. But I'm adamant. I say, "No! I want those kids in bed! I want your arm around me and I want us to sit on the couch and be alone together." So I can understand how Troy would get frustrated, but it's not like your children were hanging out watching *Wheel of Fortune*. They were doing stuff.

Mattie: That was a hard time and it led into their late night habits still doing homework.

Eve: Rock-n-Roll babies, that's what I call them.

Mattie: I have been very blessed to have a second chance. I married a man whom I thought would never ever exist in my life because I always looked at a man like Troy as being somebody else's husband. I always looked at Troy as...

Eve: If he was for someone else, not for you.

Mattie: Yeah because he had it all...a college education, a really great job...

Eve: Very handsome.

Mattie: Very handsome and always tries his best at everything. He loves sports.

Eve: He's an overachiever and very neat too.

Mattie: And he's completely awesome and I never thought I would meet someone like him, but I did! I think God put him on Divine assignment to find me because I wasn't looking and he certainly found me. So now with our marriage it's a blended family because I had my children from my first marriage. It's been a lot of work to make sure everything went smoothly with the girls and Troy. Over time Troy and my oldest daughter, Gia, really match wits very well and Gabby and me...

Eve: Well, Gabby is your "mini-me!"

Mattie: Identical mind set.

Eve: Unbelievable. Gabby is physically and in every other aspect like Mattie. Mattie birthed herself. It's a trip!

Mattie: I did. I birthed myself with Gabby. It's been about balancing the dynamics with my family and then diving in with managing family. I haven't been really good about taking time to be with Troy. I haven't been the best person to be a partner with Troy. It's been more about a balance. I've been more of a balancer than I have been the partner or the ear that would sit and listen to him. I came into this marriage deciding that I wasn't going to be a nagging wife. I'm not going to say...

Eve: You can't do this and you *have* to do that.

Mattie: Or, "You have to be home at this time!" He hasn't given me any reasons to say those things or to nag. If he wants time to do the NFL Draft, I let him do the NFL Draft.

Eve: Mattie says with a deep heavy sigh.

Mattie: One day I'll get it.

Eve: But for now, you just leave the house.

Mattie: When I know the draft is coming, I plan to leave the house and take the kids out to do something fun. I just don't understand the draft, but I'm working on it. Anything having to do with sports has not been my favorite thing. Sports have always been a part of Troy's life.

Eve: Sports are to Troy, like music is to you.

Mattie: So it took me a while to get used to the sound of a football game on the television, which is still a little hard for me to listen to. But baseball, I can listen to a baseball game, no problem.

Eve: That's love! It's that give and take and learning to pick your battles. What if you were to put your foot down and say: "Never again do I want to hear a football game on the television!" Well guess what? You'd probably lose your husband if you said that. I'm not a big sports fan myself. "Hey, who won the Super Bowl?" It's not important to me, but I can appreciate that you love him enough to give him that space and to know that's going to make him happy and if you have a happy husband he's going to want to make you happy. He's going to be thinking, "Gosh, I have the coolest wife; she loves me so much she lets me be a guy and have my friends around and do my thing. I think I'm going to go get her flowers." Are you reading this Troy? I think it's diamond earrings she's always wanted.

But seriously, it's the little things that break up a marriage. It's the little things that are poisonous that get in and start rooting like those weeds in your garden. If you don't get rid of them right away they're going to be there and you're stuck.

Mattie: Speaking of the little things that tear a marriage apart, I think it's also the little things that can start to put a marriage back together. We want to encourage women who are married to do your best to stay married. Constantly try to find a renewal in your marriage. Choose your battles wisely. Can you take a deep breath and let go of the problem that's nagging you?

Eve: Have you ever been at the point where you bit your words back? When they almost came out of your mouth but you kept them back. Then you waited a minute and realized, "Hey that wasn't so bad and my world hasn't fallen apart and everything is okay!" This really is a decision you make in the moment to keep moving things forward. This is an everyday matter you have to stay on top of. It's hard work!

Mattie: Marriage is like brushing your teeth, you have to tend to it every day and if you ignore your teeth...

Eve: They'll go away.

Mattie & Eve: Thank you Dr. Selis!

Eve: It's the little things that help make a marriage work, like leaving a love note on the pillow or putting a little something in their wallet and waiting for them to find it. Just so he knows I'm thinking about him I'll call my husband up and say, "Thank you for being such a great guy, such a wonderful man. A man I respect and can fall more in love with every day!"

It's like what you do with your children, Mattie, when you call out to them and say, "Hey!" and they answer, "What Mom?" And you say, "Did I tell you that I love you today?" Those are the things that make a difference. If you can stop someone on a dime like that they really get it. It makes an impact.

Mattie: Have to water the flower every day. Like I mentioned earlier, Troy's out on a trip right now but when he was packing the night before he left, his luggage was sitting on the floor in the closet and I thought, "I'm going to slip him a little note in his pocket." So I did. I grabbed a Post-it sticky and wrote "I love you" on it and I saw a pair of pants I knew he was going to be wearing this morning so I slipped the note into his pocket, deep down into the pocket. He found it this morning and called me and said, "I got your note, I love you too. Thank you."

I think we are all here to lift each other up. It's hard enough living in this world and seeing marriages get destroyed left and right. It takes everything in our power to keep our relationships working beautifully and harmoniously.

I want to share with you my wedding vows. This is from an e-mail Troy sent to me before we were married. There were so many times when we were dating that I wasn't sure what I was doing. Single mom, should I be dating? What am I doing with my life, yadda, yadda, yadda. We went through a lot before we got married. One evening he wrote me this beautiful e-mail and included this poem called "I Will Stay." It goes like this:

If you feel like loving me, give me your heart, I will take care of it
If you want to trust me, give me your faith, I will honor it
If you think you need me, give me your hand, I will guide you

If you see how to guide me, show me, I will follow
If you desire affection, give me yours, I will give it back
If you seek understanding, talk to me, I will listen

149

If you know you want me, tell me, I will be with you
If you want a life together, show me, I will stay.

Eve: Oh my God! Tissue! Please! That's so beautiful…he wrote that?

Mattie: He wrote that to me before we were married and I had a copy of it in my car for a while. One day I was talking to my minister who goes by the name Bear, (I love Bear) who was going to marry us.

Eve: Anybody with a name like Bear, you know it's all about hugging!

Mattie: I asked him about special wedding vows and he asked me if I had anything I had written or maybe Troy had written. I realized at that point I had a copy of what Troy had written to me. He read it, looked up at me and said, "These are your vows! We're doing it and we're not telling him!"

Eve: Ooh, sneaky, sneaky!

Mattie: So at the wedding when it was time to say our vows, Bear said to everyone, "I want you all to know these are vows that Troy wrote for Mattie and he doesn't know this yet, but we are going to use them as the official vows for their marriage." And Troy gave me this look like, "What are you doing?"

Bear started with, "Repeat after me" and Troy and I were so filled with emotion it was very special. He did look at me at one point and said, "That was a dirty trick!" but we laughed and I got to say the very same words and everyone at the wedding was moved.

I have to share one other story about Troy before we were married that pertains to our wedding ceremony. One evening Troy had invited me to his apartment for the first time and as he was giving me directions, he asked me to park in his parking space so he moved his car to a different area because it was all assigned parking. I remember it was late in the evening after one of my gigs. So I parked in his space, got out of the car, shut the car door, and looked down on the ground and saw a rose on the pavement. I thought to myself that somebody must have dropped the flower. So I left it there and continued walking past my car and on to the path leading to his apartment. As I was walking I noticed a rose on the ground every four to five feet leading all the way to his doorstep. When I got to his door, there were about two dozen roses lying on his doormat waiting for me! So on our wedding day he surprised me with a path of roses leading to the altar! We really had a wonderful foundation and beginning of our life together.

At this point I feel I have to do a little more to make this marriage work. Maybe I've gotten a bit comfortable with routine. I think many women slip into this habit, getting comfortable with the routine of the life of being married. Wrapping yourself up in your children's activities you can get sidetracked with so many other things that take priority over your husband. Lately I've found myself caught up in this cycle of doing everything I can to make sure the family is functioning without problems. In the morning when everyone has gone to school and Troy has gone to work, I take care of my baby Morgan; I get busy with laundry, dinner, and errands. By the time everyone comes home my goal is to have dinner ready, coffee in the coffee maker set to go for the next morning and Nate and Morgan in the bath. Before I know it, there hasn't been much conversation with Troy.

Writing this book has helped me take a look at where I stand right now with my marriage. There are some important changes I need to make because I desire to live a long life with a happy ending. It's up to us, each individual, to make a difference in our marriage. I've had this thought about God and how He did not intend for us to live with our parents for the rest of our lives. How long do we live at home, seventeen or eighteen years? But yet you look at married couples and there are some who have been married for sixty-five plus years! I see this all the time when I'm singing at wedding receptions. How do these people do this?

Eve: One day at a time.

Mattie: One day at a time. And being the largest demographic in our forties we have the opportunity to change a statistic. To remain married women who will work on having stronger marriages and less divorce.

Eve: We are on this path in our lives for a reason. We chose the path of marriage so we need to follow it through the best way we can. It doesn't always have a happy ending. Our first marriages are proof of that. Mattie and I have certainly made our share of mistakes. Fredrik Nietzche says, "It's not a lack of love, but a lack of friendship that makes unhappy marriages." When I think about my husband and our relationship, I realize we are each other's best friends. I can tell him anything and I know he's my biggest fan and he can tell me anything and he knows I'm his biggest fan and I'm standing on the sideline in my cheerleading outfit yelling, "Go Tom Go!" Sometimes when I'm being silly I'll put my hands together and clap and do a cheer for him just because I want him to know that I care.

There are things each of us does that drive the other crazy. But there are so many more wonderfully deep, important, fulfilling things we do for each other that wipe away the negative. It's when you say, "I'm in this, I made this choice, and whatever it takes I'm going to see it through to the right end." And the right end means, "Oh here come Mr. and Mrs. Mills for their sixty-fifth wedding anniversary." You owe it to yourself because your children and your family and friends stood by and watched you say on your wedding day, "This is what I believe to be true forever!"

Mattie: Work at your unity and try to keep it as fresh and alive as you possibly can for as long as you can. Life is basically about an attitude. It's about where you keep your faith and trust. You have to have faith. What about you women out there who get together with two or three friends for coffee or wine and end up talking about your husbands? Is it a rag session or a brag session?

Eve: What you said about attitude really struck a chord with me. You make a choice. Things do happen yes, but you can choose to stay honorable and united with one person or you can choose to go off and have affairs. It's a choice. There are a lot of reasons why things happen in relationships.

I think I might have mentioned this to you in a phone conversation, but the longest my husband and I have been apart in our marriage has been about two weeks. I might be touring and he's at home doing his thing and we're away from each other and it's very hard. Tom and I are very kissy, lovey dovey. When we are away from each other we're obviously not there to kiss each other so we get out of the habit. I remember coming home one time from a trip and I was so excited thinking about the homecoming and kissing him. I just couldn't wait to kiss him and when the moment finally came he had a horrible cold! I couldn't kiss him because I had to perform again the next day and I might catch his cold and lose my voice. This is something that Mattie and I have to be cautious of when we are around other people who are sick. So Tom and I didn't kiss for about three weeks. I remember it was torture!

I remember thinking at the time, "Oh this is how people get out of the habit of intimacy." You stop doing it. And then three weeks turns into a month, which turns into two months and then six months have gone by and you haven't kissed or touched or done anything. I always wondered how that would happen because Tom and I are not like that. We are very physical and show our affections. But honestly, I didn't understand it till we were apart. It's the daily practice of intimacy that keeps it going. I know you can get to a point where words don't mean what they mean because maybe you're just saying it out of habit and you don't want that either. Maybe some days you feel it more than others and maybe some days, murder is what you feel and not love. But you get through it, you work through it and the intimacy is there.

Mattie: I agree. It's those habits we slip into. We got into a really bad habit for which I think I am to blame, of just falling asleep and not saying goodnight. I think because of my crazy, crazy, busy schedule with motherhood, four children, husband and life in general for several weeks I was falling asleep with all my clothes on. At least I would take my shoes off, but I would wake up with my jeans and t-shirt and socks still on my body. I was exhausted. All this happened after I had my last baby. It could have been that whole year of being forty-five and going through postpartum in a different way. I think we all experience it differently. Now that I think about it, that's probably what I was experiencing. I was so tired at the end of the day I would wake up the next morning with all my clothes and jewelry on, fully dressed.

Eve: How convenient, just brush your teeth and hair and you're ready to go!

Mattie: Well in a sad sick way it was very wonderful because all I had to do was slip on my shoes and get the girls up and take them to school. I was dressed and ready to go, threw my hair back in a ponytail, who'd care? But in another way, it was a bad habit that I was forming because I wasn't kissing Troy goodnight.

Eve: Right.

Mattie: I recently said to Troy, "You know, I haven't been kissing you goodnight and I know I'm the one to blame and I'm really sorry. I would like to start kissing you goodnight again." And he agreed to "accept the challenge" and so now we have...

Eve: Child number five? No, you don't have to type that in! I'm teasing, I'm so teasing!

Mattie: I'm going to throw up! So now we make it a ritual to kiss each other goodnight. I usually go to bed and watch a little television but I know the minute I do it's like a drug and I fall asleep. Television in bed is a tranquilizer to me and I'm out in two minutes. So I really try to kiss Troy goodnight before I go to bed. There was one night a couple of weeks ago that I fell asleep and I didn't kiss him goodnight and he said, "You know you didn't kiss me goodnight last night." And I felt really bad and I said, "I am so sorry."

Eve: You should have said, "Let me give you two or three right now to make up for it!"

Mattie: That might seem like a little tiny thing if you're reading this but it's not. Those little things are huge.

Eve: It's being true to your word. You said you were going to do something and you didn't do it. It's so easy to fall back out of habit. You didn't do it on purpose, it just happened, but he wants you to know he noticed.

Mattie: That's one of my challenges I am working on at home. A kiss goodnight! Because it's so easy to leave him working at the computer while the girls are in their rooms doing their homework and the little ones are asleep and I'm so dizzy I want to pass out. And I have to stop and take the time to kiss him and follow through with what I said because it will make ours a more successful marriage. I suppose he could have kissed me on his own knowing that I was so tired. It *is* a two way street.

I think in a marriage couples need to figure out each other's matrix. How can you get along in your relationship? What is that thing that makes our partners tick? We put ourselves to the challenge of being married so now we put ourselves to the challenge of extending outside of ourselves to better understand our partner, like our second skin, more than we've ever known anyone. Well, like our children. We know our child really well. That's a "no-brainer."

Eve: It's unconditional love. They look up at you and they expect it. And you give it freely. And why is it so different with a husband or wife?

Mattie: Because you don't need to talk about finances with your little kids.

Eve: There's a Bible phrase that always used to bug me until I understood it and I bet you'll be able to find it. It's the one about how a wife should serve her husband.

Mattie: "Be submissive to your husband."

Eve: To be submissive. That word would always get me. "What are they talking about, don't they know what century this is, submission?" I finally realized in my forties what it meant to me. I need to give my husband what he wants and needs from me as a wife, friend, lover and companion, by submitting it to him and serving him and making him happy. What is there left for him to do other than turn the mirror around and reflect it right back on to me and give me all those things too. It doesn't have to be "Why should the wife do it, why not the husband?" You both go into a relationship knowing you're going to give and take and give some more. If you give someone what he or she needs, they'll give you what you need.

Doesn't it feel like now that we are in our forties we're finally getting it? When I was in my twenties and thirties it was never about what I wanted in a relationship, it was always about what I didn't want. "Well, I don't want to go through that again! I know I don't want that!" What do I want? Well I think I want this, this, this and this! But then I kept choosing the same type of person and I finally went to counseling. I was asking, "Why do I keep choosing the same type of person that's not right for me?" I finally worked through all those bad choices and now I realize I'm with the right person. But you can't put your marriage on "auto pilot." You have to work through every day. How do you make a marriage work? One day at a time!

Mattie: Yep!

Eve: Did you find it? (Mattie's looking through the Bible)

Mattie: I didn't yet and I know it has to be Matthew.

Eve: It is Matthew. Let's check.

Mattie and I found it through her concordance in the back of her Bible. And she has it underlined.

Mattie: Surprise! It is Colossians 3:12-14 and it reads:

> *Therefore, as God's chosen people, holy and dearly loved, clothe yourselves with compassion, kindness, humility, gentleness and patience. Bear with each other and forgive whatever grievances you may have against one another. Forgive as the Lord forgave you. And over all these virtues put on love, which binds them all together in perfect unity.*

Then I move down to Colossians 3:18 and it reads:

> *Wives, submit to your husbands, as is fitting in the Lord. Husbands, love your wives and do not be harsh with them. Children, obey your parents in everything, for this pleases the Lord. Fathers, do not embitter your children, or they will become discouraged.*

It's all right here basically.

Eve: Let's face it, Mattie, you can't see anymore. You didn't put your glasses on.

Mattie: I actually had to sit up on my knees to read the words because I can't see. So anyway, it says it right there. It's right there in the Bible.

Eve: That's what I was trying to say. You submit and they will love you and they submit and then you love them. It's about the give-and-take. It's that perfect combo that sometimes happens so synergistically you think the other person is woven into you; they're part of your fabric. And then sometimes it's a real challenge, sometimes it's like they're speaking Russian and you're speaking Chinese and neither of you can understand the other. But I guess that's life. God made us the way we are.

Mattie: That can be with anybody not just your husband! You're going to find that conflict with all types of individuals. It's just that when it's the person you have to go to sleep with at night it makes it even harder because you've got to wake up the next morning and face it.

My sister brought this up to me the other day and I remember discussing it with a friend. I was explaining that life is about an attitude and faith and trust. When the junk is going down you can use the metaphor that when it's cloudy or really stormy in your life, you have to know that above all those clouds the sun is shining. God is there waiting for you to clear that up and make some space to let the sun shine through. That faith, hope and trust are there as long as both of you have it in your heart and you can be guided through hard times. This is not only with marriage but also with people in general. It's learning how to maintain your faith and knowing that God's got a handle on this, He really does. This is what I believe.

Eve: And being grateful for what you have and telling people that. Sometimes we take people for granted in our lives. There are many times when I will call my husband and tell him how grateful I am for all that he does for our family and me and I think it goes a long way. I think verbalizing what is obvious and the reason they are doing it is important. Saying "thank you" means I love you.

Mattie: If your husband's at work, why don't you send him an e-mail saying, "I'm thinking about you today and I love you and I hope everything's all right." Be your husband's e-mail partner. I e-mail my husband at work and sometimes we joke with each other and it's a fun way to get out of that everyday communication box. How often do we thank our partners for what they're doing? I don't remember my mom *ever* calling my dad to say those things back in the 60s!

Eve: Well, it was expected. This is what men did and that is what women did. And now the game is completely different and we all have different roles.

Mattie: And nowadays it's hard enough for a man to be a man. A man should be allowed to be a man, a "gentle man"; and a woman should be allowed to be a "gentle woman." And we should respect each other more.

Eve: Love is precious. Shouldn't the people you love be treated as precious? I feel this generation of young girls needs to understand they are worthy of being treated with respect and shouldn't be degraded. A perfect example is popular music videos where girls are barely wearing anything. The danger here is that young girls start believing that it is acceptable to be treated like an object. It creates low self-esteem!

Mattie: Hopefully you readers understand what we are saying. Because most of us were raised with the ideal of a man being a gentleman and a woman being loved for being a woman, it was just so sweet.

Eve: Mattie and I are romantic idealists.

Mattie: We are!

Eve: We'll be the first ones to say it can happen.

Mattie: It can!

Eve: It's like we said before, it's all about attitude.

Mattie: It can happen in your marriage. Just stop trying to take over being the boss of everything. How we handle certain situations in our marriage has everything to do with what we can expect from our marriage. I believe it is possible to love someone till the day you die, to love someone so much that you know them so well, like you never thought you could know someone, someone who is by your side until your dying day. I believe this can happen and I believe we are the generation that has the opportunity to keep marriage together, stay united, and to keep it precious.

And try to avoid, if at all possible, tiny arguments. I love my husband so much and we're both clean freaks. We like to have our areas clean, not perfect, but clean.

Eve: Everything has its place.

Mattie: Everything has its place pretty much. I was calling the carpet cleaner to come to the house every six months because we do have a lot of people in and out of the house all the time and the carpet does tend to get really dirty. And when it's dirty it starts affecting me emotionally. One of the biggest things that used to upset me usually occurred the day after the carpet was cleaned. My husband would walk up the stairs like he normally does with his cup of coffee every morning and I would find a trail of little spots of coffee all the way up the stairs into the bedroom.

Eve: Grrrrrrr!

Mattie: Now I choose to let that get me angry enough to where I made him pay for the carpet cleaning. I thought, "Maybe that will teach him a lesson!" But you know what? I haven't had the carpet cleaned in almost a year.

Eve: Good for you!

Mattie: Is it almost a year?

Eve: She's letting go!

Mattie: And the carpet looks horrible! Up the stairs there are drips.

Eve: Does it bother you?

Mattie: And drips and drips. It bothers me because I see it every day and it's dirty. The stains are getting darker and bigger and Troy made a comment to me a couple of days ago, "You know I'm really proud of you for not making any comments about how dirty the carpet is."

Eve: So he noticed that you noticed, but didn't say anything?

Mattie: I couldn't respond to his comment. I just smirked and looked at the carpet and said, "Maybe the next time we get carpet it's going to be the color of Starbucks House Blend Coffee!"

Eve: Oh that's a classic line. That should be in a movie!

Mattie: I'm just changing the color of the carpet that's all it is. That's my magic formula.

Eve: And that's the quick fix. But you're doing the deeper fix by learning to let it go. Picking your battles, letting it go. It's not *that* big a deal.

Mattie: Yeah.

Eve: It's like the little details you remember and noticed that might have gone wrong on your wedding day. We're always so much more critical of what we felt made our day not so perfect and other people are thinking, "Really? I didn't even remember that."

It's the same in everything we do in life. We are always so much more critical of our own body, of our hair, of how we made dinner and other people respond, "Really? You're stressed out about that because I thought it tasted great!" "Wow, it was really good!" I think the bottom line in a lot of relationships is just putting the effort and the work in.

I had a boyfriend once who spent so-o-o much time playing and practicing and holding his guitar. I got to this point where I said, "You know, if you spent as much time on our relationship as you did on changing those guitar strings and cleaning that guitar and practicing to make sure that note was perfect, we'd probably be married and have a happy life together!" It's about finding the connection or an analogy like, "Do you know how much time you put into A, B, C or D? If you were able to generate some of that energy towards us, wow, what would happen?" And just leave it as a question.

Life is life. You're exhausted some days and you're going to fall asleep and forget to kiss your husband goodnight.

Mattie: With all your clothes on!

Eve: I used to lie every night on Tom's chest. We have a king sized bed and there's a reason because I sleep like an "X." I need the whole thing and he gets the end. I need my space when I sleep. I get so crabby when somebody wakes me up or I haven't gotten a good night's sleep. Oh, I get so crabby! Everyone in my family always says, "Don't wake her up!"

I would lie on Tom's chest and fall asleep and then when it was time to really go to sleep he'd start snoring and I would move over. Well, he started becoming allergic to my hairspray and so I would be lying on him for about twenty seconds and then he would start sneezing or coughing. So I would move away and say goodnight. Now we don't do that anymore and I miss it!

You mentioned earlier that you were going to kiss Troy every night. Lying on Tom's chest was something we did and it was ours and now we don't do it and I really miss it! I need to either wash my hair before I go to bed or I need to brush it through or I need to change my hairspray. I really want to start doing that again with Tom for that closeness. It doesn't always have to be about sex, it can just be about holding and that intimate feeling of "I think you're precious."

Mattie: Yes, it's that comfort, reassurance and love that ties it all in. Troy runs at a temperature of about one hundred and eighty degrees Fahrenheit and I'm about thirty-five degrees below zero. I am so freezing cold at night and he's so hot.

Eve: He's a furnace.

Mattie: I sleep with so many blankets, as many as I can and he starts sweating so we can't cuddle unfortunately (that much) unless there are no sheets on the bed.

Eve: It's that give and take and you know that about each other so you have to make it up in other places.

Mattie: Exactly.

Eve: So therefore he buys you coats and scarves for Christmas! "Oh look, it's thirty pairs of socks, the really thick ones. I love you, honey!"

Mattie: It's a temperature thing with us. But once he gets too hot and he can't stand it anymore, we'll move apart and then through the night I'll feel his foot extend to touch my foot and I'll think, "Ah, he's touching my foot!" And then I'll get my foot and try to touch his foot and then I'm happy. There's at least a toe contact or a leg or something like that. That kind of stuff speaks volumes to me because with love it's just so nice to have that reassurance with your partner.

Eve: There's that old cliché, "Actions speak louder than words." Don't give lip service, although kissing is good! Prove it, show it, and don't be afraid. Especially in this world today there are so many things to keep us apart. Take computers, for example. They're actually designed to bring us together, but most times you work on your own.

If you love to read, reading is a solitary activity. You can't read with someone else unless they're reading to you. But there's no reason why you couldn't sit on the couch together and cuddle while reading separately. Just finding those ways, those little things that keep tilling the soil and rejuvenating your relationship.

I have to say this drink says it all right here Mattie. (Eve holds up a bottle of Kombucha.) Can you read it?

Mattie: Rejuvenate, restore, revitalize, replenish, and regenerate your marriage.

Eve: The five R's! We give you the five R's. I've been drinking this Synergy Kombucha drink and those words are on there and I've been listening to you talk and thinking, "Oh my gosh, its all right here! It's being marketed at Whole Foods!"

Mattie: Folks, it's being marketed on organic drinks at health food stores. You can market it yourself at home. Eve and I are basically saying we are in full support of old-fashioned marriage.

Eve: Allowing people to be who they are, that's key. You can't get mad at someone for being who they are. Don't try to change them, learn to love that crazy little thing that drives you nuts. Learn to giggle about it, learn to find a way to smooth over those rough edges and make things work. I have to read this quote because it just cracks me up. It's Socrates: "My advice to you is to get married. If you find a good wife you'll be happy, if not you'll become a philosopher." And Mattie and I are *not* trying to become philosophers.

We got "that second chance" and we are trying so hard to make it work, maybe because our first marriages didn't work. We want to make it right. We are willing to work harder the second time.

Mattie: So make your marriages successful! Remember, marriage is "one day at a time."

7

HOPES AND DREAMS

Eve: Been an interesting morning hasn't it, Mattie?

Mattie: Yes, it has, and the saga continues with the lump in my right breast. The surgeon called me this morning and said it needs to come out right away and he does not want me to wait. Eve and I write this chapter with anticipation of hearing from two different surgeons and their availability.

Eve: So we're shopping around.

Mattie: For lump removers!

Eve: Got a lump? We can remove it!

We're both disappointed. Yesterday after Mattie's appointment I told her I was disappointed because I was so sure the doctor was going to say, "Ah, that's nothing! Oh and you want it out, okay we'll take it out!" But he was a bit more conservative with his answers, which is scary because they see this kind of thing all the time. And you're left wondering, "What the heck is this?" But of course he doesn't know what it is. Nobody knows what it is until he takes it out! Mattie was already going to ask to have it removed because like my mom says, "It didn't come with the set!" At least the doctor got a giggle out of that.

We'll go on from there. It is ironic that we're sitting here talking about hopes and dreams with this cloud of "unknowing" which can only be fear. And that's what fear is, it's the unknown. Yet we just aren't going to go there. We won't go there!

Mattie: Anything is possible. We're experiencing a lot of uneasiness right now over a personal matter, yet I made the choice to get together today because that's all I have—hope.

I also have the faith to know that everything is going to work out just the way God wants it to. And I have the support of my best friend in the world with whom I'm writing this book and love very much. We've been on the phone with our friends and family, the word is out and the prayer circle is going. I am hopeful and I am very blessed to have that.

Eve: They're praying in Nashville, they're praying in Arizona, they're praying in San Diego, California. I've got them praying in Florida.

Mattie: They're praying everywhere. I'm blessed, I really am! It's an example to all that if you truly believe in your heart and desire the goodness in your life to happen, it really can. Through prayer with friends, and through surrendering it, whatever miracle it is you need to have happen will happen. There's hope all around you. I'm not saying this is going to turn out the way I have envisioned it. I could end up with cancer. But I am satisfied knowing that if that's the outcome, I am confident God has used me for a reason and I accept the challenge and the responsibility. Because that's all I have and prayer is good, prayer pulls people together.

Eve: Prayer is the *action* of hope.

Mattie: Yep.

Eve: Don't you think?

Mattie: Yes it is!

Eve: Faith and hope. You pray hoping God hears you, but faith tells you He does, you know He does.

Mattie: He absolutely does.

Eve: We've got to be looking inward, particularly because we're getting older and things are breaking down and slowing down, especially in our joints. I've got a shoulder problem that has been bothering me for about six months and darn it if it isn't going to turn into some kind of arthritis. I'm trying to deal with it now while it's treatable and not ignore it.

You have to start taking care of yourself, mentally and physically and spiritually too. These are the most important things in our lives. There are so many factors out there that are going to affect how you feel. Without hope, without the belief that "I'm going to be okay, I'm hopeful for the future, I'm dreaming big, I'm looking ahead!" you'll become lost. It's all there for you as long as you continue to look inward and develop spiritually and keep growing as a wonderful human being.

Mattie: A wonderful whole person. I'd like to share a quote from my sister Margie, who in my life has been my mentor. I have always gone to her for prayer and guidance and I thank God I've had her since my mother passed away over twenty years ago. It's so great to have someone in your family you can get support from. I was talking to her about this chapter and she said, "I want you to share with everyone the affirmation I say every day, every morning, and that is simply: "I love the life that I have!" She affirms this when she's stressed, when things are going great or when things are going not so great. She says this first thing in the morning and the last thing at night. It's a positive, simple, powerful phrase. Even in the middle of your darkest hour simply saying, "I love the life that I have!" bends God's ear because He gave you the life you have. And you're affirming that this journey on earth is one that is totally meant to be, one that is guided by God. Our life might not go the way we hope, but it's important to love our life along the way, through our journey, through good times and hard times and challenging times.

Eve: This goes along with Frederick Buechner's "All moments are key moments!" I love my life! All moments are key moments. Mattie is teaching me how to be less impatient in traffic, how to be grateful for the moment and to say a prayer, "Thank you for getting me into this traffic and keeping me safe." You just never know, around the corner may have been an accident I would have been involved in. There's a reason I needed to be right here because maybe I'm going to meet somebody when I get out of my car at my destination that I needed to say something to who needed to hear it.

I like looking at it this way. It's a very enlightening feeling, it causes you to realize this has all been planned and you're just the actor on stage; you're going through all these things that have already been planned out for you.

Mattie: "I love my life!" "All moments are key moments!" Say that every day.

You can look at your life on a broad scale and obtain a concept of what you want to accomplish. You can set out a planned itinerary, but as you move through life, keeping the faith tells you this course you've plotted has already been mapped out. I'm not saying your wants and hopes are for naught because you have to have your wishes and dreams to get you through. And you can only hope and pray that on a grander scale the way you see your life through your golden years is the same plan God has for you. Somehow along the journey I think you can't help but feel, "I have to change my plan and go this way." Don't be discouraged about the shifts because this really is all being guided for you as long as you hang on to your faith.

Eve: And know your truth. You have to do things that are within your grasp. Like you said, the path is laid out for us and we're just following it. Wherever it leads us is where it is supposed to lead us and there's always a lesson to learn that's going to get us closer to our dream or live our dream as it morphs into something else!

When a person knows their truth they can face their reality. "I guess I can't be a professional basketball player, but loving the sport as much as I do, I'm going to find a way to get myself involved with the sport as a career." Your dream does a metamorphosis and you still have the giddiness of "I'm doing what I love to do!" A quote from Allan K. Chalmers reads: "The grand essentials of happiness are something to do, something to love and something to hope for."

Mattie: Wow!

Eve: Yeah! That's a good one. "Something to do, something to love and something to hope for." And there it is—the secret of life. I guess we're done. The book's finished!

Mattie: Think back when you were ten, twenty and thirty. We had these dreams set out for our lives. When I was eight, I wanted to be a princess, a queen.

Eve: O-o-oh very nice.

Mattie: And my dreams changed a lot because the reality of knowing I wasn't anywhere around royalty and the fact that I lived in Yuma, Arizona, made it impossible to live out *that* dream. I used to use...what are those things you use for your bathroom that you put around your toilet? Is it a toilet rug? I used a toilet rug as my cape.

Eve: Very chic!

Mattie: I realized, as time went on, that I was never going to be the queen of any country and I was okay with that. Fortunately, childhood thoughts mature and gel and we realize, "Okay the reality of the whole thing is this isn't going to happen." But sometimes I *feel* like a queen when I do things for myself like take time to get a pedicure and a manicure. When I think about what I wanted back in my childhood, I really didn't want to be a queen of anything. I had lots of hopes and dreams as a child and they made me happy, they made me feel special. I would think, "What if this really happened? I could wear a huge crown, get a better toilet seat rug for my cape and be really cool!" Then you get into your high school years and your dreams become about your career.

Eve: What am I going to be when I grow up?

Mattie: And everyone is asking you that same question. And there's a lot of pressure. "Well I think I'm going to be an attorney." You don't know! You may think you have an idea and many people follow through with those ideas, but there's usually something else nagging at you. Maybe you're an attorney by profession and an artist at heart. Maybe you aspire to be an artist one day after you're done being an attorney. You secretly wish for the day you can set up your easel by the ocean and paint a nice wave. Or play in a band or whatever. Those kinds of dreams and hopes cheer us up and make us happy, give us hope. They change our outlook about how we view life when we're in the thick of dealing with life.

Eve: We were talking on the phone yesterday about today's chapter and we both expressed how we came from families and friends who encouraged us to dream and to dream big. We were both told, "You can be whatever you want to be and you can do whatever you set your mind to doing." And that gives you license to dream outside the box and dream "unrealistic" dreams and actually make some of them come true because you don't know any better. When you're young people tell you things you accept as truth. You don't realize people might be pacifying you or they might be humoring you; you just accept that's what it is.

When I was quite young we were having a family concert and my grandmother said, "Eve's got a great voice!" I was seven or eight and I thought, "Wow, I can do something!" And here I am all these years later singing for a career. She whispered it to my dad, she leaned over to him and I just happened to hear it. Or did I just happen to hear it? Was God there saying, "This is where you need to go, Eve!"

You were saying earlier how you wanted to be a princess when you were younger. When I was younger I wanted to get married and have sixteen kids! Yeah. Dreaming big! And then I found out how you had kids and I didn't want any! Isn't that funny? And then being raised Catholic I thought I wanted to be a nun. Did you ever want to be a nun?

Mattie: You know, I thought about it for at least five minutes.

Eve: It doesn't last long once you realize you can't be with boys?

Mattie: Never mind!

Eve: Too much of a sacrifice! Ha!

Mattie: So what dream did you have that you can share with us? One you remember thinking about, dreaming about, and it finally happened, little or big or in-between.

Eve: When I was young, I would actually pray about this to God. I would have these business sessions with God and barter back and forth. I would say, "If you do this, I'll do this!" And my dream was to be famous. I wanted to be famous, that's all it was, and it's such a childish immature dream. But when you're younger, you don't realize what any of that means; you just know you want to be noticed.

I was one of eight kids and you really had to be the squeaky wheel to be noticed. It's not a surprise then that it's the path I went down. I clearly remember praying about it and asking God, "Dear God, please, if you let me be famous, I promise I'll help needy children. I'll start orphanages and I'll try to make the world a better place." You know all those big huge dreams. When you're young they are just words that come out of your mouth and the reality of what they mean doesn't come into play until you're older and you start doing fundraising for example. You realize, "Boy, this is hard work!" That's why there are people who have a calling for this, who specialize in fundraising and who are very good at what they do and God bless them.

As I got older I realized it was a very selfish, self-fulfilling dream. Wanting to be famous just really didn't mean anything. It just meant I wanted to be rich and recognized, which is so shallow. Then life goes on and I think, "Well, I want to sing, so I'm going to sing." So I moved to L.A. to pursue my big dream. When you embark on a path and really focus on it you say to yourself, "This is what I've got to do to make this dream come true." To become a doctor you have to complete four years of college, then four years of medical school and then an internship and residency before you can become an M.D. There is no set path for becoming a successful singer. You just start walking down the road hoping you're going the right way and maybe finding yourself in the process.

Mattie: You have been successful in your own right singing and performing, traveling and touring and fundraising and helping others. And along the way God was saying, "Okay Eve, this *is* your hope, these *are* your dreams and this *is* how I'm going to help mold you to be an even better person than you think you could ever possibly be." You can hope for something but that doesn't mean you're going to get it exactly the way you asked for it. You need to look more deeply at your request and rely on your faith because realistically, God has His hands on your life. You are setting a pace and following the steps.

Eve: God uses us in mysterious ways. When we're younger

we have the energy to match those big huge crazy off-the-wall dreams. As we start getting older hopefully we get wiser. We've come through our turbulent twenties and the "I think I'm pulling it together" thirties and now in our *Forty Schmorties* we're saying, "Okay, I'm on this path, I'm still dreaming and hoping and God's showing me every day how I need to look deeper, how I need to *see* what's most important is invisible." It's the fine print; it's what's inside that counts. And it's as if God's holding your hand and leading you back into yourself. "Look here!" You're reaching out saying, "What about my dreams and my hopes?" And He's taking your hand and He's putting it back onto your heart and saying, "They're all right here." You've got the ability and you can do all those things, but you've got to work on the inside first, you have to be the person you are supposed to be. It just hit me when you were talking. I wouldn't be the person I am today if I hadn't gone down all those roads, side streets and back alleys that weren't on the path I wanted to take. But God was leading me to get here. I would have missed my husband, Tom! Had I become famous when I was in my twenties and a has-been by twenty-three and a druggie at twenty-five, look at all the people I would have missed knowing in my life. I would have missed my baby girl, Sarah. It's all those "What ifs?" I look back and think to myself, "Wow, there's a reason I'm here!" There's a reason I'm sitting in Mattie's kitchen writing this book with her. We would never have gotten to this point.

This journey has been incredible for us. It has given us insight into each other and insight into so many aspects of life; it has filled us up. I might not have been able to be here so strongly for Mattie during this cancer scare, but because I went through it with my sister Gay, I'm here to help any way that I can. As I'm sitting here talking with Mattie I realize how many people I know who have breast cancer. And part of me is thinking, "If this scare is cancer, we've got it licked, we know exactly what we're going to do. And if it's not, then were going to say some prayers of rejoicing and gratitude. We'll transform all this energy and put it elsewhere and use it! There's a reason all this is happening. God is going to show us our path. Maybe this will lead to our *Forty Schmorty* Breast

Cancer Fundraiser Rock-a-Thon. Why not?

Mattie: Our intention was to help others, but as we go along writing, it is really helping us! My cancer scare is an unexpected interruption on my list of "Hopes and Dreams." Obviously, this wasn't on my list, it just happened. I think I can speak for both of us when I say our faith has grown even stronger and it has been a life changing experience. We're working on ways to have a better life, a stronger marriage, more quality time with family and how to become a better friend.

Eve: I think I called you on the phone the other day to read this to you. It's a quote from Dana Reeve who recently passed away from lung cancer. She was not a smoker and her husband, Christopher Reeve, passed from complications from a spinal chord injury. She is quoted as saying: "Gravity will make you fall, and it will keep you on the planet. It's how we respond to the tragedies in our lives that give them meaning." You can also carry this over to your hopes and your dreams. It's how you respond to them that give them meaning. It's what you do right now with this cancer scare that's going to give it meaning. And you're the kind of person, Mattie, that's going to find the positive. If you focus on the negative it will make you even sicker. But if you focus on the positive, you can actually prevent yourself from being sick.

Mattie: I totally believe that!

Eve: You've got a book that I love written by Louise L. Hay, *Heal Your Body*.

Mattie: Yes, it's a wonderful and very interesting book containing lists of ailments with reasons why you have that ailment – all due to poor thinking. The best part is the little prayer the author includes to help you change your way of thinking. I agree with you when you speak about attitude and the challenges we face in life. Perhaps something we hoped for didn't come to pass. What do you do? Well, you have to believe there was a reason for it not happening just like there is a reason for everything that happens in this world, sometimes unexplainable. This is all a big test of our faith. We have so much ahead of us in our lives and as women in our forties we have to start looking to the positive. I truly love the life I have. Are you in gratitude when you wake up in the morning? What kind of attitude do you have when you wake up? Believe me, there have been many mornings I have awakened thinking that my day would go one way and it goes completely in the opposite direction. And it's okay!

Eve: This whole book got started on our hopes and dreams. We were asking, "Is this where we thought we would be in our forties? Is this where we thought we were going to end up?" And out of that conversation new hopes and dreams sprouted. Now here we are writing a book together about our lives and what we see as our challenges, and how we've worked through them up to this point. There's nothing set in stone declaring that the path you have chosen is not the right path. I remember asking my friend Kim, "Didn't you have bigger dreams for your musical career? Didn't you think you would be selling millions of records?" And she answered, "Just because we didn't choose the path that U2 or Madonna or Sting chose doesn't make our path any less valid or any less important." This to me was a very nice way of turning the prism of thought to see it in a different, positive light.

So what are you saying about all these gifts God has given you? "It's not good enough God because this was not the dream I had. My dream was to sell a million albums and all you've given me is this?" No! You are exactly where you are supposed to be. I wouldn't be here right now in your kitchen (I had only seen Mattie's house a couple of times this year before we started writing). I don't even know if you've been to my apartment? Everything happens the way it needs to happen. The dreams and hopes you have are tools. It's what you do with them, how you look at them and how you mold them.

My friend Patty, a musician, has been on this same path and believe me, the life of a musician is not the easiest life. There's a lot of rejection and struggle that leaves you thinking, "Am I good enough?" She told me she threw out to the universe her thoughts of becoming an attorney. She loves the law; her dad is a State Supreme Court Justice, but she wanted to follow her love of music and the creative side of her brain instead. So she took the law school entrance exam thinking, "Well, if I pass the test, then that's a sign." When she didn't hear back from the law school she decided to follow a lifelong dream of performing in England figuring she probably wasn't meant to be an attorney. Three months after returning from her tour she receives a letter of acceptance from the law school! So now here she is, in her late thirties starting a completely new path, going back to school to be a lawyer. And I said to her what I said to Mattie when we started writing this book, "Wouldn't it be ironic if by completely changing our point of view and focusing on something else, our initial dreams happen to come true along the way?" And it certainly has become evident with this book that coming from our hearts, trying to be really truthful and honest, and trying to believe and dream together, we have bonded tighter than we ever could have imagined. Whether this book comes in hardback, paperback, or ends up covering our kids' textbooks next year, it doesn't matter. We've accomplished so much by dreaming it and living it and hoping it. Maybe that's what it is; maybe hopes and dreams are an everyday living thing.

Mattie: Yes, they truly are!

Eve: Is that an epiphany? I'll be back in a few minutes, Mattie.

Mattie: Okay, you go away for a while, Eve. I'll move along by sharing a little story about dreams and wishes. I've been performing with the same band for almost twenty years called The Heroes. We're based in San Diego and play for many corporate events and private parties all around the world.

Eve: Weddings, bar mitzvahs.

Mattie: Every once in awhile we'd play wedding receptions at the Four Seasons Aviara Resort in Carlsbad, California. It is such a beautiful resort. Every one of these weddings was amazing, filled with beautiful flowers, wonderful food, great people and happiness everywhere. It was like being in a modern day fairytale, standing up on stage and singing with the reception room gracefully perfumed with the scent of tuberose and stargazers—so intoxicating! I always loved watching the newlywed couple dance in each other's arms as I sang their special song for the first dance. I would think to myself how fantastic it would be for me to marry at the Four Seasons Aviara and be that bride on the dance floor with a very handsome husband and happy people all around us. This was a huge dream of mine. Every time we would play a wedding reception at the Four Seasons I was thinking how wonderful it would be to have my own wedding there. Then I met Troy. We fell in love. He proposed and it was my chance to set up the wedding. So of course, the first place I thought of was the Four Seasons Aviara. And I finally get to this point and suddenly it seems impossible because of the cost.

Eve: "Did we mention the cost?"

Mattie: But we met anyway with the special events coordinator and go over all the details of a possible wedding for us. And with the help of a few trade-offs and discounts on some items we were able to make our special day at the Four Seasons a reality!

So there we were on our wedding day exchanging vows at the Four Seasons Palm Garden (a beautiful outdoor garden) with brilliant palm trees covered with red bougainvilleas at the base, the clear blue sky, heavenly music and happy people. Everything about the day was my dream come true. I was finally that girl on the dance floor with her gorgeous husband, holding him in her arms and looking lovingly into his eyes.

Eve: Two dreams happened to you that day. You got to have your wedding in the perfect place and you got to be the queen!

Mattie: I got to be the queen!

Eve: Dressed up in a beautiful gown.

Mattie: I even had a little tiny crown on my head. I did, it's true! We have to take the time to stop and recognize that what we've hoped for and what we've dreamed about, although perhaps not in exactly the form we envisioned (wanting to be a queen for example) has actually manifested. I am actually the queen of my domain here!

Eve: The star of the show here, baby!

Mattie: Right here in my house I make sure that my countrymen are all getting along and living a peaceful life in my mini-country with a roof. So my dream when I was eight years old did come true!

My sister Margie once told me that making a list of your wishes and desires could assist realizing your dreams. Back when I thought I was ready to find the perfect man in my life Margie said to me, "Make a list! Get a piece of paper and make a list!"

Eve: Of what kind of man you wanted?

Mattie: Yes. I made a list of things I wanted him to look like, what qualities he would need to have, how tall he would be, and the list went on meticulously describing my wishes. I remember starting the list then I decided to make it up in my head. When I gathered up all the qualities of the man I desired he eventually came into my life! When I was least expecting him. And of course, I thought he liked you!

Eve: You did! In fact, I remember the day you met and I said, "Oh Mattie, you are so blind, he is interested in you. He doesn't want anything to do with me!" Well, you couldn't believe it. And I knew right away he only had eyes for Mattie!

Mattie: That's when Eve and I were singing together in the band.

Eve: A dream! Carl Sandburg said "Nothing happens unless first a dream!" Did you ever dream of Prince Charming riding up on his white horse to save you?

Mattie: Oh yes!

Eve: I've had that dream many times. I was always looking for Prince Charming and I found him and you found him too! He came along on his white horse and he saved you, but he also enriched and fulfilled your life. So your dream is multi-faceted. That's the exciting aspect of our dreams because we never know how many people in our life they're going to affect. You know your daughters are two specific people whom it affected the most. Adding Troy has affected their lives and now you have two more children and their lives are all connected. You're all related now through the kids and it's amazing how the picture keeps getting bigger and bigger through all the people you touch with one dream.

Mattie: This experience actually completed me. Troy had me at "Hello!" I highly recommend making a list of all your hopes and desires.

Eve: Here's a wonderful dream quote: "To accomplish great things we must not only act but also dream, not only plan but also believe." Make your list, plan it out, believe it's going to come true, then act on it. And keep dreaming!

I remember when I became pregnant with Sarah it was a dream come true. I always wanted to be a mom. I remember someone telling me that having a baby was the end of my music career and that my dream was over because now I had a child. And I thought to myself, "Really?" Wow, I always looked at it a different way. I felt having a child would make me want my dreams to come true even more because now I have somebody to share it with, a gift to go along with my dream.

My parents told me I could do and be whatever I wanted and now I pass that on to my child as you have passed this philosophy on to your children.

Mattie: I grew up with a mother who told me things like, "Mattie, don't ever worry about money, it's only money."

Eve: That's why you and I don't have money! Because we don't worry about it! We always have enough though, don't we?

Mattie: We do always have enough, but I actually worry about it too much. It's chronic for me and I need to get over that. I'm always hearing Mom's words in my head. There are times when I ease up on the worry; something always comes through for me.

When I was born I was told (my sisters are ten and twelve years older than me) that my mom had specifically said, "I want this child to be a free spirit. I want her to be able to accomplish whatever she feels she can. I want her to understand the sky is the limit." I am very thankful for my mom's attitude because it shaped me into the person I am today. It enabled me to dream dreams that have allowed me to help all the people I love. And I've tried to pass this on to my children.

My oldest daughter is finishing her senior year in high school. We're looking at colleges and getting ready to fill out applications and anticipating visiting some schools. Will she go back east or stay in California? Well, she came to me the other day and said, "Mom, I've been thinking about majoring in theater and literature and I have an opportunity to audition for Yale." I looked at her calmly and said, "What a great idea. Go for it!" Yet inside, in my heart I was thinking, "Oh my God, I never as a senior in high school ever dreamed...I don't even think I knew about Yale!" When I graduated from Yuma High School (home of the mascot The Yuma Criminals) it was either Arizona State University or the University of Arizona. "It's an in-state college.

Those are your choices, so pick one!" said Dad. And that was it. I chose the University of Arizona and went for two weeks.

So I found myself encouraging my girls and saying, "Listen, the sky is the limit. Go out and try for whatever college you want even if it seems like the impossible dream and even if you have to take your S.A.T. test for a third time. Do it, just go for it. What have you got to lose?" And it comes back to me with Gia thinking about auditioning at Yale!

Eve: Just ask. All they can say is "No." There will be other options and that's the beautiful thing about dreams. They can always morph into something else. George Bernard Shaw wrote: "You see things and you say why? But I dream things that never were and I say why not?" That's a very famous quote we've all heard. We really don't have anything to lose. You just have to be yourself, find your bull's-eye and go for it. Focus on what you want and you'll get there, whatever that path is, you'll get there.

Mattie: If there's something you truly desire and really want and you know you can get it if you ask, then ask for it! Asking is free! When you wake up in the morning tell yourself, "I love my life, every moment counts and asking is free." If I really need something I can always ask. Nobody is going to charge me for a question, unless of course, it's an attorney.

Eve: And listen for your answer because you are being answered every day. God's answering you every day and He's saying, "I love you no matter what. I'll always be there for you no matter what." We've all heard about people who have become successful on their chosen path and they say it's the journey of getting to success that's meant much more than the actual success itself.

I've been back and forth to Nashville for many years now and as you know Nashville represents the music capital of the world. Los Angeles and New York have the same feel, when you go there you can smell the success (and the competition). I haven't had what one would call "physical success" like getting a huge recording deal, but I've had wonderful success at songwriting and with musical friendships. And I had this little chip on my shoulder whenever I'd go back to Nashville, which was completely knocked off one day by a bellman at a hotel. He asked, "You're a singer?" I said, "Yeah, I'm a singer." And then he said to me, "Well, enjoy the journey because it doesn't matter how successful you become, it's a path you're on. Enjoy it while you're on it!" This was like God whispering to me saying, "Hey, every day you wake up is a good day." I often recall that day and think, "Okay God I hear you." I believe God used him to talk directly to me. I think if I would have looked deep into his eyes I would have seen God right there nodding, "Yes, it was Me."

Mattie: T.S. Eliot is attributed with saying, "The journey, not the arrival matters." Look at this, it says it right here on my coffee mug!

Eve: Every time we get together to have these conversations, we learn more about each other and discover that we're on the right path. I get so excited! There's much excitement here people! I think I'm actually going to feel depressed when we're finished with the book.

Mattie: I'm a better friend because of this experience. Everyone has a fascinating story. I know I've said this many, many times to so many people and finally, one day I heard myself and I said, "I need to be the one to write a book!" I'm telling everyone else and nobody is really acting upon it, so I might as well go ahead and do it...with Eve.

Eve: I know! This was not one of my dreams.

Mattie: This wasn't on my list, but I consider it a wonderful interception in our lives.

Eve: Hopefully this will encourage others to realize their own personal story is not over. They can change their dreams and do other things. Here are two moms who have children, carpools, laundry, gigs, dreams and hopes that got together and wrote a book. So where does that leave you in your life? Maybe you can do that one thing you've always wanted to do. I don't know, mountain climb or start a clinic in a poor neighborhood or volunteer time, whatever that dream is. Hopefully you'll realize you *can* have it all. You can have a family, have a career, and have your dreams and hopes fulfilled. The key is to remember that the "all" is constantly evolving. Some days you're going to be totally immersed in family and sometimes you're going to be totally immersed in your career. There's no human being out there who can do one hundred percent of ten things in one day. So you figure out where you're going to put your energies and you get through it. You know there's always tomorrow and you are going to continually grow. It's simply a matter of changing your way of thinking and going for it.

I'm very happy with the quotes I've found on dreams. Here's one from Gloria Steinem, a famous publisher and founder of *Ms.* magazine: "Without leaps of imagination or dreaming we lose the excitement of possibilities. Dreaming, after all, is a form of planning." At the end of this chapter we are going to leave two blank pages, one labeled "Dreams" and the other labeled "Hopes" to give you a chance to write down every single dream and hope you have for yourself. If you don't do it anywhere else, we encourage you to do it here in this book and share it with a friend. There's strength in numbers.

Mattie: Share it with a friend and get together with your friend once a week. Make a commitment to becoming a better friend to your friend. What does it take? Give yourself the gift of time it doesn't cost a thing.

Eve: Then there's the famous speech from Martin Luther King, Jr., "I Have a Dream…" What a truly powerful, inspiring and wonderful dream! Although he died before the dream came true he set that dream in motion and it *did* come true.

I just read a biography on Queen Elizabeth the First and her life back in the 1500s. She had a great dream for her country, England. She hoped that during her reign as England's first queen it would become one of the strongest nations in the world. She set the plan in motion five hundred years ago and here we are in the year 2007 and England is stronger than ever. Dreams have lives and energy. That energy goes somewhere just like Albert Einstein said, "E=mc2." Energy equals matter squared which means energy never goes away. So if dreams are possibilities and hope is energy, it's an act and we're doing it!

And then there are the lyrics from John Lennon's song "Imagine." "Imagine all the people, living life in peace. You may say that I'm a dreamer, but I'm not the only one. I hope someday you will join us and the world will live as one." Such a great song! A dream set in motion through song. It *can* happen.

Mattie: I'd like to reiterate the importance of affirming your hopes and dreams and wishes for life by saying every day: "I love the life I have! Every moment in my life is a key moment." And always remember to ask for what you want because asking is free and God does hear you.

Eve: Dream big! The bigger the dream the more chances of coming close to it. There's another saying I love: "Reach for the moon. If you fall short you still have the stars!" Anything is possible. Like you said, Mattie, "Asking is free." Ask for help with making your dreams come true.

Hopefully, by now we won't be afraid to ask for help. "I *do* want to be a painter!" "I *do* want to start a dance studio!" "I *do* want to build a bowling alley!" Maybe you're a great cook and you want to start baking pies. It can be anything, just ask for help. Ask your friends. "Success is when opportunity and preparedness meet."

Here's a perfect quote to close this chapter by Mark Twain:

> *Twenty years from now you will be more disappointed by the things you didn't do than by the things you did do, so throw off the battle lines, sail away from the safe harbor, catch the trade winds in your sails, explore, dream, and discover!*

HOPES

DREAMS

HEALTH, BEAUTY
AND FITNESS

Eve: I thought it would be perfect to start off with a health update from Mattie because Friday she had surgery.

Mattie: Well they performed what was called a wide excision of the right breast mass, a surgery about fifty minutes long. I was in, I was out, and I came home and slept the rest of the day. I felt a little woozy for the next couple of days. I still don't really know the outcome. I can only hope I'm cancer free because I haven't heard from the doctor. I go in tomorrow to find out the results of the biopsy and the pathology report.

Eve: It's benign, we know it is.

Mattie: In the meantime, there's nothing like not knowing for sure. I can only speculate that things are fine and I look forward to moving on with my everyday normal activities without having that nagging thought in my head about where my health stands.

Eve: I'm very hopeful because when my sister had her lump removed, the minute she woke up from surgery the doctor told her she had cancer. Surgeons can usually tell by looking at it whether they think it's cancer. They can have the pathology report done then and there and know before you're out of anesthesia. So since they didn't tell you that, and since the doctor didn't even stick around to talk to you afterwards, I have a really good feeling he thinks this was a routine mass needing to come out. My mom told me to tell Mattie: "Take it out! We don't want it in there to give it a chance to grow into something ugly."

Mattie: That's right! "If it didn't come with the set..." I've spoken to a few people about my situation and they each felt I did exactly what I needed to do. I found it on Mother's Day and I moved quickly. I had a doctor examine it and he immediately gave me the name of a surgeon to consult. The surgeon didn't want to waste any time testing the lump and I was glad for that. It's been almost a month since I found the mass and now it's out of me and I'm waiting for the results. I've prayed so much harder. I have a circle of friends I don't normally talk about faith and prayers with, but now I'm reaching out to them and asking, "Can you please hold a good thought for me and say a prayer for me?" I've asked them to pray that everything is going to be okay and taken care of. I think this whole procedure wasn't just about me, but also about the circle of friends needing to come together to find their faith for a moment.

Eve: I think it also shows how it ties into wellness, because wellness is a state of mind. Having a strong faith and believing everything is in God's hands and that you're going to be okay can really change how your body reacts to things. I'm a strong believer that having a positive outlook can make a difference in how things turn out. Even if it's the worse case scenario, having a positive outlook is going to make everything okay in the end. The waiting is the hardest part. Did your sister Margie go through this a couple of times?

Mattie: Kay.

Eve: Oh, Kay, I'm sorry, your other sister. Your sister Kay has had a couple of lumps removed and they were benign. So that should give you a sense of well being. Does breast cancer run in your family?

Mattie: My mom had it.

Eve: Oh, your mom had it?

Mattie: And my aunt had it.

Eve: I thought your mom had...

Mattie: And it came back as bone cancer.

Eve: AHHHHHH!! Aye, yi, yi. I see. So there's a scare here. Red flag! And your sister Kay had this happen a couple of times.

Mattie: Yeah.

Eve: And they were all benign.

Mattie: Right.

Eve: This is not going to be cancer.

Mattie: Right.

Eve: This is not. I won't allow this to happen!

Mattie: We'll continue to find new exercises, new diets, new health drinks and new ways of sustaining a healthier life. I truly believe that the foundation of a healthy life begins with the wellness of mind, body and spirit.

So where do we start? What things do we tap on? We started off with my situation involving the breast mass and surgery. And you know I'm sitting here waiting to hear the results. How can I move on from this? Well, life goes on. And I really have to put all my trust in God and know He is in control. He put me here for a reason, with this particular circumstance, and I know, regardless, I'll get through it and have a conclusion to it and move on, at whatever degree. I'm willing to accept it and in the meantime, the sun will rise and the sun will set.

Eve: Well, I think its no surprise or "CinciGod" this happened right now in your life. You are at a place in your life where you're able to deal with it differently than when you were in your twenties. In our twenties we think, "Ah, heck, I'm gonna live forever." You don't take good care of yourself, because your body is still...well, there are no children (chuckle).

Mattie: Everything is tight!

Eve: Everything is tight, your stomach is flat, and you remember you have muscles under there. And then in your thirties you're more focused on the kids and the babies and everything else in your life. And now you are in your forties and you're realizing how important it is to stay on top of your health and to stay in a place of at least status quo. I think that's the most important thing I've learned in my forties. "Do the work now!" You're going to find out it's very hard to get yourself back into shape in your forties. You've got to be diligent. And now we have some financial stability so we can spend money on a personal trainer, or join a gym. Maybe we have a little more time on our hands than we used to or maybe we don't because of our busy schedules. But because it's so much more important now, I think we must find the time. I know some people who get up at 4:00 a.m. so they can be at the gym by 5:00 a.m., be done with their workout by 6:00 a.m., shower, get back home, make the kids' lunches, and get the kids to school. And I'm thinking to myself, "Are you insane?" But that's what they have to do to make it work.

Mattie, I don't think it's a coincidence this health issue happened now. You're in your forties and it happens at a time when we are writing about our life experiences. It could actually be, "Hey look! This isn't just a reality check, this *is* reality!" This is actually happening now along with all the things we've overcome up to this point in our lives. I can only imagine what you have gone through and what my sister went through, when you hear that dreaded word "cancer." Your heart starts pounding and the black hole opens up and everything comes to a screeching halt. But I swear to you, I have felt those things by virtue of my connectivity with you. I woke up from a nap thinking, "Oh my gosh, no!" And then realizing, "Oh, it's not me, it's Mattie!" And then I think, "Oh God, it's Mattie! How can I help?" I don't know what's worse. Is it the helplessness of being in the situation or the helplessness of being outside the situation? Either way, what can I do to make a difference?

Mattie: Well you certainly made a difference! I don't know what I would have done without you. You, Eve, have totally inspired me with the strength of our friendship, God-given friendship. I have found strength in the love of a friendship for a fellow sister. I found the courage to surrender and cry. It felt good to cry. Instead of feeling like, you know, sometimes when you cry in front of a guy, you feel, "Man, I shouldn't have done that!" I think one of the worst things I can do is cry in front of a man because I always think guys expect women to cry. But I've found strength and comfort in my friendship with Eve. I've been able to turn to her and call her anytime when I really couldn't call my husband who's working at his new job and is completely busy. Sure there were the times I have stopped and said, "God, could you listen to me for a second," but it is so important for women to find and maintain a good healthy friendship. We really weren't meant to do it alone. You can't expect your children to be your "buddy pal friend" because you really need an adult to lean on. I truly learned how beautiful a friendship can become by waking up the "sleepy giant" friendship we've had over the last fifteen years. I had no idea our friendship could have such a huge impact on my life at this time. This was one of the biggest CoinciGods I could ever imagine.

Eve and I didn't know we were going to be doing something like this three months ago. This book sprouted from a telephone conversation. And we decided to take our life experiences, our stories, and put them down on paper for others to read. Hoping they would feel beautifully normal and agree, maybe cry or respond by saying, "Yes, I feel the same way. I'm not alone!" We're here to support, edify, help, and say, "Look this is where we are, all of us, we are human."

I don't get up at five in the morning and I don't go to the gym. I don't walk every afternoon with a dog. I don't even have a dog. Nor do I stroll with the baby, and I have a baby I can stroll. I often watch these people in wonderment. I highly commend you folks out there! All you women who make the effort to get up regardless of what your schedule holds, to do something about your health, and to really make that work. It does become addicting once you get yourself into a schedule; you actually look forward to it. I know this to be true for a lot of people. Myself, I used to enjoy long distance running. I couldn't wait to run. That's all I looked forward to, running until I couldn't run anymore. That was the best feeling in the world. I hope you're now thinking to yourself, "Yeah, maybe I should get up and do this, and maybe I should do a little more to live a healthier life." Because there are women out there who are making a concerted effort to do something about their life, to do something about their health. Then there are those who don't do much, they're sedentary, those who feel that housework like cleaning and laundry is enough exercise. But it's not.

Eve: And it only gets harder.

Mattie: E-e-e-e Yah!

Eve: The longer you wait the harder it is to get started, just like anything in life. Your friends are your resources. I'm a very curious person, I ask questions. Sometimes I don't ask enough questions. And through my friendship with you, Mattie, being such a curious person always reading the paper, watching the news, and gathering information, you've had some great ideas. You've come up with things I never would have thought of or didn't even know of because I wasn't in that space. So don't be afraid to go out there to your friends and say, "I'm having problems with (fill in the blank). What do you do in your workout routine to help this area of your body? Do you have varicose veins?" By asking questions you'd be surprised at the answers you'll receive: "Oh, you know what, my doctor told me this and it's worked so well." Or "Could we try this?" And "Oh, you've got low energy? Well this is what I've been doing and it's really helping me!" You get tons of information just by using the resources in front of you and then branching out information into other areas. The Internet is simply amazing with the options it offers. You start with one subject then all of a sudden you've gone to six different websites and you're finding out all these great tips.

With your close friends you can say, "Oh my gosh! Okay, I just can't stand it anymore. I will not, *will not*, WILL NOT buy bigger jeans! I need to fit into the jeans I'm wearing." So, what are you doing to stay in your jeans? I'll tell you the secret. It's not just diet, and it's not just exercise, it's both, especially in your forties. In my thirties I was a sloth. I thought I was moving enough on stage and sweating up a storm and I thought I did enough in my life to keep me in shape. I figured I would just let my body stay where it was and starve myself, or do whatever I needed to do to stay in those jeans. Well, it worked until my metabolism changed again when I hit my forties. And now I'm saying, "Uh-oh! Not only am I going up a size, but there's also fat that won't go away." So I figured it out, you have to do both. You have to eat healthy; you don't necessarily have to diet and starve yourself, but eat healthy *and* exercise. It will work together, but it won't work one or the other. So if you're in your thirties DO IT NOW. Change now and you'll find the transition so much easier.

Mattie: Exercise and diet with a friend.

Eve: Ah yes!

Mattie: If you're home every day watching Regis and Kelly after the morning news like I do, or maybe getting caught up at the computer, there go your opportunities to do anything for that day. Sometimes I feel like I don't even want to leave the house, I'm just happy being at home.

Eve: Because everything's c-l-e-e-e-an in here!

Mattie: I don't want to go out there. It's too expensive to drive.

Eve: It's too messy.

Mattie: My baby needs her nap and the other kids are at school, yadda, yadda, so why bother going out? Boy, I really need to start changing my thought pattern. Watching my husband with his diligent workout schedule has inspired me. I thought it might be a great time to join him at the gym and see what I can do for myself. By the way, this has all happened within the timeframe of writing this book. At the gym I have signed up for "Gravity" classes. Gravity is this innovative program that provides full body conditioning through resistance training. So far I have only attended one sixty-minute class and it took me half an hour to recover afterwards. I needed water and I needed air and I knew at that moment "It was love!"

Eve: And were you sore?

Mattie: Yes, but I got over it.

Eve: That's just your body talking to you. I used to teach aerobics, back in my twenties when I had more energy. I'd say to my class, "No pain, no gain!" Pain means your body's telling you something, it's saying, "Hey! You're out of shape!" And if you're in pain that means you're challenging your body to step up a level and get back to where it needs to be. Soreness is OK, but not if you pull a muscle and you can't walk straight for a month. So pain is good, but not pain from an injury.

Mattie: If you can't afford to go to a gym and you can't afford a personal trainer or a special class, go to the library and check out some workout videos or DVDs. Start with yoga or start with something easy and simple. I'm not saying that yoga is easy, but it's not going to challenge you like a high-speed aerobic workout. Stretching is a wonderful start to warm up your body. Try a little bit at a time. Work your way up the ladder. Try checking out a workout video/DVD for pregnant women even if you're not pregnant because if it's a little bit too much for you, you'll think about the pregnant woman who really *is* doing the exercises. Get yourself out of the house and try anything! Especially if it's the dead of winter or you're in Fargo, North Dakota.

It all starts with you and your attitude. You have to tell yourself, "I'm going to make a change. Yes, I'm in my forties and yes, I might be about twenty-five pounds overweight, but I am going to make a difference in my life." Sometimes it's not about losing the weight but about getting yourself back into shape. If you label it by turning it into a huge weight loss project it could become a slippery slope into problems like constantly standing on the scale and watching where your weight has gone in the last four hours. Insist that your thoughts begin with wanting to be healthier and feeling better about yourself. If you make that a priority over how much weight you've lost you might find losing the weight is actually a lot easier. It's all about shifting your focus and developing a healthier attitude.

So many health issues can arise in our forties. There's bone density that can decrease and introduce osteoporosis, or maybe it gets harder to sleep at night because of leg cramps or snoring or your arms fall asleep. Are we stressing out more than usual? I looked up "women's health tips/sleep deprivation" on the Internet and found a few interesting facts about things that can cause a lousy night's sleep. Here's what I found. Arguing with anyone before you go to bed is not a good idea. Just a side note, I saw a sign in front of someone's house the other day that read: "Don't go to bed mad, stay up and yell all night!"

Eve: It will exhaust you and you'll get a great night's sleep.

Mattie: Don't let the sun go down on your wrath, take care of all those difficult matters before you go to bed.

Eve: Good advice!

Mattie: The list I found stated items like caffeine and sugar as being big culprits that might keep you from having a great night's sleep. Take a hot bath before you go to bed and have a cup of hot herbal tea.

Eve: Chamomile's the best.

Mattie: Grab a glass of milk, read a book or magazine to help you relax. Getting back to that bath before bed, you could put some lavender oil in your bath water and even dab a few drops on your sheets.

Eve: Or you might be thinking, "I never take the time to do those little things that make such a big difference in my life." It starts to creep up in your forties, five pounds, ten pounds, and all of a sudden you're fifty pounds overweight in your sixties. It happened to my mom, she said she couldn't take it anymore and the idea of buying bigger clothes was out of the question so she decided to try the Jenny Craig diet. Unlike the quick fix, lose weight fast programs, this diet worked beautifully for her because it was disciplined and it was a gradual process. But the main thing she did that worked for her, was buying a workout video that trains you to walk a mile in your home. She said she was drenched after working with the video, walking around her house doing the various step routines and *that's* what got her going!

The diet was perfect. You know how sometimes you see immediate results in the first week when you start a diet and you think, "Wow, this is going to work for me!" But nothing kicked in and was consistent for my mom until she did the walking around her apartment. Then she got the next tape, which was three miles. My mother takes care of my brother's two younger daughters so she had to wait before she could put Jessica (the youngest) down for a nap. She would put her shorts, t-shirt and bandana on, put the tape in and start walking. Mom would say, "If I didn't do it then I wouldn't get it done, it just didn't happen. Jesse had to have her nap and I had to have my work out!" And it worked beautifully for Mom.

My mother-in-law, Noreen, loves Weight Watchers, goes to

Curves five days a week and walks two miles a day, that's what works for her. I think every one of us in our forties has probably tried just about every diet out there. We've tried the juice fast, we've tried the Hollywood Diet, and we've tried Atkins and South Beach. South Beach is what worked for me; I hated Atkins. South Beach is very similar, but the difference for me was that it taught me about "good carbs" versus "bad carbs." So I could still do my sweets but do them the right way and it all seemed to work for me; it clicked in. The Atkins Diet worked beautifully for me the first time I tried it. I lost twenty pounds. Boom! I looked great and I was in my thirties. Then I just got bored with the whole thing. I was thinking to myself, "If I eat any more meat, I'm going to die! I have to eat something else, pasta, give me something else!"

So I encourage you to experiment and look at all the different options. I was so impressed with my mom; she lost thirty pounds with Jenny Craig. It took her six months. She had a motivational goal, she was going to her fiftieth high school reunion and wanted to lose the weight and look good. She still felt like she needed to lose more weight, but because she felt great, everyone at her reunion thought she looked fabulous! When you feel good it shines through and people pick up on it, "Wow what are you doing differently? Did you change your hair?" It's all about attitude, that *Forty Schmorty* attitude! Jump on this bandwagon and say, "You know what, I'm not going up a jean size. I'm not going to worry about those lines on my face. I'm going to do all the things I need to do to get back to a place where I *feel* great and people are going to think I *look* great and it's just going to be a self-fulfilling prophecy."

Mattie: You have to feel great. You have to have the attitude that you want to feel good about yourself and eventually you convince yourself, "You know what, I *do* feel good!" And people *do* notice. It's as if you have a huge lightbulb on top of your head and people want to know, "Wow! How did you get that thing up there?" It's because I feel good about myself inside and out—mind, body and spirit.

I had a baby fifteen months ago. I gave birth to my fourth

child at age forty-four and two months later I turned forty-five. Here I am in my mid-forties with my youngest child being an infant and my oldest child a teenager learning how to drive. Not to leave out my two other children, ages four and fifteen, and all the challenges that go in between. Vitamins and daily supplements are two important things that keep me going. I'm not going to list all the supplements I take, but I encourage women to do some research on the best vitamins to take suited for you and your own busy life. Consult the Internet or ask your local health food expert at any health food store. And make sure what you do end up taking is easily absorbed into your system.

Eve: And you're not peeing them out!

Mattie: Exactly! They have to absorb easily. One of the natural approaches I tried in my late thirties was wheatgrass. I bought a wheatgrass machine and I had a tray of fresh wheatgrass delivered to my home once a week. It's pretty weird because it's just grass (well, wheatgrass but it smelled like grass). I would put it in my juicer and make enough to put into a small jigger and drink it down the hatch. I think about it now and to this day I still shudder at the thought of drinking it. It's so great for your body.

Eve: But it tasted like grass!

Mattie: It tasted like grass. Every time I smell a jigger of wheatgrass juice it reminds me of the days when I was attending high school in Yuma, Arizona. In the latter part of August in the 100 plus degree temperatures all marching band members, cheer and song leaders (I was a song leader who marched and danced with the band during football games) and football players had to practice on the football field. The field was always freshly mowed and smelled like, well, freshly mowed grass. If you know that smell you know what wheatgrass tastes like. You're drinking the grass out of your lawn mower. But wheatgrass is great for your body. Let's look at the drink we are drinking right now, Kombucha. My sister told me about this stuff and then Eve found out about it.

Eve: My hairdresser, India, told me to get this because I had a yucky stomach. Then I started reading the label on the bottle and was blown away.

Mattie: G.T. Dave is the guy who developed this drink, Kombucha, and it reads, "He began bottling this drink in 1985 after his mother's success from drinking it during her battle with breast cancer. He is committed to bringing you the freshest, purest and most potent kombucha available." I'll tell you what. Eve and I are drinking this right now and I just may drag out another bottle.

Eve: Read the definition of kombucha.

Mattie: Oh yes. "Kombucha, pronounced 'kom-boo-cha' is a handmade Chinese tea that is delicately cultured for thirty days. During this time, essential nutrients form like active enzymes, viable probiotics, amino acids, antioxidants and polyfenals. All of these combine to create an elixir that immediately works with the body to restore balance and vitality."

Eve: I drank this because I had a bad upset stomach that lasted all night long and into the next day. My hairdresser said, "You have to go to a health food store like Whole Foods or Jimbos (local San Diego health market), or wherever you go, and get this drink." So I went to the store, I did what Mattie said, I asked somebody for help, because to this day, even in a bookstore I have to ask for help. I can never find anything! Don't be afraid to ask, don't be afraid to ask what you think might be a stupid question.

Mattie: Asking is free!

Eve: And there are no stupid questions. I mean people might make you feel stupid for asking, but if you don't know, ask. The woman at the store showed me my options; I went for this drink right here, the one we're talking about. It's not the greatest tasting drink but within a half an hour my stomach felt better and I was sold. When my husband came home that night with a stomachache he drank some and a half an hour later his stomach felt better. My stepson came home from school two days later not feeling well with a headache and a stomachache and I made him drink it. Of course I said, "I'm sorry, Jake, this is going to taste a little bit like wine." Then his eyes perked right up, he's fourteen, "Wine, huh?" And I think that's what made him drink it! He told me later that his stomach felt better. This stuff works. Whatever is in this elixir is in there for good reasons. It even has the Five R's on it.

Mattie: "Rejuvenate, restore, revitalize, replenish and regenerate."

Eve: We mentioned the Five R's earlier. It's organic and it's raw and it's good stuff people so check it out. This is our gift to you because we found it and we're sold.

Mattie: Check out the website: www.gtskombucha.com. Thank you, G.T. Dave!

Eve: By helping his mother, I'm sure one of the most important women in his life, he's helped a lot of others. I'm sure these stories are told to him all the time, but we couldn't have found it at a better time in our lives.

Mattie: So go to your local health food store and get some fresh organic food, even frozen organic food. It's nice to see that even regular supermarkets are beginning to carry brands of organic food. Buy healthy food you can stock in your pantry and eat or snack on later. I like raw almonds; those are always great to snack on a little at a time. And speaking of a little at a time, it's a good habit to eat small amounts of healthy food throughout the day. Eating healthy has been a big change in my life, now more than ever before. There are so many changes happening in my forties.

Eve: Let's look at menopause. I know many women in the midst of going through menopause and they all tell me weight gain is a major side effect because your hormones change. And the weight will not come off! So if you're already struggling with weight issues, guess what? Not only is it harder to get back into shape, but also there's weight that won't leave your body because of your physical makeup and the changes you're going through. I'm going to tell you one of the most important things you have to do. The number one word you have to think about when you're *Forty Schmorty* is WATER.

Mattie tells me all the time, "Water, water, water, water, water, water, water!" Yesterday I was working in Las Vegas and got so dried up from the air conditioning, cigarette smoke, the extreme heat outside and the dryness of the weather. I was making conversation with the makeup artist who was on the backstage staff for the show and told her about the book we were writing. I asked her if she had any helpful beauty hints for women in the world. "Water!" she replied. She gave me a really great tip. She slices cucumbers and puts them in her water. The flavor of the cucumbers diffuses into the water and gives it a crisp fresh taste that actually makes her want to drink more water.

I told her my problem with water is that I have a tiny bladder and I hate being in the bathroom all day long. She said, "That's good. Your body is processing and getting rid of all the bad things." Six 8-ounce glasses of water a day is no joke. There are experts who say you don't need eight ounces, you can get by with six ounces. I don't care what it is, just start drinking because as we get older our skin starts getting dryer and we need the extra moisture. That's why they always give you water at the spa; drink, drink, drink! Even after you get a massage they ask you to please drink more water.

I have been working out with my sister Lee and her trainer for three years. My sister got pregnant during this time (at the age of forty-three) and had her fourth child. She invited me along one day to do a double training session, just like you were saying, "Work out with a friend." Well, a sister can be a friend and my sister has been a great friend. I thank her every chance I get for giving me this opportunity to work out with her. One of the most important things our trainer does at the beginning of our session is to give us water. She refills it throughout our workout at least two or three times and makes us drink. When you're working out you concentrate on lifting the weight, doing the exercise right and making sure you're not hurting your neck while you're doing your crunches to "de-jelly your belly!" You're drinking water throughout the workout and you don't realize you've had the equivalent of four 8-ounce glasses. Water rejuvenates you.

Mattie: If you don't drink water your blood can thicken to a sludge consistency. To test your dehydration pinch the skin on top of your hand and if the skin stays up in place grab some water fast. You're dehydrated! Get liquefied!

Eve: Another sign too is if you get a headache and it won't go away. Grab some water. I'm at a point in my life where I'm really trying not to medicate. If I don't need to take Tylenol or Ibuprofen I'm not going to take it. I'm going to suffer through and tough it out and get through it because I want to try to heal myself. Sometimes I just can't do that so I get help. Water is so important. Oh, and did you eat today?

Mattie: I'm the biggest one to blame for eating poorly. I have not been a great eater in the past. Like I said earlier, stock your pantry with good healthy snacks in many varieties so when that time comes to fulfill your hunger you can go to your pantry and grab something quick and healthy. There are many times in the past when I would stand at the doorway of my pantry glazed over with hunger waiting for something to jump out at me. I would usually end up going for a carbohydrate. I needed to make a healthier change with food so I try now to have a better plan for stocking my pantry. Eating for me was never a priority; I guess I was having too much fun with life. Taking the time to sit down and eat took away precious time. I can't believe I lived my life like that.

Eve: Food, the gasoline for the car that is your body.

Mattie: Yeah, I get it now.

Eve: I am still on the South Beach Diet. I read the book and it talks a lot about eating small portions all day long. When you're hungry, feed yourself so you don't eat too much at one sitting. You'll eat less at one sitting if you eat little bits during the day. I never realized how important that is. The book also recommends making healthy choices when you're eating, like eating almonds or peanuts even though peanuts have a lot of calories in them. Eat twenty peanuts in one sitting (count them out), wait ten minutes and you'll be surprised—your hunger is gone. This might only last an hour, but then eat an apple or a pear. A pear is even better, because there's more fiber in a pear than in an apple. I've learned so much about fiber. Fiber makes your body work harder to get the sugar in the food you eat because your stomach has to separate the fiber out before it can get to the sugar. By the time it's digested and into your system your body hasn't grabbed the sugar. One of the popular tips you hear now is to eat fiber fifteen minutes before a meal. If you do this you won't eat as much because you'll feel full. I always think about the fiber content of foods when I'm eating a meal.

Broccoli is a perfect fiber food. I love broccoli now because my husband makes it tastes so good (he's a great cook) and I know it's good for me and it's making my body work harder to get to the nutrients in food. Sugar is generally bad, though there are some good sugars, like the sugar in fruit. Another thing I learned from the book was very eye opening. When you want something healthy to drink you think, "Oh I'll just have a glass of juice." And juice is definitely a healthier choice than soda, but in one glass of apple juice there's about five or six apples. Would you sit down and eat five or six apples in one sitting? No! You can't because your body gets full and the reason your body gets full is because of the fiber in the skin and in the meat of the apple. The drink is all sugar! Now it's the good kind of sugar, but way too much of it at once. If you want to have juice, pour about a quarter cup of juice into a glass and fill the rest up with water. You'll still get all the healthy juice but you're not getting all that sugar.

Mattie: Low-fat yogurts are a great snack to keep in the fridge. Dried fruits, like raisins, you can take with you in the car.

Eve: String cheese. Believe it or not string cheese is a healthy snack if you eat it once a day. You'll be surprised how much it fills you up.

Mattie: I like really good healthy protein bars.

Eve: It's important to read the nutrition label and look at the grams of protein and the grams of sugar. The label will tell you the percentage of each and you can decide if it's a good choice.

Mattie: I went to the health food store and bought a variety of health food bars just to see which ones the family likes best. So they're sitting in the pantry available for a quick-snack-grab food. Another quick-snack-grab food is the Star-Kist brand tuna and albacore packets. They fit nicely in your purse or backpack and all you have to do is remember to include a fork.

Eve: I love those teeny tiny cans of tuna; they're a perfect size. Oh, how about the new item from Kraft Foods called the 100 Calorie Snacks? Those are great. They measure out for you a one-hundred-calorie snack, like a little packet of Wheat Thins for example. And they have sweet snacks too. Sweets are a problem for me. If I eat one M&M I have to eat the whole bag and maybe half of another bag. So instead of that, I try not to eat sweets at all. Then I'm denying myself, so I've had to find something else to satisfy my sweet tooth. The 100 Calorie Snacks are great because you get just enough sweets and you know you won't overdo it.

Sometimes however, you think you're eating something healthy but you've really had six hundred calories because of the sugar content. Those little snacks are a great way to get just the right portion, eat it and wait ten minutes. For me, it's also about the waiting. Once I wait ten or fifteen minutes I notice my hunger is gone. It's really important to listen to your body. I tell you what, I never listened to my body in my twenties and thirties and I think I'm listening now in my forties because I'm physically slowing down.

Mattie: And I think now more than ever before we are all much more health conscious.

Eve: And there are products the food companies are partnering up with because they've been proven to be healthy. The South Beach Diet for example has a variety of products you can buy. So when you're shopping and you see a product with the South Beach Diet label you know it's been approved by that diet and you'll be eating something healthy. But check the portions because sometimes they might be bigger than you really want to eat.

I agree we are all more conscious about our healthy diet. I think the health insurance companies are realizing, "Hey, maybe we should go about health with a different attitude. Instead of helping people when they are sick we can help them stay healthy and then we won't have to pay out as much money because people will stay healthy longer." It's all about the preventative measures we need to take to stay healthy instead of running ourselves ragged and getting sick. The preventative maintenance route is really about doing yourself a favor.

I've been going to my dermatologist for interesting weird side effects since I went off the pill. She told me research studies claim it is very unhealthy to continue taking the pill in your forties. I've been taking it for many years for ovary issues. Unfortunately, now that I've stopped taking it I am breaking out all over just like a teenager. My dermatologist is also a plastic surgeon and they are looking at their whole industry with a different approach—preventative. Why wait till everything's broken down? If you've got sun damage or wrinkles, there are so many things you can do to maintain the quality of your aging skin to keep it as healthy as possible.

Mattie: So if I want to make an appointment with a dermatologist, does insurance cover that?

Eve: Yes, but it depends on your coverage. In the long run you'll see the advantages of staying on top of keeping your skin healthy. I'm reminded of the article on Susan Sarandon where she was quoted: "Start working on the inside because the outside is a losing battle!" She wasn't just talking spiritually; she was talking about health too. Your face is going to start looking older. Guess what? We're forty. Mattie and I are in an industry where we have to stay on top of the way we look constantly.

Mattie: I need to make an appointment with a dermatologist because I want to know how healthy my skin is from exposure to the sun. It seems like a good idea to make regular check-ups for sun damage and weird spots as part of the program for maintaining healthy skin. Here's something to think about when you're driving in your car. Your left arm and the left side of your face gets more sun damage because of its exposure to the sun. My sister Kay lives in Arizona and is in her car a lot. She has an arm sleeve she wears on her left arm to protect her from the sun while she's driving.

Eve: What a great idea! I've been to the dermatologist and had a growth removed; it wasn't cancer, it was pre-cancer. The test results came back benign, but if I had let it keep growing it would have turned into skin cancer. By the way, that was on the left side of my face.

Mattie: Find yourself a great sunscreen lotion to wear every day. Not only for your face but also for the parts of your body that are going to be exposed to the sun. Are you wearing flip-flops? Put some sunscreen lotion on your feet. Do you have short hair and wear t-shirts with a scoop back? Put some sunscreen on that area. Get yourself into the habit of using sunscreen before you leave the house every day. The sun isn't like it used to be; the burn seems to have a bite. If you need to have a tan, get it in a bottle and spray it on.

Eve: When we were kids, we used to put Crisco Oil Shortening on our skin to get a dark tan. We would fry like chickens. My sisters used to take tetracycline and lay out because you could tan darker. There's a reason why we weren't supposed to do that. We weren't protecting our skin from the UVA and the UVB rays. So now one of my sisters (who is in her forties) through the help of her plastic surgeon and modern technology has received a procedure called Fraxel® Laser. She has received three out of four treatments in an office procedure. Her skin looks amazing and the beauty is it has tightened up her skin and her sunspots have faded. She looks younger and a lot of her lines are gone. So go see your dermatologist, examine your sunscreen to be sure it has zinc in it and that it also contains titanium. If it doesn't have both ingredients, it's not doing the best job for you.

Mattie: Why is that?

Eve: The zinc and the titanium deflect the sun. One or the other only protects your skin; it doesn't deflect the sun so you're still getting the rays, you're just not getting them as much as if you didn't have anything on your skin. I find beauty products are now containing SPF. So when I put my makeup on in the morning I always start with my sunscreen for my face, then I put my makeup containing SPF on top of that. Start using these products now. You may have the sun damage from years past, but you can still protect your skin from getting worse. If you have teenagers, tell them now to get into the habit of using sunscreen. My stepdaughter just turned nineteen and I asked her to start using SPF and she said, "Ah, why do I need it, I'm young and my skin is fine." I said, "Yes, but why not keep it that way for as long as you can?" When we were in our teens we thought we didn't need it and look at our skin now. If you've got teenagers have them start using the SPF 30 with zinc and titanium now and their skin will look gorgeous when they're forty.

Mattie: Growing up in Arizona I used to walk barefoot on the hot concrete sidewalk in 115 degree temperatures. SPF? What's that? I should wear a straw hat? Who needs that? The scary part of the whole thing is there was not one drop of water I would think to drink. I don't know how I survived growing up? Somehow I made it through.

Eve: Did you drink a lot of iced tea maybe?

Mattie: A lot of sun tea. We would make the sun tea outside and that was it. I didn't drink water or use any type of sun protection back then. I used to use Johnson's Baby Oil. That would give me the deep tan like your Crisco.

Eve: Did you eat a lot of fruit during the summer? For me, fruit meant summer had arrived! There were peaches and apricots and cherries. They would all come out during the summer. My mom would have bowls and bowls of it out, there were eight of us so I guess that's the way it had to be. Another thing to mention is that when we were younger there weren't as many preservatives in our food, toxins in the air or as many fertilizers for the crops as they use now.

Mattie: So the fruit we were eating back then still had all of its nutrients.

Eve: Today you go to a health food store for organic fruit. The fruit at Whole Foods is unbelievable. You know you're going to pay twenty cents more per pound but you're getting all the stuff you need from it. It's organic, it's fresh, and it's better for you. And we're in our forties and we can afford it. My twelve-year-old daughter doesn't like vegetables, but she loves fruit so I stock up on fruit from Whole Foods. I'll keep doing this till her tastes change. You couldn't pay me to eat vegetables when I was a kid, but now I eat them like they are going out of style.

Mattie: You can also mail order organic fruit and it comes right to your door—fresh!

Eve: Ooh, what a great idea. There are so many resources out there. I get *Fitness* magazine, I love that magazine, and I get a couple of others like *Shape* and *Self*, but *Fitness* is my favorite. It always has good tips and great ideas about what you can do to change your diet. They have testimonials from people with all different types of lifestyles and that's one thing that resonated with me about dieting. There's something different for everybody. Some things work better for one person and not for another. It's empowering to realize there are so many options available. Just keep trying until you find something that works because when it works it all starts clicking. Then you can change your focus from losing pounds to wanting to be healthier. You start feeling better, you'll want to eat better then you start losing weight and your focus shifts. You'll pay more attention to your face and hair, all of which starts coming together once your attitude is better. *Forty Schmorties,* man! We need to change our attitude and our attitude needs to be Wellness!

Mattie: And moms, it is possible to do this with kids and family life. You *can* do this. You can make yourself the new priority. Take brief moments out of the day to pamper yourself. Busy moms tend to put all their focus on their family and forget about themselves. I'm telling you, you can pull your focus on yourself fifteen minutes at a time during the day.

Eve: If you're not helping yourself first, you're no good to your family. Or you're only there fifty percent because fifty percent is depleted; your own personal needs are not being met. Even if you're not realizing it, subconsciously it's making a difference in everything you do.

Mattie, you love to cook. You have your cookbooks and you share recipes with friends and family over the phone and via e-mail and you're a fervent Food Network "Foodie." You have even written and co-produced, directed and co-starred with our great friends, Laymon Davis and Jeremy Sykes, six cooking shows that aired in San Diego called *MusiCuisine.* This reminds me of something I found out about when I was visiting my cousin in Indiana. It's a different take on frozen food meals. TV dinners were a great idea when they first came out for busy families or moms who didn't cook much. Unfortunately, they weren't the healthiest meals. Well, there are two women in Indiana who are great cooks who would always have dinner parties and people just loved their food. They had neighborhood friends and family from all over who wanted their food and recipes all the time. So they came up with the idea to cook fifteen meals in one day. They would prepare enough food for ten families. They would invite their friends over and have them choose the meals they wanted. Once a decision was made the prepared meal was packaged along with a list of directions for reheating. Everyone already knew the food was healthy and tasty so this launched their career making healthy meals for busy families with a business called Dream Dinners.

I thought this would be a great resource for de-stressing my life. I can't cook but my husband loves to cook. There are days when these meals would be a wonderful way to give my husband a break from cooking and help my family eat well. When I was in Indiana visiting my cousin she offered to heat up one of these meals. Let me tell you, it was delicious and all she had to do was put it in the oven and turn it on! A really cool feature included with the reheating instructions was a suggestion for a side dish. How difficult is it to make a salad or heat up your favorite vegetable? Isn't that a great idea? I think this might be more popular in the Midwest and on the East Coast than it is in California.

Mattie: It's funny you are mentioning this because just the other day I heard about a couple of places in San Diego offering this very service. In fact, one of the places lets you use their cooking and food prep facilities so you can do it all yourself, package it up and take it home for the freezer.

Eve: These meals are very economical because they're made in bulk. My cousin was paying fifteen to eighteen dollars to feed a family of four! You can't buy a meal for a family of four at a restaurant for that price. What's even better with these meals is that you know what's in them because you put it together yourself.

Mattie: So we've talked about fitness, health and beauty. What about our hair? Eve, you have a very fabulous hairstylist, India Chaney. And I love my hair stylist, Tony Fiorentino, whom I have been going to for the last fifteen years. I love my appointments for the amazing job he does on my hair and our wonderful conversations. I'll say to him, "Do what you want to do with my hair. Make it fabulous because people know where I go to get my hair done." And he always does a great job. Maybe you know someone who hasn't considered putting a little color in her hair to hide the grey or maybe they like the grey? I know there is a way to enhance your grey to make it shinier and silky looking. I say, "Dare to be and try something different!" Make an appointment with a hairstylist and try something different and fun. Do this for YOU. I don't know your hairstylist yet, Eve, but from what you tell me I already love her.

Eve: Everyone I have recommended her to adores her and loves what she does to their hair. Her name is India and immediately you get a spiritual, mystical feeling about her just from her name. Then you meet her and you know she's in the perfect business. She can give you a hug and you instantly feel better about yourself. And she knows hair; she's an expert in her field.

Mattie's hair is thick, beautiful, wonderful and full. Then there's my hair, which is thin, balding in one spot and very fine. I get one "good hair day" a month and Mattie and I are in the same business so you can see the challenges here. Every time India styles my hair I look at it and say, "It's just a miracle what you do with my hair!" She is so happy that I am grateful. India shared this great story with me the other day because, of course, I tell my hairdresser everything. I told her about this book we are writing and all the dreams and plans we have for it so she told me a story about a client of hers who had just turned fifty. Her client came in for an appointment and she was feeing melancholy. Her shoulders were rounded forward and she had this ho-hum look about her. She stated she should get a conservative haircut now that she's fifty. India said, "What are you talking about? You are in the prime of your life. You're energetic; you've got a wonderful career and children that love you. I'm not listening to you and I'm going to change your hair!" So she gave her this cute, short, zippy, fun great hairstyle with a little bit of color and the woman was nearly in tears with joy. She walked out of the salon like she was walking on air! Her head was held high and there was a spring in her step and you could definitely tell she was not the same woman who walked into the salon earlier.

That's what hairdressers do. They take whatever God has given you and make it better. Fortunately for me, there are so many products out there. My hair is nothing without hair products!

Mattie: Getting a great haircut is key for most women. All I have to do is wash my hair, dry it with the towel, run my fingers through it, flip it back and forth a couple of times and voila! Instant hairdo! That's the kind of cut Tony gives me and I love its versatility. During the day when I'm at home I can throw back my hair into my mommy ponytail, complete with various hairclips to keep my bangs back. Towards the end of the day when I know Troy is coming home out comes the ponytail. All I have to do is mess it up with my hands and the hair falls into perfect place. I don't know how Tony does that! I think it's important to look good for your husband when he comes home from work. After all, he's been working all day and you don't want to look like the cat just dragged you in. Throw some fresh clothes on and brush your teeth!

Eve: Oh very important! And always greet your husband with a kiss. When he walks through the door my husband says, "How ya doing?" and I say, "Better now!" I do, I get so happy when he comes home from work. This is all a part of the wellness, feeling good inside and out. I am so lazy when it comes to makeup and hair because we have to be made up so often for our work being on stage. Any chance I have not to wear makeup I'm taking it!

Mattie: I'm with ya!

Eve: Most fashion magazines show gorgeous and perfect movie stars and models. Everybody knows those photos are touched up, airbrushed and manipulated with the help of computer programs. Super models can afford to have a makeup artist every day. If I could afford it, I would too, what the heck? A few times I have worked with a makeup artist, Michelle, who does such a good job. When she's finished I look in the mirror and think, "Who is that looking at me?" I'm the reason makeup was invented, I'll tell you that right now.

Mattie: Models to me are like living art. I heard a model once say that some designers design clothing to look like it's on a hanger not on the model. That is such an odd way of thinking. People need to be celebrated for the beautiful individuals they are. It's that simple. I think designers need to start becoming more realistic with their designs for the everyday person. Models will continue to be models and that's great for them, but to me they will continue to be art.

Eve: Part of a model's beauty is painted on, sucked out, stretched over, and if you've ever seen those shows with the models behind the scenes, they are pulling and tucking and pinning everything! Nobody can do that in real life. How would you get through your day? You'd need ten people around you and a fan blowing. Living art is a great way to look at it. Accentuate the positive and accept the negative. If you accept it, it has no control over you. It is what it is, you can't change it, but you can try to improve on it, and work around it. It's empowering to know what your strengths and weaknesses are and to mesh them together and simply be who you are. I love that "living art." You said earlier you are the "star of your show" and you're the star of your health and your beauty too. There's nothing wrong with not having a perfect body, we're all there. Let's look at the things these super models have to do; what society says is a perfect body. Some suffer from bulimia and have eating disorders. Some models fast just to make it through a photo shoot. It's not healthy and it's not a good way to live.

Mattie: This is part of a personal destruction, and an unhealthy way of being and thinking. We must start celebrating who we are.

Eve: Start accepting who we are. This is a self-awareness self-confidence issue. I'm reading a wonderful book written by Jane Fonda called *My Life So Far*. I highly recommend it. She has a lot of advice about what she went through in her forties, but one of the issues she's struggled with was her sense of not being good enough and being imperfect. Guess what? We're all imperfect. She even says it in her book. "We're mortal and mortal means imperfect!" Perfect is for God; perfect is for the afterlife when you shed all the weaknesses of being human and you move on to a spiritual being.

If hair is your best feature, then build on it and "let it shine." Hair is not my best feature. But I found somebody who can make my hair look the best it possibly can. I always get compliments on my hair and my hair color and it's because India does the best she can with my really, really (trust me) bad hair. So you *can* make the best of what you don't have. There are shows on television that explain the different body types and the bathing suit you should buy to accent the best part of your figure, whether you're pear-shaped or any shape. I have no hips; I'm straight up and down so I have to find the suits that have fuller coverage to make me look like I've got a waist. There are tricks; ask your friends what they do. And don't be afraid to ask a stranger. You would be surprised what it will do for someone's day if you go up to a perfect stranger and say, "You have the most beautiful skin. What products do you use?" You'll see them light up and they'll respond, "Really? You think so? Well I use this, this, this and this!" You might be amazed at some of the stuff they're using. You made their day and you got some information that might work "beautifully" for you.

FORTY Schmorty!
...life keeps happening

9

THE "C" WORD

Eve: It's Wednesday, June 28, 2006. We took a couple weeks off from writing and now we want to talk about everything that has happened.

Mattie: We discovered back in Chapter Four that I found a lump in my breast. My story has unraveled slowly through this book, chapter by chapter, about our findings and we now know that I have breast cancer. Since our last chapter I've had surgery to remove the lump. The pathology report determined that I have invasive ductile carcinoma and a second surgery was necessary to clear the margins.

I had a second surgery the following week where much more breast tissue was taken out along with the sentinel lymph node. It was tested for cancer and it was positive. At that point he removed a fatty patch where there were more lymph nodes and discovered a microscopic measure of cancer had gone into one of ten lymph nodes. I was diagnosed with stage two breast cancer and now I am a survivor.

This is nowhere near where we thought this book would be

going, but how appropriate it is for women in their forties to know more about some of the things we are not expecting in our life, like breast cancer. So now we're taking this time to stress the importance of self-examinations, regular mammograms, and having your doctor check you. With all this we are here to tell a little bit of the story because our book has been diverted by what we feel is, for all intent and purposes, a good reason for it to go this way. We want to help and encourage other women who just might be going through the same thing I'm going through. Eve and I feel this is all part of being in your forties. *Forty Schmorty*!

Eve: Mattie and I were talking earlier about me being on this side of the chair, she's on that side of the chair and cancer's in the middle. It's a weird place to be. You don't know what to say, you don't know what to do, but you want to be supportive. Maybe we're just going to discover this together. I do a lot of fundraising for breast cancer because my sister Gay had breast cancer. One of the things I found was that almost everybody on this planet knows somebody, either in their immediate family or their close friends, who's had cancer. That's astounding! And we don't talk about it. Unfortunately, breast cancer is on the rise and the numbers keep going up every year. I'm sure researchers are going to find out why that is. Is it a food issue? Is it a stress issue? Is it an environment thing, some thing that has caused this to happen? Is it a certain place where you grew up? I don't know what it is, but they're going to find out what it is and we're all going to go "Aha! That's why!"

Right now I'm sitting here in a chair with Mattie who's going through the worst thing you can hear from a doctor. "Yes, you have cancer." And I'm asking, "How can I help? What can I do? How did we get here? What's going on? Whatever you need I'm here for you." And the hardest part for me in these last two weeks has been that I've had work related travel so I've been away. So I'm calling and asking, "How's Mattie? What do we know? What's the latest?" I've been a long distance pest because I couldn't be there physically to be a pest in person. I've been calling on the cell phone and hearing the wrong information because I hear one thing and get caught up in the emotion and miss the rest of the information. And I don't even have cancer and I feel like I do. I feel like this is our cancer. I know your family feels that way too. We all pull together as a community and say, "Okay, we're going to get through this together." It's scary. I'm scared. I know Mattie's terrified. I know her kids are scared.

The amount of people praying for Mattie right now is unbelievable. We have sent the word out there asking people for prayers. So many people are concerned about her life, health and future and we're here to say, "Mattie *is* cancer free." In our minds they got all the cancer out and now we're just going to go through the next step. I'm going to let Mattie talk more about that because it's not going to be fun. We'll do what we need to.

Mattie: Knowing now that I have breast cancer, I have so many questions and so many things I want to know. It is by far one of the scariest things in the world. I might as well have been handed a death sentence. That's how I felt when I was given the news. It was *very* unexpected. I went in to get my pathology report with my four-year-old son and my one-year-old daughter. I thought I would just slip into the office and the technician would read me a quick report on my first surgery and everything was going to be fine. It wasn't.

Suddenly my life flashed before my eyes. I have to say first and foremost that one of the biggest and main things keeping me going through this has been my faith and belief in God. I cannot begin to tell you how important it is to have faith in your life. The prayer support of everyone out there who knows about my condition has been so comforting. And for me, I am really challenged every day by looking forward to my life, looking forward to when I'm sixty and seventy and eighty. Looking forward so that I *can* look back and see where I've come. It is *so* important to visualize complete health. Visualize your life having what you desire. Like children for example, or a partner or a husband to be with you for the rest of your life. Visualization of my future has been important, one of the utmost things that has sustained me. Sometimes I don't get a really good picture; sometimes my thoughts are so crumbled with fear I have to pull myself back, take a breath and say, "I've *got* to get through this." My intention is to live. My intention is to be a long time survivor of this and to be someone who can push forward and make changes to make it better for other women who are going to have breast cancer in the future.

I am discovering so many things so quickly about this disease. There are the women who have had breast cancer who share amazing stories about their survival and then there is the importance of what Eve and I have talked about, regarding the community of friends you make, and the community of friends you rely on in times like these. It's so easy for us to continue and go on with our lives each day and manage our routines with our children or with work or whatever it is we need to do. We forget to have friends and we forget what it's like to have a friend come over for a cup of coffee and just sit and talk. We've talked about that in these past chapters and I am the one who's been guilty of not practicing friendship, not inviting friends to come over for that time. What time? I don't have that time! I've got four children. I have a husband. I've got to shop and clean and take care of *everybody*, but me, at the end of the list. I'm the one at the bottom of the list making sure I put on my pajamas and don't fall asleep wearing my jeans.

When you receive shocking news about your health like I have you can't help but review your life; you can't help but look back to your childhood and go back to certain key moments. As we have said, every moment is a key moment. It's been nothing but a constant replay. Looking back at how my life has been and checking, "Where did I go wrong? Why did this happen?" I have to say that I am *really* practicing *so* strongly the importance of gratitude and the importance of knowing that God has a reason for me to go through this trial. My community of friends has grown so much and people I didn't think cared or have been out of my life for a certain length of time are coming back and I'm able to have conversations with these people and pick up where we left off.

I had a girlfriend call me two days ago whom I haven't spoken to in almost seventeen years. Deep in my heart she has always been a dear friend of mine. Even when she stopped communicating with me, she always remained special. I got a phone call from her and she said, "Mattie I'm so sorry for calling you under these premises." And I jumped right on it and said, "Where have you been? What did I do? What's going on? How come you stopped communicating with me?" I took care of it right from the top and I completely understood her point. I understood her life at that time when we stopped communicating was upside down. I did have to make sure we were okay so I said on the phone, "So are we okay? We can talk now? You'll call me back?" And she said, "Yes, I will." And I know she will.

So many wonderful people have come forward with concern and prayers. People I know that *don't* pray are praying for me. There's a huge amount of people in my circle and it's changing *their* lives. I pray for the best and I ask God every day to make me a surviving example to others that this particular type of cancer can be beat and it can be done successfully and with gratitude. I know more than anything I *have* to give back to the community of people who know me and on an even grander scale, the people who don't know me but who are clinging to every word I'm saying and looking for that little bit of hope, that probability they too can be breast cancer survivors. I'm here to say, "Yes!" Everyone's telling me, "It's your attitude." You've *got* to have a good attitude. You've *got* to keep yourself in the positive mode of knowing, "I'm *going* to beat this! I'm *going* to turn around and thank God for this journey and this healing."

We have now entered into summer and I can expect that from summer into fall I'm going to be a hairless wonder. I've prepared myself for chemo and I continue to do so every day. I'm preparing myself for the pain and the weakness and I'm preparing myself to be, gosh, the strongest I've ever been in my life. This is beyond labor and delivery. This is more than going through natural childbirth and I am really looking forward to meeting other people who have been through this because I think it's really important to talk to those people. I think it's important to have strength and respect for each other and to carry that torch for others. If *I* can do that, if even *I* can make a difference then I think we've done an awful lot. Already the people we've communicated with, that we've made telephone calls to, have made an impact. It's just the beginning.

Eve: Yeah. Oh, my goodness. It's been such an emotional roller coaster. We stopped and listened to the tape on Chapter Four when Mattie first found it on Mother's Day, and I have to tell you it feels like a lifetime ago. We have been on the emotional roller coaster of cancer. We had a celebratory breakfast because nothing showed up on the mammogram and we were so sure everything was going to be fine. Then Mattie had the first biopsy and the doctor didn't even stick around to talk to her. So I said to Mattie, "If you have cancer he would have stuck around." Even *he* didn't think it was cancer. We were just so sure it wasn't cancer, and then we got the news and I feel like all we could do was pray, pray, pray, pray and get the word out.

So many people have stepped up offering advice. Mattie found out that there were survivors surrounding her everywhere. People are bonding together saying, "You can do this." I think the hardest thing for us right now is the not knowing. I feel like we know we're going to beat this, but the fear comes in from the unknown. The doctor says, "Okay Mattie, you have to have chemo." And Mattie says, "Okay, I understand and accept I have to have chemo and I know it's not going to be pleasant." But I guess until you get through your first treatment we won't know what to expect for the next four months. It's taking those baby steps each day one day at a time that are going to get you through this, Mattie.

At the time you had your second surgery I was out of town and I was *so* upset that I had to be *gone*. My sister Jeanne said, "Eve, just go and do what you need to do. Mattie would want you to go. So you do that for her because she needs to know you're okay. She can't worry about you. She has to worry about herself right now." Still, it was so hard for me to be away. I'd be in airports landing in different cities calling when I could: "Please call me back before we take off." I wanted all the information I could get and all I wanted to hear were positive things and of course I was thinking, "What does this mean now for Mattie?" First of all, there needs to be more people working in pathology 24/7 so someone doesn't have to wait three-to-five days to find out if it's cancer. And then if it *is* cancer, and there is another surgery that needs to happen, it takes three-to-five more days to find out what kind of cancer and what stage it's in. This is just ridiculous! You should be able to know *within* twenty-four hours. That was the hardest part, the waiting and the not knowing.

Mattie and Troy got the pathology report after the second surgery and found out that the cancer was only in two of the lymph nodes. I had been praying so specifically for only those two. I only wanted one, but out of eleven there were two. That's good. That's great news! And I was so grateful. I told her, "I just didn't pray enough." I started crying I was so happy. Then I asked myself, "What would Mattie do right now? What would Mattie do?" Mattie would say, "Be grateful!" So I start thanking God for everything! I was thanking God for good hair days, for family, friends, life, birds, happiness, peace, harmony and happy endings. It was a ten-minute prayer of gratitude. During this whole time I was going back and forth to my hybrid SUV grabbing CD boxes out of the trunk. I was on my third trip back to my car when a small sparrow flew by me into the underground garage, which is uncanny because I have an issue with birds flying near my head.

I walked by the bird as he landed up above on a small water pipe next to my car. When I opened my trunk and I looked up the sparrow was inside my car. Inside! My whole body tingled because I *knew* it was God. I *knew* God sent that bird to reassure me, "I told you it was going to be okay. You have to trust me. You have to believe me. I didn't say it was going to be easy. I didn't say it was going to be a piece of cake. But I did say it would be okay. I'm here with you. I will never leave you." That bird looked directly at me and just stared at me for thirty to forty seconds. This seems like a really long time when you're face to face with nature. Especially when you live in the city and you don't get much nature, you know? And then the sparrow sang a little song and flew away. Every day I look for those little signs. Like our girlfriend Marti calling today saying, "My mom's a twenty-five-year survivor." And our friend David told us his mother is a forty-year survivor. Imagine what they did forty years ago. They just removed your breasts and said, "Good luck." They didn't have chemotherapy forty years ago. Then there is my friend Annie in New York. I was telling her all about our book *Forty Schmorty!* and what we're going through right now and she says, "You have to get this book by Robert Buckman, *Cancer Is a Word Not a Sentence: A Practical Guide to Help You Through the First Few Weeks.*" It's not a death sentence. It's just a word and it has no power over you unless you give it power.

Mattie: Yes, I agree!

Eve: It's so important to surround yourself with people who are constantly going to be giving you positive energy. It's been two weeks since you were diagnosed, right? At this point, everyone is concerned and calling often. But what's going to happen a month from now? Where are those people going to be? They're going to be living their lives, which is as it should be because that's what people do. Life goes on and we get back into the day-to-day of our lives. What I'm trying to say is it's imperative for friends to continue supporting one another through difficult times.

Mattie: I have a friend who is a breast cancer survivor that has been wonderful and very adamant about me getting a second and third opinion and finding a place that has a breast care center. When I look back at my interview with the first oncologist, I was surprised that after the appointment I was not handed information about a breast cancer foundation indicating, "We're here to help!" Or told, "Here's a brochure, call these people." There was no counselor on staff to help me get through the shock of what I was to endure. Every woman who goes to the oncologist is in there with her life on the line and is depending on the doctor to save her. You expect to be treated as if you're the *only* patient who has ever had this. You want that doctor to focus in on you. It was during my next interview with a different oncologist that I chose Dr. Sabina Wallach. I completely connected with her and had no hesitation putting my life in her hands. She was referred to me by a friend and described as being "The salt of the earth." I was at peace with my decision and felt absolutely blessed.

I received a lot of really good information about my case, about the cure…

Eve: The prognosis.

Mattie: Yes, the prognosis and about what we were going to do for my treatment. I now know that when a woman is going into the oncologist's office for the first time it's the scariest thing in the world. You don't know what kind of treatment you're going to need, how long it's going to take, who's going to be there with you, what they're going to do with your body before, during and after? There are so many questions. Eve and I both agree we don't want this to be a book on cancer because we started off as two women in our forties with a lot of spunk saying, "Hey, we're twice as twenty." We've got a lot of energy here, we've got a new lease on life, we're getting ready for our fifties, but hey, let's enjoy the sun while it's shining right here and make our forties worthwhile. Let's make being in our forties something that's going to rejuvenate us like a springboard into our fifties and sixties and seventies. We want to be encouraging and bring promise and hope, joy and tears and laughter to every reader, male or female. This cancer diversion is a fact of my life. This turn in the road is a part of being forty.

Eve: This *is* a cancer survivor story, which actually makes every other chapter so abundant with life's rich pageant. We're saying, "In the blink of an eye life can be taken away."

You can get in a car accident. You can get sick from food and die. And so for me, with all that Mattie is going through, each new day is underscored with a highlight pen saying, "Life means even more now because it's so precious."

I guess we don't realize how many people's lives we affect until tragedy hits. There's a quote from Dana Reeve that says, "It's how you deal with the tragedies in your life that makes them meaningful." Having cancer is a tragedy, but it's not a death sentence. Mattie, your story is a survivor's story about how you give meaning through your personal journey. I know you'll give back to the community any way that you can.

Maybe Mattie's journey will help shed light for anyone reading this who might be experiencing the same thing. This is life and this is what we're going through and we're going to get through it with grace, and mercy and with prayer. The power of prayer is the most amazing thing. I have seen it and I have felt it. Since this has happened my mom has told me, "Okay, Eve, tell Mattie that my friend Carol is in a 200-person prayer chain in Arizona and they are all praying for her every day." My friend Kim has introduced Mattie into her Tuesday Night Prayer Group. Mattie has told me, "Eve, I can feel it. I can feel them praying for me."

Mattie: Praying for each other is so important whether we are sick or in good health. All of us have our own personal ailments and diseases, be it of the mind, body or spirit, we all need to be there for each other even though we might not be there on a day-to-day basis. When Eve was gone on tour in England, I was blessed with so many other people that wanted to help. My sweet friend Kathleen came to my house to spend an afternoon with me. She brought her daughter to play with my son. They played all day long and went through two big rolls of scotch tape and an entire ream of paper, taping pictures all over the walls of my house. Kathleen made dinner for my entire family that night and I was in gratitude for the blessing I had received. I had good company, good laughs, and we watched our children play together. She cooked a beautiful meal and found her way through my kitchen incredibly. She even found an old kitchen knife that had been missing for three months. I was in gratitude for that! I was wondering, "How could I lose a serrated bread knife for three months?" But somehow she found it.

Eve: Ta-da!

Mattie: Kathleen gave unselfishly of her heart and her own family's time to come over and be with me. I know there are others out there who would love to do the same thing and I'm grateful for that. I marvel at their unselfish love. The bottom line to all this is there are good people in this world.

There are so many things going on in my mind right now and what I know for sure is that over the next few months I'm due for a surgery. My question is "Should I have both breasts removed?"

Eve: Is there an advantage to remove both?

Mattie: I'm feeling it would be an advantage the way things are now. What if cancer returned to my other breast? I believe reconstructive surgery can be done at the time of the mastectomy and I'm looking at that because it's a huge option. Troy and I are meeting with Dr. Wallach again on Monday and I have to say I've been blessed with how quickly things have gone since Mother's Day. We're already heading into the end of June.

Eve: Amazing!

Mattie: It's only been five weeks and already I've had two surgeries. I know there's a lot more to go, but I'm hopeful because it's been moving so quickly. I'm looking forward to the treatments. Really, I'm looking forward to knowing that they are going to heal my body. The closer I am to being cancer free FOR GOOD and never having it return excites me greatly because I know I've got a whole life to live.

Eve: We don't know where this is going to lead, but we do know this has been a life changing experience for both of us. We comment to each other often how we had no idea this would happen. I didn't realize by sitting down with Mattie and sharing my thoughts and feelings and trials that I could evolve so much. Not only with our friendship but also as a human being. Mattie and I were just listening to Emily Richards' *Peace* podcast where she said, "There are no endings, only beginnings." That fits in so perfectly with what we were saying. Is this book going to end? I don't think this book will ever end. We'll finish writing the book, we'll publish it but our story doesn't end there!

My initial reaction to Mattie's cancer was, "I wish I could go through it. I wish it could be me. God, let it be me, not her." But that's not how it's happened. Mattie is the only person who can get Mattie through this. But she knows she has a huge support group of family and friends who are going to be there for her every step of the way. She is going to be able to get through this huge life changing experience—life before cancer, life after cancer. It's going to be something she'll be able to share with many other people. There are *so* many people out there who have already gone through this. She knows if they can do it, she can do it. Mattie will be saying to herself, "Each day is more precious because of what I've been through and what I now have to offer. Even if I'm just standing next to somebody and holding their hand and saying, 'I *know*, I know what you're feeling.'" But it's so frustrating for me being on this side of Mattie's experience because I can't say I know what it feels like. As a friend I feel guilty. I think, "Why did she get cancer? What did she do differently? Was it the food? Was it the pork rinds?"

Mattie: It might have been!

Eve: Whatever it was, who knows? We can get through this together.

Mattie: Yeah.

Eve: It's okay when you don't feel well to let other people take care of your kids, cook meals, and pick up the slack. Mattie, you need to start saying, "I can't do it all because right now I need to put myself first and focus on being healthy."

Mattie: And for the first time in my adult life I got a house cleaner.

Eve: Yeah!

Mattie: She came to my house for the first time last week and I was so thrilled to have her there and have somebody there keeping me company knowing that she was cleaning and I could still take care of the kids. When she left I gave her a hug and started crying.

Eve: So sweet.

Mattie: I said to her, "You have no idea how much this means to me!" The feeling was mutual because she really needed the work and I really needed the help. It was a beautiful thing. I'm sure there are people out there who have had housecleaners for years. I'm forty-six and this is my first time hiring help because no one else could do it better than me. But, by golly, she did it exactly like I would.

Eve: Yippee!

Mattie: Those little things are very helpful. For the first time in my life I have felt what it is like to be in such dire desperation and experience a little bit of hope. Receiving an ounce of hope through a good word means so much. It's like being in Death Valley and...

Eve: Finding water.

Mattie: Yes, finding water! Every ounce of good news I hold onto and think, "I'm going to take these words and ride this wave." I've heard good news and great stories about women and *men* who have conquered breast cancer. Bill Griffith, a local news reporter in San Diego, is a breast cancer survivor.

He's very active in the community speaking at fundraisers and bringing awareness to the fact that men can get breast cancer too.

Be prepared in your life to take the challenges God sends your way. Try not to respond to those challenges with anger and disgust, but with grace and gratitude and say, "You know what, God? You're throwing me a curve ball. I'm going to take it and use everything I know to keep my faith strong, pray and know you are never going to leave me. I won't be afraid because you are with me." The Bible tells us this. The Lord said, *Do not fear. Know that I am with you.* It's mentioned in the Bible 365 times! That's every day of the year.

Eve: Wow, isn't that interesting!

Mattie: I thought that was noteworthy.

Eve: What about leap year? I'm sure that's covered!

Mattie: You get an extra one.

Eve: Bonus.

Mattie: It's a bonus day. I have nothing else to do but walk through the storm with my head up knowing that God stays with me. I plan on surviving and continuing on with my life *cancer free*! I'm going to continue being a mom, a great wife, a great friend, and a better person.

Eve: All you have to do is understand the trials in your life.

Mattie: And even though they come across as trials, they're blessings. They are there to fortify, to strengthen and to help you move on so you can help others. You know what folks? We're all here for each other. We have our routines, we've got our busy schedules, but we're here for each other. Try to touch a life out there. Try to make a difference in someone's life.

Eve: The perfect challenge.

Mattie's Footnote:

Once the initial shock of my diagnosis had passed I soon accepted that I had breast cancer and kept it in my mindset that I was going to make it to the "other side" of my life. These 127-plus days of treatment paired up with a total of five surgeries in a span of fourteen months were the hardest darkest days I could ever walk through. As dark as it may have seemed, however, the whole entire time I always had a light of hope. I always knew deep in my soul that I was going to make it through and that I was going to survive.

I got closer to God. I could hear people praying for me, hurting for me and I felt love all around me. I was wrapped in a blanket of love from everyone, even from total strangers. I cried and suffered many days. Some days all I could do was sleep. I now know what it's like to have the body of a ninety-year-old woman. It hurt to walk and it hurt to stand up straight. I lost everything that physically identified me as Mattie Mills. My breasts, hair, fingernails and ten-plus pounds were all gone. I was so weak death tried to take me one afternoon.

I remember having intense pain in my hips and legs. My bones ached like I imagine acute arthritis must feel and I suffered severe dehydration several times. One of my dear friends and caregivers, Diana, was by my bedside one afternoon asking me to drink every five minutes or so. It was hard for me to sit up because my body was depleted and I wanted to sleep. It was early September and I remember my room being very hot because we have no air conditioning but I could feel a fan blowing in the distance. My bedroom windows were open and I could hear our neighbor's child practicing her piano. Up and down the scales she would practice and I didn't mind because to me that was life out there and it sounded beautiful. I was lying on my right side facing my window barely able to move because of the pain, and then all of a sudden I felt my pain going away and the sound of the piano was getting faint and I was feeling better. I realized that I was starting to die. Not wanting this to happen I began to bear down somehow and pull myself back from dying. Every time I tried this the excruciating pain came back. I prayed to God in my head and said, "Please keep me here, I'm not ready to leave. I want to be with my family. I want to live, please, please!"

Somehow in my desperate plea I made it through that afternoon and was taken to the hospital to receive special care. I was there for four days recovering and regaining strength. I am grateful to be alive. I am grateful for the pain I endured. I am grateful to be on the other side thriving and living the life I begged God to give me back. Now, I cannot let a day go by without being grateful. I cannot let a day go by without making sure I did the best I could do with whatever situation was handed to me. I am different. "I GET IT NOW!" I get this whole thing about life.

Eve's "Appendage":

One of the hardest things to do in life is to find beauty in tragedy. I think hearing the words "You have breast cancer" might be one of life's ultimate personal tragedies. And yet, when Mattie heard those words spoken she chose to look at this tragic circumstance in her life with gratitude. I knew that this was going to be the hardest thing she was ever going to go through and that it was going to affect every aspect of her life. I also knew that she would have a very difficult time singing and performing and that her recovery would take at least six months. How was Mattie going to help provide for her family if she couldn't work? At that realization an idea grew into an event. I decided to put together a benefit concert for Mattie and her family with the idea that the money we raised would give Mattie the opportunity to focus on healing with the peace of mind that comes from financial security. I put together a team of friends and advocates and this event grew into *Music for Mattie: A Benefit Concert and Survivor Celebration*. With just the mention of Mattie's name and need an entire community of musicians and local San Diego leaders came together to make this benefit concert a huge success. We were able to give Mattie enough money to support herself during this horrible time as well as donate a portion to "Susan G. Komen for the Cure."

Every single person who was a part of *Music for Mattie* came away from that event blessed and better for it. There was a sense of community and a spiritual bonding that lifted our hearts and soothed our souls even if it was just for those few hours. The beauty we found was our connectivity to love; love of a sister, brother, friend, mother, father, to all of us. We are all in this together!

Once Mattie was back on her feet we decided to take the *Music for Mattie* concept and pay it forward. So the following year we focused on a beautiful woman named Sarah who had been fighting breast cancer for nine years. *Music for Sarah* brought an outpouring of support and concern from businesses and individuals who didn't even know her but wanted to assist in any way they could. The idea of incorporating music and breast cancer survivors to help someone in need strengthens the bond of a community and heightens awareness of this insidious disease. When we know someone with breast cancer it becomes personal and what starts regionally can spread nationally. Why can't *Music for a Survivor* become a nationwide event?

10

CATCHING UP

Eve: All right, we're back together. It's been awhile. I think it's been at least a couple of months. Has it been four months or three months?

Mattie: *(Counting on her fingers)* July, August, September, October, November, December, January, and February. Eight months.

Eve: Well it's been more than a few months!

Mattie: It's been eight months and today is March 1, 2007. The last chapter I spoke about cancer. I was diagnosed with breast cancer and here I am eight months later. I finished my chemotherapy, my hair is growing back and my nails are growing back. I have a new attitude; the journey through that whole process was difficult, but beautiful.

When Eve and I started to write this book we didn't set out to write about cancer or survival or anything of the sort. We got a detour. We planned out this book meticulously. We had ten chapters and all of a sudden the book and our lives started telling us where we needed to go. So now I am cancer free. I am a new person. I am still in my forties and I am ready to motivate and spread the word.

Eve: If we backtrack a bit, July was the last time we got together. It might have been the end of June actually, because I left on the fifth of July to tour England for three weeks. While I was gone you had your double mastectomy.

Mattie: That's right.

Eve: So much has happened. When I got back in August that's when you started your chemo and that's when I found out I was pregnant.

Mattie: In the earlier chapters you were talking about your desire to have another child. And Eve is now pregnant. She is beautifully pregnant! She's seven months and we know the baby's a boy, we've seen the sonogram. So life keeps happening!

Eve: Yes, life keeps happening! We were getting together just about every week and working on the book. Then like you said the book took over and it's telling us where to go. Of course our lives keep happening. Cancer has come and gone and now a baby is on the way and we have this circle of life. When cancer comes into your life all you can think about is, "Oh my God, I'm going to die!" That's probably a person's first thought but that's not where Mattie went with it. That's not how she went through her journey. It wasn't "I'm going to die, I'm going to die" every day, it was, "I'm going to kick cancer's ass!"

Mattie: Yep!

Eve: And you did! You did it with grace and with humility and look at you now. You look so good!

Mattie: I'm sitting here *without* a scarf on my head. I have a nice layer of hair, but very close to my head. My attitude the whole time was "I'm going to live, I'm going to live, and I'm going to spread the word and I'm going to encourage. And we're going to make women feel better about themselves and we're going to help as much as we can with what we know and with what we've learned."

It was a year ago this month I was cleaning my kitchen sink and told Eve we needed to write a book. Now we can look back and see all the changes. We became best friends forever; we decided to write this book and my life took a complete about face. I ended up turning my life around and learning so many things. Eve, now you're pregnant and we're going to have this baby in May. Life is happening and it's great!

Eve: This book has taken on a deeper, richer meaning because of what we've been through. You've lived through cancer and I've got this new life growing inside of me. A year ago our lives were completely different. Maybe that's part of the grace of being forty. We've lived through our twenties and thirties and now our life philosophies are more certain. Faith, combined with family and friends, has helped us through our journey and we realize how precious life truly is. I say, "Our lives are a journey not a snapshot." Here we are sharing glimpses of where we've been this past year, but what's the reason? Why did this happen? Why did we experience this? Did we need to go through this to be able to finish the book?

Mattie: Purified and refined! I am a person who a year ago did not have a "best friend." I have learned the importance of fellowship with a sister, a friend. I think we all need that as women. We need to stop and take a moment to put everything that's driving us crazy aside and go out to lunch or go for a walk or meet up with a friend somewhere just to give her a hug. That's what I did yesterday for Eve. She needed a hug so I just showed up and gave her one. It's those precious beautiful moments that have changed my life. I've made the effort to be a friend and it has opened my eyes to see the importance of women coming closer together and helping each other out. Try what we did. Get with a friend and journal your lives for a year or six months. Get together and talk, see what happens and how life changes through your time together. You will find it is quite an awakening. It's pretty funny when we go out together. I'm bald, she's pregnant, and we get people's attention. It's a very unique experience for both of us and we're not even rock stars. People want to know what's going on with us.

Eve: We're very non-threatening in this present mode. When people come up to us it's as if they have a sense we know something. Maybe it's slowing down and savoring each moment. Prioritizing; for example, leaving my cell phone in the car for a couple of hours while I do something for me because *I* need the time. Sometimes it seems to me like I'm on a treadmill: "I've got to do this and I've got to do that!" If I keep busy then I don't have to stop and look inside and find out what I'm afraid of or find out what's keeping me from growing. When a person is lying sick in bed day after day all they have is time to think. Time to think and ask, "What? Why? How? When?" What an experience for anyone to endure. I wonder if you were mentally overtaken or if it was a day-to-day battle?

Mattie: It was one day at a time. While you were talking I was reflecting about chemotherapy in the middle of the summer. We have no air-conditioning; it was blistering hot in my bedroom where I'd been lying in my bed for four months. Chemotherapy knocked me out, it made me so weak and during those days when I was in bed recovering I could hear children laughing and playing outside. The sound of happy music resonated from my neighbor's home every afternoon as if they were celebrating the glorious summer days. They built a fountain in their back yard and sometimes if I listened closely, I could hear the water cascading. There was lots of life and happiness in that family. The summer of 2006 was exceptionally beautiful. I told my two older daughters to "Go to the beach and enjoy. Live and be happy and in 2007 I'll be out there with you enjoying it all!"

Eve: Looking hot I might add.

Mattie: Yep! My breasts are reconstructed and all I need are nipples.

Eve: As our friend Joanne said, "You need a nipple-on-to-me!" Not a nipplectomy, a nipple-on-to-me!

Mattie: That's my next surgery, a nipple-on-to-me! And we are moving forward one day at a time. I look at our worries and think humans thrive on worrying. I think we dwell too much on the "what ifs?" and the unknowns. I'm here to tell you what you worry about does not exist. What exists is the moment you are worrying about.

Eve: I have a quote from Mark Twain. "Do the thing you fear most and the death of fear is certain!" And that's exactly what you just said, Mattie. It's about how so many people worry all the time. What does that do for them? Absolutely nothing! Worrying is obstructing the view. But we had tremendous fear when you were diagnosed with cancer. That's got to be the biggest fear you will ever have in your entire life, wondering, "Am I going to live?" I know there must be different stages of fear once you hear the word "cancer." The fear of losing control is frightening, the realization sinks in and then you go into warrior mode.

Mattie: I think there's a little control freak in every one of us. My fear of cancer started to subside after I wrote the chapter on my diagnosis. That entire chapter was about fear. I was scared to death but I made the conscious decision to tell myself, "Look Mattie, you only have this day and this moment. You are going to beat this, you are going to live." Guess what, I have big things to accomplish and I need to be here for a while!

Eve and I went out to lunch the other day and as we were sitting at our table a woman approached us, looked at me and said, "Excuse me for asking this, but did you have breast cancer?" I was caught of guard for a moment and answered, "Yes I did." And she said, "I just had a mastectomy. Can I talk to you?" I looked at Eve, my heart sank and I knew at that moment this is what we were called to do. I invited the woman to sit down at our table and her best friend came over and joined us. Our appetizers came, our drinks came, our lunch finally came and we were still talking. I was doing my best to encourage this woman who, by the way, had just turned forty and had her surgery ten days prior and was scared to death. I was carefully trying to give her words of encouragement. I wanted her to walk away from our table feeling so much better than she did when she first walked up. I kept thinking, "God help me say the right thing. God help me. God help me!" I believe seeing me with my very short hair encouraged her. I told her to see her whole body healed from cancer, a very bold thing for me to say to her not knowing her diagnosis. I looked at her and said, "See *yourself* healed!" I suggested she get a fun, sassy haircut because her hair would be falling out and she might as well have fun with it. I told her, "Make this a time to invite change every second of your life."

My words are not just for cancer patients; they are for everyone. If you feel like cutting your hair off short and sassy, do it! You want to spend an extra few bucks to get some extensions to flip your hair around then do it! Feel better about yourself. You will encourage everyone around you. Because you made the conscious effort to make those changes for you and your life instead of hanging out in your own pity party saying, "I'm in my forties. Now what am I going to do? Oh God, my life is changing!" Instead you want to be saying, "Thank you God, my life is changing for the better and I am on fire! I am going to be the best I can be in the world!" Somebody asked me once if I ever wanted to be famous. I answered, "I am already famous. I'm a star in my home. I am a rock star to my husband, my daughters, my son, and I'm happy! I don't need to be the rock star of the world." All women of the world are stars in their own homes. You are famous right where you are.

Eve: You can apply this to anything and I have applied much of what you've said to my pregnancy. I have said from the beginning that everything is going to be okay with this baby. I see a healthy baby! When a woman is pregnant in her forties there are so many health warnings. There are tests needed and doctors will give all the possibilities of what can go wrong. Yes, there are some risks. "Hey, life is a risk!" But I saw myself in the beginning having a great pregnancy and I have not been sick one day. Now I certainly had some challenging times in the beginning with my exhaustion, but I actually am in better shape now than I was in my thirties when I had my first child.

You're right, Mattie, what you are saying can be applied to anything in life. See yourself healed; see yourself having a healthy baby while you're going through it. You're going back to school to get your degree? See those straight A's. Our friend Kim McLean graduated with top honors, going back to school for four years in her forties! Know that it's okay whatever you decide to do and that it's going to be what you choose it to be. When we were talking about control I remembered this mantra I say every once in a while: "When you release you are released, when you control you are controlled." When I first heard this it hit me hard, it made such an impact in my life because I had a huge fear of flying. At that time, Mattie and I were singing together but she was unable to travel because she was pregnant.

Mattie: Of course, I was pregnant.

Eve: It was a two-month tour and we flew all over Europe. Most of the flights were on military airplanes where there are no windows and no cocktails are served. They pull down a little bench for you to sit on and then hand you a bag containing two earplugs because it's so dang loud in there. I remember sitting there and thinking to myself, "Okay, just release it! If this plane's going down, I'm going with it. I can't fly. If this plane lands safely, I'm landing safely. Why worry? Why let it ruin my time? I chose to go on tour. I chose to get on military airplanes. Let it go, let it go."

Mattie: I believe it's that change in attitude that allows us to live the life God wants us to live.

Eve: Very true.

Mattie: We get in the way of God's graces and we are our own worst enemy. I truly believe that now.

Eve: I'm on a Mark Twain kick and I have another quote that I love. "Wrinkles should merely indicate where smiles have been." Let me tell you in the past eight months Mattie and I have a few more wrinkles, maybe a few more than we'd like to have, but it's okay because there was a lot of laughter and a lot of tears too. It's nice to write again and get caught up.

Mattie: So it's March 2007 and Eve's baby is due in May. We are preparing for a beautiful baby boy. We will share the experience of the delivery later on. I might even go in the delivery room. I don't know...

Eve: You're invited! Anyone can come. Oh wait a minute; I think they said I could only have ten people. Sorry, with my family you'll have to get a ticket. Mattie's going to be in there, that's all I know.

Mattie: I'll be there with a tape recorder.

Eve: I'm going to have my kids in there, hopefully they will all want to come in and witness the miracle of life. There's the miracle of new life growing inside me. And there's Mattie, the miracle of new life sitting across from me. Mattie you are on fire, you are glowing. You got your life back but you chose a different life. You didn't want the life you had before. No. You're a new person with a new attitude and a new vision. You have things to say to people and you're not holding back.

Mattie's quite good at giving advice. I've been in a grumpy mood since I returned home from the three-week tour in the UK, which was great, but not really the best thing to do when you're six months pregnant. The entire trip was wonderful and now we're going to Vegas for a couple of weeks to perform. I know it's going to be fine. It's the whole "being gone" that's hard and I was concerned about my client's reaction to my pregnancy. So I got into a little funk and then Mattie says, "All right, what's going on?" Because she knows me so well she was able to pick away the leaves, find the root of the problem and show it to me. "Here's what's giving you this funk." And I'm amazed. She's absolutely right! Why am I worrying about what somebody else is thinking or feeling? I can only worry about what I'm doing and I'm having a baby and it's the most beautiful amazing gift God can give. I'm not going to worry about what other people think. If they have a problem with it, it's their problem.

Mattie: Exactly!

Eve: Wow, was that a lift off my shoulders! Thank you, Mattie!

Mattie: I feel lighter just hearing that again. Did I say that?

Eve: You said all of that. Looking all "hot mama" you just got your nails done, you're looking good and just ahhh!

Mattie: I've got nails. I've got everything. I'm getting my groove back!

FORTY Schmorty!
...life keeps happening

11
NIPPLES

Mattie: It's Wednesday, May 9, 2007. I'm in my car on my way to Mary Birch Hospital to witness the birth of Eve's baby boy. I am filled with anticipation, I have butterflies in my stomach and I can't wait to see this child. He has become such a symbol of transition, joy and new beginnings. I love this boy so much and I haven't even met him yet!

Eve has been a stellar example of how a woman in her forties can go through an entire pregnancy and have success at staying healthy by exercising and eating right, getting enough sleep and learning how to say "no" at all the right times. I am so proud of my best friend for working so hard and being prepared for the delivery of her baby. Eve worked out three days a week. She was always very conscious of her diet, got rest when she needed it and she's forty-three years old! What an inspiration to women who feel they want to have a baby after forty. And I'm here to tell you that you can do it. I had my youngest daughter when I was forty-four and I didn't exercise like Eve did. I'll tell you she's in much better shape than I was. I could barely walk and this girlfriend can walk all over the place. I am so happy for all the support and love she has received from everyone during her pregnancy and I am so blessed she is my best friend.

When I called Eve at 11:00 a.m. she told me the doctor had induced labor at about 8:00 a.m. and that she was feeling some fairly strong contractions at that point. Eve's husband and her mom are at her side and I'm on my way. I have just left my house and my two youngest children are with their sitter, Lindsay. I made a "vat" filled with Mac 'n' Cheese for them to survive on, which really consists of two boxes of Kraft Macaroni and Cheese. Thank you Kraft and God bless you for creating Macaroni and Cheese! I did two loads of laundry, straightened up the house, put on a little makeup, and called Ty at our production company, Gorilla Soapbox, because we will also be filming a podcast of "The Adventures of Eve Having Her Baby." What a great day! The sun is shining, it's seventy-five degrees, the sky is clear. I'm on the freeway and I can barely see out my window because my car is so filthy dirty. I've got bug splotches all over the place. I see a layer of dirt on the hood of my car and I don't care because we're having a baby today and that's all that matters.

1:13 p.m.: I just hung up the phone with Eve. She's dilated to a two and is now on some mild medication to take the edge off of the contractions and she feels really good. As I was talking to her she told me very nonchalantly, "Oh, I'm having a contraction and I can't feel it!" So that's wonderful. She's in great spirits and I'm pulling up to the hospital in the next two minutes. I'm picking Ty up at the front of the hospital and we are heading back out on the freeway to film our podcast. This is crazy. Then we'll get back to the hospital and crack down and get serious about getting this baby out and into the world. This is so cool! There's the hospital. I'm driving on I-163 looking to my left directly at the hospital. I'm going to be there in a few minutes, Eve, to see you and your baby. This is great. Just great!

1:50 p.m.: Ty and I just finished filming the opening segment of the podcast and now I'm parking my car at the hospital parking garage. I turned off the tape recorder and went about all the necessary business needed to get to delivery room #319. I was in the company of Eve (of course), Eve's mom Sally, her husband Tom, best friend Phoebe, daughter Sarah, stepson Jake and nurse

Alana. On the Mac laptop computer sitting on the table next to Eve's bed we can see Grandma and Grandpa Gulotta along with Aunt Chrissy (Tom's sister) in Florida, anxiously awaiting the birth of this new life. Modern technology is simply amazing!

It was about an hour and a half of waiting, talking and watching contractions come and go with the excitement mounting over Sweet Baby's arrival. Eve was getting tired and was ready to receive her epidural. At that point we were all asked to leave the room so she could be given her medication and take a brief nap. While in the waiting room I continued filming the podcast with Ty and prepared for the closing minutes of our show. Megan, Eve's stepdaughter and the last of all the family members attending this blessed event, finally arrived. Within minutes Tom emerges from the delivery room and hails us all to follow him because it was time.

The delivery room felt smaller than before with all the family members and friends present, minus Jake who stepped away for a moment. Now adding to the mix was our hero of the hour Dr. Dana Chortkoff preparing for delivery. Eve was getting instructions from nurse Alana and Dr. Chortkoff on what to expect, as she got closer to delivering the baby. There was so much commotion going on in the room as we all tried to find our position around Eve's bed for the perfect view. Tom answers his cell phone and explains to his best friend, "We're getting ready to have the baby!" then says goodbye."He then starts instructing Megan on the best position to video the delivery.

At the same time nurse Alana is asking Eve if she's "feeling it?" "You're having a contraction now so let's just see how you do with this first one. All right, big breath in and push down." Nurse Alana counts to ten and Eve exhales. Tom cheers her on and the nurse asks her to breathe in one more time and push again. This time a few more of us join in on the counting out loud. Eve is instructed by nurse Alana to breathe in one more time and push. By this time everyone in the room is counting!

Nurse Alana: Good job.

Tom: Good girl.

Nurse Alana: Won't be long at all.

Eve: I can't believe this, I'm already crying. I'm crying because I'm happy, Sarah, I'm not crying because I'm in pain. I don't want Sarah to think I've been crying because I'm in pain; I can't feel a damn thing!

Nurse Alana: Can you put your foot down here because I'm actually going to have you lift up just a little bit?

Grandma Sally: Might want to watch when Jake comes in.

Eve: Yes, we're going to skooch him over. I don't want him to be scarred for life!

Grandma Sally: Skooch him over to the corner.

Mattie: This will be the best sex education he'll ever have.

Eve: I know!

Mattie: Can't get this in the classroom. My daughters have been through this twice and they're okay.

Tom: Here he comes!

Grandma Sally: I know, your son! Oh Tom!

(At this point, I turned off the tape recorder to let some time pass. There was very little talking in the delivery room, as the birth was getting closer.)

Dr. Chortkoff: Count it down.

All: One, two, three, four, five.

Tom: Good girl!

All: Six, seven, eight, nine, ten.

Nurse Alana and Dr. Chortkoff: Breathe.

Tom: He's got hair, black hair!

Eve: Black hair!

Nurse Alana: Breathe in.

Dr. Chortkoff: Now push down and out.

All: One, two, three, four, five, six, seven, eight, nine, ten.

Phoebe: Breathe, baby.

Nurse Alana: Good job, do it again.

(Eve takes in a deep breath.)

All: One, two, three, four, five, six, seven, eight, nine, ten.

Phoebe: Breathe, baby, breathe!

Dr. Chortkoff: Don't push your legs back this way. Keep them relaxed.

Eve: Oh, okay.

(Someone's cell phone is ringing in the distance.)

Dr. Chortkoff: Let's do it again *(the doctor counts alone this time)* one, two, three, four, five, six, seven, eight, nine, ten.

Mattie: Good job, Eve, good job, good job, good job. Can you feel yourself pushing?

Eve: I am having a hard time feeling it.

Mattie: Yeah. Just make the face.

Tom: *(Calling out to son Jake who's just entered the room)* Jake, if you want to come in the corner you can.

Megan: Shut your eyes!

(Jake enters the delivery room and carefully "skooches" over to the side.)

Dr. Chortkoff: Breathe in again.

(Eve takes in another deep breath.)

All: One, two, three, four, five, six.

Mattie: Go girl! Seven…

All: Eight…

Dr. Chortkoff: Great!

All: Nine, ten.

Mattie: Good job, all right, all right!

Phoebe: Big breath.

(Eve takes in yet another deep breath.)

All: One, two, three, four, five, six, seven…

Tom: Ahh! *(He sees the baby crowning more.)*

All: Eight, nine, ten.

(Everyone in the room exclaims with "Ah's!")

Phoebe: One more?

Dr. Chortkoff: One more!

(Yes, Eve breathes in again!)

All: One, two, three, four…

Mattie: Good job Eve go, go, go, yeah!

All: Five, six, seven, eight, nine, ten.

Mattie: Excellent! *(Singing quietly.)* He's down there; he's down there!

Grandma Sally: Come on, baby!

Dr. Chortkoff: Relax your legs. I'm going to step out and give a report on my other patient to her nurse. I'll be back, okay?

Eve: Okay, all right. No problem.

(Tape recorder is shut off briefly as we pick up counting again.)

All: Four, five, six, seven, eight, nine, ten.

Nurse Alana: Breathe!

Mattie: Take a breather, whoa, whoa, whoa!

(I'm suddenly taking in deep breaths with Eve as I find myself caught up in all the instruction on breathing and counting.)

Mattie: Okay.

All: One, two, three, four, five, six, seven, eight, nine, ten.

Nurse Alana: Breathe!

Tom: Ah man!

Eve: Okay. *(Takes in a breath.)*

All: One, two, three, four, five, six, seven, eight…

Mattie: He's coming!

All: Nine, ten!

Mattie: My God! Okay!

Eve: He's right there, man!

Tom: Yeah!

(Everyone in the room lets out a soft laughter of excitement. Small conversations continue, filled with anticipation. Dr. Chortkoff returns to the room.)

Grandma Sally: We had one while you were gone.

Dr. Chortkoff: I know. I was watching on the monitor and saying, "She's going to push!"

Grandma Sally: We just did three like you do.

Dr. Chortkoff: Okay, perfect!

Megan: I think this just ran out of batteries. *(Referring to the video camera.)*

Eve: Oh no!

(Discussion continues about the filming as I lean in closer to Eve and whisper the following.)

Mattie: We always have Ty to film the birth. He can stand right here, he's done this before.

(Eve starts explaining to Phoebe about Ty.)

Eve: Yeah, he does this for a living. There's a company that films our podcast called Gorilla Soapbox. They film surgeries for a living.

Phoebe: Awesome!

Mattie: Well, if worse comes to worse…

Eve: We do have the…

Mattie: Extra battery? Perfect.

Eve: Battery adapter.

Mattie: Okay, good!

(About a minute passes filled with more small talk and anticipation. A contraction is on the mount and Eve goes for the big deep breath once again. We all start counting.)

All: Four, five, six, seven, eight, nine, ten.

(Couple of people say, "Great job, Eve!" and she breathes in again.)

All: One, two...

Dr. Chortkoff: Down and out!

All: Three, four, five, six...

Dr. Chortkoff: That's it, that's it!

All: Seven, eight, nine...

Dr. Chortkoff: Good job!

All: Ten!

Mattie: Great, great. Breathe, breathe, breathe.

(At this point you could hear everyone in the room take in a deep breath for Eve as she prepares for her push.)

All: One, two, three, four, five, six, seven, eight, nine, ten.

Phoebe: Breathe, baby!

(Voices of praise to Eve are getting louder in the room accompanied by the small beep of a monitor.)

Mattie: *(Singing)* Good job, you're doing great Eve! You're the best pusher I've ever seen!

(Answering to someone in the room.)

Eve: I know I can't feel my legs to lift them up. They're all tingly and heavy.

Phoebe: They're supposed to be.

(Tom turns to the laptop and calls out to his parents.)

Tom: Are you still there?

(More small talk continues with everyone in the room. Mattie and Phoebe are talking about the deliveries of their babies. Tom is briefly saying something to his parents via video chat. Another minute or so has passed and it's time to, yes, start counting. Here's where we pick up.)

All: Five, six, seven, eight, nine, ten.

Dr. Chortkoff: Great, one more time.

(Eve breathes in.)

All: One, two, three, four, five, six, seven, eight, nine, ten.

Nurse Alana: Breathe!

All: One, two, three, four, five, six, seven, eight, nine, ten.

Nurse Alana: Breathe.

Eve: Are you okay, Dana? *(Dr. Chortkoff.)* Is everybody okay in here?

Dr. Chortkoff: Aha!

Tom: Yes!

Mattie: Everybody's great!

(The other people in the room nod and smile and Dr. Chortkoff gives instruction to make a little more room. More small talk ensues as we wait for Eve's next contraction. We pick up with Dr. Chortkoff giving instructions at the beginning of the next contraction.)

Dr. Chortkoff: Push as hard as you can. Push, push, push, push, puuuuush!

All: One, two, three, four, five, six, seven, eight, nine, ten.

Nurse Alana: Breathe.

Dr. Chortkoff: Push, push, push.

All: One, two, three…

Tom: Ah, there he is!

All: Four, five, six…

Dr. Chortkoff: Excellent, keep going!

All: Seven, eight, nine, ten!

(Eve exhales harder and breathes in.)

Phoebe: One, two, three, four, five…

(For some reason everyone stopped counting except for Phoebe. It was very possible the baby could be seen, but was not quite out. I decided to join in on the counting.)

Tom: Come on, baby!

Phoebe and Mattie: Six, seven, eight, nine, ten!

(Eve let's out an exhale with a small cry in her voice. I know at this point the baby is just around the corner.)

Dr. Chortkoff: Great job!

Mattie: Good job Eve, good job!

(Three pushes in a row, success! This time Dr. Chortkoff instructs Eve to hold her legs when she gets ready to push. Tom and Grandma Sally are there to hand Eve her legs since she can't feel them.)

Dr. Chortkoff: And he's almost out!

Tom: Oh boy!

Dr. Chortkoff: I might need to do a little cut, we'll see.

Eve: That's okay.

(Small talk continues as we wait for the next contraction. Eve remembers that Sarah had a big sized head when she was born and had a feeling this baby's head was smaller. Sally, Eve's mom and mother of eight children claimed she really couldn't remember very much of any of her grandchildren's births. She only attended twenty-one out of the twenty-six deliveries and a small relief of laughter fills the room.)

Dr. Chortkoff: Okay, here comes another one. Pull your legs back, hands behind your thighs, big breath in, down and out, down and out.

Nurse Alana: Two, three…

All: Four, five, six, seven, eight, nine, ten.

Dr. Chortkoff: Chin to your chest. Ready? Go!

Phoebe and Mattie: One, two, three, four, five, six, seven, eight, nine, ten.

Phoebe: Breathe!

Mattie: Breathe!

Nurse Alana: Breathe in.

Mattie: Go!

Phoebe, Mattie and Nurse Alana: One, two, three, four, five, six, seven, eight, nine, ten.

Phoebe: Breathe, baby!

Dr. Chortkoff: Big breath again.

All: One, two, three, four, five, six, seven, eight...

(The volume of nine and ten swelled like a huge wave in the ocean. His head was coming out! Squeals of excitement from all of us follow as Eve starts to cry with joy.)

Dr. Chortkoff: Okay, big push again.

Nurse Alana: Push.

Phoebe: Push!

Mattie: Go Eve, come on!

Dr. Chortkoff: Take a breath, take a breath.

Tom: Hold on, hold on!

Nurse Alana: Wait, wait!

Dr. Chortkoff: Okay, push. Now big push, big push!

Tom: OOOH! OOH!

All: OH!

(Everyone in the room is simply overcome with joy. It sounded like we were all on a roller coaster ride heading down that final dip with our arms straight up in the air screaming and laughing and crying with

tears of happiness. A baby boy! Wow! Nurse Alana and Dr. Chortkoff were quickly cleaning him up when we all finally heard that beautiful cry.)

Baby: Wha wha whaaaaaaa!

Tom: Ah, there you go, there you go!

(I'm having a great cry with Eve at this point as Grandma Sally exclaims.)

Grandma Sally: Five o'clock!

(More ooh's and ahh's in the room as Eve is handed her baby for the first time.)

Eve: Oh sweet boy, sweet boy! It is a boy isn't it?

Tom: Oh, it's a boy! All boy!

Eve: Oh my sweet boy, oh my sweet boy!

Sweet Boy: Aaaah, aaaah! *(He really did say that!)*

Mattie: Wait, here comes Florida!

(The laptop is being passed over to Tom so Aunt Chrissy and Grandma and Grandpa Gulotta in Florida can get a closer look.)

Tom: Can you see him?

(Sweet Boy starts crying a great sturdy cry.)

Eve: Does he have a butt chin?

Grandma Sally: I don't think he does. I didn't see it.

Mattie: Oh, he's so beautiful!

Tom: Ahh, he's perfect! Look, his eyes are open already!

Eve: Oh, he's so aware!

(Sweet Boy lets out another cry.)

Sarah: Henry, right? Is it Henry?

Eve: I don't know. Hey Sweet Boy, oh Sweet Boy!

Mattie: Okay, it's time to sing him "Happy Birthday!"

(Mattie leads as everyone in the room joins in)

All: Happy birthday to you, happy birthday to you, happy birthday dear Sweet Boy, happy birthday to you!

(I stayed for about another thirty minutes and left the happy family to enjoy their beautiful new life. We pick up back in my car.)

Mattie: A baby boy, a beautiful baby boy. Wow! What an experience to be on the other side of a delivery. I had the chance to witness the birth of a baby that wasn't my own. Everything that went on this afternoon was a miracle from God and I am so happy. The grandparents from Florida even got to see the entire birth because Eve brought her laptop and set up a video chat with them through the hospital's wireless Internet connection. They were with us the entire time. When it was time for the delivery the laptop was held up for them to see a side view. They even got a first hand peek at the baby's weight and cleaning. How cool is that!

The birth of a baby is a wonderful thing and we are so blessed to bring this Sweet Boy into the world who at this point does not have a name so that's why I keep calling him and we all keep calling him "Sweet Boy." Now I am on my way home to pick up my son and together we are going to a mother/child tea at his preschool in honor of Mother's Day. I will fly into the house, pay the babysitter, get myself dressed, get my boy in the car and head out to our afternoon tea. And at the same time Eve and her son are having some afternoon teet! What a great life!

(Later the next morning, Sweet Boy was named.)

Henry Isaac Joseph Gulotta
May 9, 2007, 4:59 p.m.
8 pounds, 13.8 ounces
20 inches long

(Now we move forward to August 1, 2007. Eve and I are in my kitchen where she has just finished hearing the cassette recording of everything you just read. I can't believe we did this on cassette!)

Eve: Well that was amazing. Now we are finishing off a good cry while blowing our noses. What an amazing experience to listen to this and relive it.

Mattie: That was twelve weeks ago.

Eve: And Mattie ended it on a perfect note saying she was going to have tea with her son and my son was going to enjoy some teet with me.

Mattie: The next half of this chapter is all about my nipple reconstruction, which I had yesterday.

Eve: How do you feel today?

Mattie: Today I feel great, but I am a little sore. A lot sore actually. This is the completion of my breast reconstruction from one year ago when I endured a double mastectomy. I have been without nipples for one year.

I was very fortunate to have a wonderful surgeon, Dr. Eugene Rumsey, Jr. and an amazing plastic surgeon, Dr. Stephen Krant, who worked together to save my life on July 18, 2006. During the surgery Dr. Rumsey removed all my breast tissue on one breast and then Dr. Krant took over and began working on the reconstruction. When he was done on one side he moved over to the other breast, following Dr. Rumsey. Dr. Krant inserted two expanders containing 100 cc of saline resting under some muscle tissue. I would visit Dr. Krant during the months of my chemo treatment and receive anywhere between 20 to 30 cc's of saline that was injected into the expander. This was to gradually pull my muscle forward and allow space for the prosthetic (silicone breast) to be inserted. The expander has a small port entry with a circular magnet around it. In order for the doctor to find this entry the nurse would pass a magnet over the general area of the port. When the magnet grabbed we were in for business! In other words, we found the port entry.

Eve: Could you feel the needle go through your skin?

Mattie: Not really. The area is pretty numb because of my surgery. However, they did numb the area before inserting the needle. Eventually I will get some feeling back. Today I have very little feeling but it's more than it was. So in February 2007 I had the expanders removed and the implants put in successfully, without nipples of course. So on top of both of my breasts there was a line about three inches long where the incision was made.

Eve: And the skin is sewn together.

Mattie: Yes, the nipple and the areola have to be removed during a mastectomy to prevent the spread of cancer in that area.

Eve: That was mind blowing to me. I'm sure most people don't understand what a double mastectomy means anyway. We understand it's removing the breast, but we don't know what that means until it happens to us or you see someone go through it. I had no idea they had to take your nipples off. Anybody I've mentioned it to didn't realize that needed to happen either.

Mattie: When I explain it to people I tell them it's like cleaning out a pumpkin for Halloween. You cut a circle on the top and you clean out the pumpkin seeds. So for a year I've had these two 3-inch incisions to look at until yesterday. It was an outpatient surgery and I was very excited about that. Actually, this surgery was originally scheduled for May. I had a 2:00 p.m. surgery scheduled, but for me there was something about going into the hospital that I just didn't want to do. I found myself waiting for noon to come around which seemed like an eternity because I had been up since 7:00 a.m. I felt anger and anxiety during my five-hour wait. I kept thinking this is my fifth surgery and the fifth time going under and I was getting hungry.

Eve: Well there's always the chance you'll never wake up. Anybody can die from anesthesia. It's scary!

Mattie: I always look forward to waking up. You're down and the next thing you know you're up and you don't realize the time that has passed. Waking up is always a good thing after anesthesia.

Eve: Yes.

Mattie: So back in May I think I was feeling angry because I had to go back to the hospital again. Even though this was my final surgery and I would have nipples and this would be the end.

Eve: And there was a little problem they were going to fix right?

Mattie: Yes, apparently with some women the muscle tissue can't hold the prosthesis very well. One or both sides sink and become uneven. This unfortunately happened to me on one side. So on top of getting my nipples reconstructed I was getting my breast pockets reinforced. I wasn't ready for the surgery emotionally or mentally and I succumbed to two handfuls of Planters Cocktail Peanuts. I was so hungry and so angry at the time I didn't care anymore.

Eve: It's almost like being robbed. You must have felt so invaded, so infuriated saying to yourself, "Again? You have to go into my body again and do something else?"

Mattie: That's a good way of explaining it. I wasn't up for the invasion. I knew I wasn't supposed to eat before surgery, at least twelve hours before surgery, so I started off with one peanut. It tasted really good. Then I thought about you when you were pregnant with Henry and the wonderful snack you used to have. Remember when you would get a banana and dip it in a can of Planters Cocktail Peanuts? Oh my God, that is so delicious!

Eve: It's a good snack, people.

Mattie: That snack is heaven! Well there I was in my kitchen thinking of that banana and peanuts snack while reaching for my can of Planters Cocktail Peanuts. I ate one, which lead to another, then another and then another. I just said, "Forget it. I'm having a handful!" Then when I finished that handful I went back and had another handful. I couldn't stop. I was hungry! I didn't care at that point. I went to the hospital, I got checked in, changed into a surgical robe, slipped on some socks and went through the routine of getting my vitals checked. Then came the questions: "Did you have anything to eat today?" I answered nonchalantly, "No, I just had five peanuts." "You had five peanuts?" she asked. "Yes," I replied. "Okay, I'll be right back." The nurse gets up very calmly and walks out of the room for about ten minutes. She comes back in and makes a couple of phone calls discussing the peanuts with someone. The bottom line was I couldn't have surgery because they had to wait at least another three hours until my peanuts digested.

Eve: Because you could regurgitate and suffocate.

Mattie: On peanuts?

Eve: Your peanuts!

Mattie: Oh God! So waiting three hours would have moved Dr. Krant's schedule, having him finish the surgery by seven or eight in the evening and that was too late. I needed to reschedule. That little snafu I caused affected between twenty to forty people in my immediate circle. True story! If I kept counting I could have found more people on the outside of the circle affected. I felt so terrible and once again so angry, but this time at myself for all the trouble I had caused my family, friends and colleagues.

Eve: It was a ripple.

Mattie: It was a huge ripple but I had to look at it for what it was and not beat myself over the head. It just wasn't *my* time for surgery. I had to remember there is a reason for everything.

Eve: What did your sister say?

Mattie: She said, "You were just handed the biggest blessing in your life today because you were not meant to go into surgery." That really stopped me in my tracks. It made me realize there's reasons for circumstances that do and don't happen in our lives. If something didn't happen for you that you were hoping for, there is a reason. If something great happens for you there is also a reason. I quickly understood and forgave myself for being angry and upset I had put so many people out.

So, I waited two months and was mentally and emotionally prepared for the final surgery. Yesterday was my surgery. My two breast pockets were reinforced and my nipple reconstruction was complete. Dr. Krant has a method of creating a nipple from the skin on the breast and creating an areola by grafting the skin from the groin area and placing it on the breast around the nipple. I don't know what it looks like right now because it's covered up with gauze. In about seven days they will be able to remove the gauze and I'll be complete.

Eve: They're protecting the area so the skin that is grafted on can take. It actually...

Mattie: Gets affixed.

Eve: Well it grows into it; it becomes a part of it and then it's just part of who you are. Take a little bit here, put it there, take a little bit over here and put it there.

Mattie: It is amazing what can be done!

Eve: What Mattie has here is tubing that's taped on her chest connected to a pain pump. She's wearing this white vest bra and there's drainage tubes under both her arms that end in a bulb which is safety pinned to the bottom of her vest bra. I agree it's amazing what can be done today.

Mattie: This pain pump numbs the chest area. It will be removed in about five days and then I'll be on my own with Tylenol.

Eve: Mattie is going hard-core here. She's not taking Vicodin because it knocks her out so she's taking Tylenol. Even after I had Henry I was asking for one more round of Vicodin because I was in so much pain. But that stuff is vicious; that's why it starts with the letter "v."

Mattie: "V" for vicious.

Eve: It is addictive. I'm a lightweight and I can always tell when the drug is wearing off and the pain starts coming back. But Mattie is toughing it out.

Mattie: But I feel good. I'm not really in that much pain. If I take a Vicodin, I'll fall asleep. *(House phone starts ringing.)*

Eve: Hospital calling. Take a break.

(Mattie answers the call.)

Eve: That was cool!

Mattie: Had to take a quick pause to answer the call from Scripps Memorial Hospital.

Eve: Checking in on you and making sure you are okay?

Mattie: That was my nurse who was with me in recovery. She was sweet to call to make sure I was doing okay—"You sound so much better!" And I am doing so much better today. So we thought we would tie in the birth of Henry and my breast reconstruction as new beginnings. I'm in a really good mood today.

Eve: I know how you feel physically. How do you feel spiritually?

Mattie: I'm happy. I'm so happy this is behind me now. I've been named Honorary Survivor 2007 for the "Susan G. Komen for the Cure 5K Walk/Run" in San Diego. I've been chosen to motivate and inspire people to walk the 3.2 miles coming up in November. I had an interview yesterday with a public relations firm that's putting together the press release for the walk. I'll soon be on television and radio and local publications to tell my story and get people to participate. This 5K Walk/Run is a week before the Susan G. Komen for the Cure National Three Day Walk. There's a local radio station in San Diego, Star 94.1 that has the *Jeff & Jer Morning Show*. Their producer, Tommy Sablan, is walking the Three Day Walk in my honor along with a huge list of women who have had breast cancer.

Eve: That's sixty miles, twenty miles a day. Geeze!

Mattie: He's training now and he's training hard. We went out to lunch so I could help him get a better idea of what I went through. I told him my whole story.

Eve: What is it like for you now to tell your story?

Mattie: It's hard sometimes to go back. It was a wretched time. But I am so grateful to be alive and well because there's this driven inner passion I have to encourage other men and women who get breast cancer to keep going. I feel like I am on an assignment where I need to go out and spread a positive word. That positive message not only pertains to survivors, it pertains to everyone. People stricken with breast cancer suffer greatly and when they get to the other side they are blessed survivors.

Eve: You're like a beacon, a shining beacon of life. Some people live to be ninety and go to sleep and never wake up. But when your mortality is thrown in your face it changes you. You're different, Mattie. You're the same beautiful person you've always been but you're different. I can see it in the glow on your face and I can see it in your curly hair. All the hair on Mattie's head is completely curly. Perfect curls!

Mattie: It's fun actually. I'm having a lot of fun with it, even though I haven't seen Tony, my hairstylist. I don't have that much hair. I want to let it grow out. I'm using hair product to make the curls curlier and wet looking. Sometimes I straighten the front for a different style, or fluff it all out and wear a headband. I have become the inspiration for a few women I know to cut all their hair off and bravely wear their hair like they never have before. They love it!

Eve: That's what happened to me when we cut our hair short last year before you started chemo. I got so many comments about my hair and how cute it looked short. And now here we are waiting for your hair to grow back. "Come on hair, grow!" What a process we've been through. What a tie-in with our new beginnings, my Henry and you. I'm breastfeeding and my nipples are killing me because he can LATCH ON! Let me tell you, he's twelve weeks old and he's already cut a tooth! So I'm not sure how much longer I'll be breastfeeding. Honestly, my nipples are killing me and it's like I've been feeling for you what you must be going through even though it's completely different. You had to go through surgery and you're in pain right now, but it's as if we're on the same plane.

Mattie: Our nipples are...

Eve and Mattie: Killing us!

Mattie: Troy says the best time to stop breastfeeding is when your son starts requesting different outfits for you to wear. That's when you know it's a really good time to stop breastfeeding.

Eve: Okay, well I'm hoping to make it to six months.

Eve and Mattie: Uh, Boy!

Mattie: I want tell you something Dr. Krant shared with me about women who have gone through what I have gone through this last year. He said, "When a woman is diagnosed with breast cancer and has her mastectomy reconstruction surgery she gets her breasts back, but when she gets her nipples, she gets herself back." I can't even begin to tell you how true that is. The night before my surgery I had a "markings" appointment with Dr. Krant where he marks with a purple felt pen on my chest everything he needs to remember during the surgery. He took notes and then taped some fake nipples with areoles for measurement onto my chest. Then he asked me to look in the big mirror to see what I thought. As I opened up my robe to see myself I felt like I was back. I was me again! It is strange to think that for a full year I accepted what was missing, but it also reminded me of what I had experienced. The other day I was taking a shower and my five-year-old son Nathan runs into the bathroom looks at me and asks, "Mom, why don't you have any pimples on your chi-chi's?" We call breasts chi-chi's. I looked at Nathan and answered in a very matter of fact manner, "I'm getting pimples next month, no worries!" He said, "Oh, okay" and ran out and was fine.

Eve: On the way back from your appointment with Dr. Krant I was telling you about when I got my breast implants. I was twenty-eight years old and I think I was still wearing a size 34 AAA bra.

Mattie: I remember.

Eve: I was flat as a pancake! All I had were nipples, just two nipples. I felt like a little girl, I didn't feel like a woman. So I went to a plastic surgeon and asked for the smallest breasts he could give me. I didn't want big breasts I just wanted some breasts. I'm coming from the complete opposite perspective, but the minute I got them I thought, "Oh my gosh, I feel like a woman!" Is that what you're feeling? Do you feel like a woman again?

Mattie: I feel complete again. I really do. I feel complete. Your breast augmentation in my mind was justified. If anyone needed breasts you did.

Eve: I did. It was so sad. My nieces, who were fourteen and fifteen, had bigger breasts than I did.

Mattie: I was so happy for you. I remember that.

Eve: Yeah, it was a big deal. I got them positioned underneath the breast tissue so I could breast feed if I ever decided to have a baby and of course, I got pregnant three months after I had my breasts done. If I had only waited I would have seen what I looked like with real breasts.

Mattie: Well we fast-forward to today and they look beautiful.

Eve: Thank you. Hey, what is it about the word nipple that makes us squirm and giggle?

Mattie: You know, I don't know. Can we call it something else? I know "nipples" does sound funny.

Eve: People say nipple and it's "tee hee, hee!" Have you ever been to a bar and heard someone order a drink called, "Slippery Nipple"?

Mattie: No!

Eve: There's a drink called a "Slippery Nipple" and I think people like to order it to make other people feel uncomfortable.

Mattie: I've heard of a drink called the "Purple Hooter," but "Slippery Nipple" is a new one for me. Mine aren't going anywhere. They are tied down!

Eve: They are tied down. They are going to be beautiful and you are beautiful Mattie. You are just amazing. I wish you all could see her.

Mattie: Here's something. I gained seven pounds in four days. I don't know what happened.

Eve: Well they gave you a lot of fluids during surgery. That's what the nurse said today.

Mattie: Well I'm very puffy.

Eve: Did they give you medicine before you went in? My doctor gave me Vicodin to take the morning of my surgery.

Mattie: I didn't take anything before I went in for surgery.

Eve: They gave it to you in the hospital?

Mattie: I was given something to relax me, then they put me out and I woke up ten pounds heavier. But I want to explain that a week before my surgery my daughter Gia and I went to orientation at her college for three days. I gained three pounds because we were all given a meal card to eat in the cafeteria. We had breakfast, we had lunch and we had dinner. We don't eat like that at home. Breakfast for me is a glass of orange juice or a cup of coffee, lunch is small too and dinner is our main meal for the day. At orientation I went to town eating three squares a day and came back three pounds heavier. Then I went into surgery and gained seven more pounds! Every time I pee I jump on the scale to see if I'm at least a half pound lighter.

Eve: You could use the extra weight, Mattie. You are skin and bones. Maybe it's God's way of plumping you up so the surgery would be easier.

Mattie: Just a little, that's okay. I'm okay with that.

Eve: This has been a crazy journey Mattie and I have been on. If you spell the word journey the word "our" is in there. We're on the road together holding hands and getting through.

Mattie: Skipping along and changing our part of the world.

12

CAREER MOVES

Eve: I want to start with a wonderful quote from Mother Theresa: "Work without love is slavery." I think both Mattie and I have felt like slaves occasionally when we've been at shows that were more work than love. Music is usually so healing and wonderful but sometimes it can be work and when it is, it takes everything you have to keeping going, to change your attitude, to turn it around and make it a positive experience.

Mattie: I think in the corporate world these days there are those who have their share of hard times and realize they've lost their love for the job. People find themselves stuck in the everyday humdrum of their position. Their growth has been stunted and when you stop growing at your job you stop loving what you do.

We want to plant an inspiration seed and encourage you to rethink your career. And if you aren't currently working, maybe you're in serious need of something different for the fun of it. The biggest "secret" I've learned about career change or finding something fresh to do with your life is to rediscover your passion. It's easy for Eve and me because we "sing for our supper" and we know we can grab a guitar, write a song and perform it in a bookstore or at a fundraiser. We've been fortunate to live our passion all along. Not so for everyone whose passion may have been sidetracked in order to make enough money to support a family or because a career was mapped out for them.

I have spoken to a number of people who have taken their passion and turned it into their second (or these days, maybe even third) career. For example, I met a retired gentleman who wanted to continue working, doing something fun and different, but he didn't know exactly what he could do. He spoke with a friend one day about his favorite personal hobbies, one being fishing, and realized he could become a fishing instructor. This would enable him to spend more time out on his boat, teach students at any age how to fish, and make money all at the same time! Eventually this became a very lucrative business for him and I believe he ended up writing a book (why wouldn't he?) about his whole venture. It's all about awaking the "sleeping passion" inside your soul. What is your most favorite thing in the world to do?

Eve: I think we just don't consider that a hobby could end up being something we can actually make a living doing. After all, hobbies are fun and work is work. Then one day we realize the potential and "Bam!" we're doing what we love, hopefully for years and years. I guess I was lucky. I found out at a very early age that I could sing. When you're younger and you realize you can do something, you get excited about it (there's the passion) and you think, "Hey, I can do something, I can sing!" So I started singing and gained the confidence to grow. I always knew I was going to be a singer and I always knew where my path was going to lead. I was able to make a living singing in clubs. You remember, Mattie, how we used to do that in our twenties, when we would sing five and six nights a week, four hours each night. Oh my gosh! We would sing in smoky clubs and get up and do it again the next night and still have a voice.

Mattie: In my twenties I sang with a band called Saddletramp in a Country/Western nightclub six nights a week. We always knew we were doing well when a fight broke out in the bar. If a fight didn't break out and the cops didn't show up it meant we (the band) weren't ringing the cash register and we were doing a terrible job promoting the drink specials. Before every break I would spin the "drink wheel" which had hilarious drink specials like Kamikazes for twenty-five cents, Tom Collins for fifty cents (you get the idea) to be sold during our fifteen-minute break. We would always encourage the audience to buy the band a round of drinks and of course, it would always be six shot glasses of something horrible. Back in those days I witnessed some gnarly fights.

Eve: I bet you did! At some point you begin to think, "Am I a singer or am I a liquor salesman?" I remember there would be times when we were performing together and we would comment, "We're just the means to an end!" We were providing the music and the songs so the people could dance and drink. That's all it was, which can certainly weigh on you if you're trying to be an artist or trying to get your craft into alignment.

Mattie: In our forties, we're changing our tune. We're singing songs of love and inspiration. We don't want fights to break out at the bar and we don't want anything to go wrong. We want people to feel good about who they are and feel good about life. And this is why we think the topic of "Career" is an important element of being in your forties. Here's another story. A woman who had just had a baby felt out of shape and was suffering from postpartum depression. She gathered a couple of her girlfriends who just had babies and started an exercise program while strolling. Today she's nationally known for her group called Stroller Strides. Check it out on line, it's amazing.

Eve: That's a great idea. She took a passion, found a need and turned it into a career. I think by the time a person is in their forties they've probably had one, maybe two, serious career moves. Now they're probably looking at their life and asking, "What am I going to be doing when I'm fifty and sixty? Is this what I want to be doing? Do I want to try something else? Do I want to work for myself? Do I want to continue to work for this corporation that may or may not be here or that may or may not downsize me and I'll have to start over anyway?" The reality of work life has changed dramatically since we were in our twenties.

Mattie: I meet so many people with home businesses. They find a way to make their business work around their personal schedule. It's nice to see that people have the option, especially moms who want to be home with their families and keep their brains sharpened.

Eve: Our careers have worked out nicely for us because we are both married, we are both moms and our jobs are mainly at night when the kids are sleeping. We get to spend our days with our children. We've certainly had day jobs too along the way and we've had several jobs at once just to make ends meet. But it's nice how it has worked out the way it has for us. I think there are a lot of women who would love to stay home but they are teachers or managers of a store or a restaurant and they have to work during the day. That's definitely a challenge! We have both gone through the morning daycare and the "take the bus to after-school care and wait for me" routine. We did whatever we could to bring in enough money to be able to do what we love.

Mattie: To make ends meet. It's difficult, but women do it. We've done it. One of the hardest parts of being a singer in a band, even though we get to be home during the day, are the days and weekends where we miss out on family events.

Eve: Oh yeah.

Mattie: I have to be the first one to leave during a family barbecue or it's somebody's birthday and we can't go to it because I have to work.

Eve: Yep.

Mattie: Eve and I both got married on a Sunday because all of our musician friends were working on Friday and Saturday.

Eve: Right! It's so true.

Mattie: That's the downside of our career, having to sacrifice family events. And now that I'm "older" it's harder to leave because these events are more precious and I want to spend time with my family. It means more than it ever has and sometimes it's difficult to compromise. But it's what we do. And compromise is what we have to do. Maybe you're in the medical field but you have a passion to write. You could split the difference between being a doctor by day and a writer by night. I think when you find your passion you'll devote time to exploring the possibilities and it becomes really fun.

Eve: Oh yes, and sometimes you have to throw caution to the wind and tell yourself, "I'm going to trust in myself and in God. I'm going to get through this and even if I'm going to take a hit financially I'm going to try!" I have a friend who is taking a sabbatical for forty days and forty nights. She's going to a place where there's no phone, no Internet and no television. She's telling me, "I can't really afford this, but there's something in me that's saying I have to do this." So she's going away to some place in New Mexico to write. She needs to be in that space and in that zone. I know other people who have wanted to write but can't find the time or make the time. Maybe because they have to get up at five o'clock in the morning in order to find a block of two hours where they're by themselves. Or they need to find seclusion, but due to family obligations it's too difficult and they're waiting for the "perfect time."

Mattie: Speaking of finding time to transcribe this book with a husband and four children, now you're talking difficult. But since I don't have that much time I wait until everyone is in bed for the evening and the house is quiet so I can sit down at the kitchen table and transcribe from our cassette tape. An hour at the computer only gives me a page or two and that's it! I have to continually stop the tape, listen and rewind, edit and rethink. Fortunately, it's gotten faster and much easier. As I recall, this chapter was originally going to be chapter four and I believe somewhere around that time...

Eve: You discovered your lump and we didn't feel like talking about our careers.

Mattie: Right and I suggested we talk about careers later. That's why we called Chapter Four "Stop the Show!" and discussed the possibility of me having breast cancer. Kind of interesting isn't it to be ending with career because in a way you and I are launching an "extension" career.

Eve: Right!

Mattie: We're not quitting our careers as singers. We will always be singing; there will always be a wedding or funeral or an event where we will want to sing. But the book and its positive outcome are an extension of our career. This project has stimulated my brain and brought me to the computer researching mounds of information. It has allowed me to read more books than I have ever read in my *Forty Schmorty* life. I know there are women who feel like me, who feel their brains are not stimulated enough with knowledge and information because they are so busy with family and everyone else. It's difficult to make time but you must try. Otherwise your brain feels dead.

Eve: You never know where or how one step is going to lead to the next step. For example, when we started writing this book we had no idea of the journey ahead. We had no clue you were going to be diagnosed with breast cancer or that I was going to become pregnant. And now here we are. We've traveled full circle with a newborn and no sleep and you completely cancer free and moving on with life. We had no idea this book would lead to you becoming an advocate for breast cancer and working with the Susan G. Komen for the Cure as an Honorary Survivor for 2007.

Along with the book, we decided to jump in and produce a video podcast, which has been fun. Who knows where that's going to take us? Doing something different and trying something new, taking chances, opening doors you didn't think existed or ever would or could open. We didn't think we were going to be on the Internet with this project, but we are. Take those chances! Take those risks! We hear it all the time but until we actually try it, we don't realize the truth of it. You really don't get things in life unless you take risks and take chances. We've all got twenty-four hours in a day. It's a matter of prioritizing. Some of us may not have as much time as we think we have in the long run. We're in our prime, our forties, but who knows what could happen to us tomorrow? Who knows? We have to take the chance and do for ourselves now.

Mattie: Do it for yourself. Act on it now. If you feel you can't do it on your own, that you don't have the support you need or want, or you're shy about taking the first step, bring a friend with you. Eve and I did; we chose to do this together and I am so grateful I had my best friend along to get this done. It started as a fun project because I felt Eve and I had interesting and parallel lives. I'm always telling people whose life story has caught my attention: "You have a very interesting life. You need to write a book!" Now here we are "walking our talk" and excited about our new adventure. Who knows what's ahead—public speaking, book signings, selling our inspirational music? And to think, what started as an idea and a desire to share now includes eight people on board the *Forty Schmorty* train.

Eve: We just opened a bank account. We're a business. Wow!

Mattie: We're an official business now. It's been a year and a half. This started off so innocently with two small tape recorders and some old-fashioned cassette tapes. We most likely couldn't do this in five years with such dinosaur technology.

Eve: Hopefully by then we'll be able to record on our computers that will transcribe while we're speaking. I think they already have software to do that.

Mattie: I'll tell you when it's going to happen. It's going to happen the day I type the last punctuation mark on the last page of this book.

Eve: Oh yes! But the bottom line is we couldn't have done this without each other. We couldn't have gotten as far as we did without building together on our original dream and desire. We've had our hurdles and wondered, "How are we going to explain that?" And then "Boom!" Mattie meets somebody at the grocery store or I run into someone and say, "Hey, we went to high school together." "What are you doing now?" And they end up being someone who can help change the course of our direction.

Mattie: Exactly!

Eve: You never know who you're going to meet or who's in your life already that you haven't thought about in awhile. Consider all the people you know, including your family, and then casually mention your project to them and they might say, "Hey, I know somebody who's doing that." Or "Hey, I've got somebody you should talk to." It's been like a game board. You land on a square; you pick up a card that reads, "Go three steps to the right!" To me the book has been revealing itself as we go along.

Mattie: Sort of like the game *Candy Land*; we have that game at home.

Eve: We have it too. I think every American home with children has the game *Candy Land*. The point is to get it out there, tell people what you're doing. The Internet has been wonderful. We've been looking things up and asking questions. We decided to do a partnership agreement. We've never written a partnership agreement so I just Googled it and found one that worked for us.

Mattie: Fill in the blanks.

Eve: Yep, fill in the blanks. It was so easy. It looks official and it will hold up in court. I want to challenge people to make their dream list and write it down, make it official.

Mattie: I was just going to say that! Create a dream list of all the things you love to do. It can be crazy; write down whatever you want. The list can be silly and/or serious, but it has to be things you really enjoy doing or have always wanted to do. Then narrow the list down to one or two things. If you went to college then you can compare your dream list of ideas with your college degree and see how they work together (or not). If you don't have a degree or you're completely removed from your major or minor, add the things you do really well then compare it with the items on your list. Outline your start-up plan and goal. Go online and look up your newfound idea. You may be quite surprised to find it with instructions for steps one through ten or certification courses. How many times have you thought of an invention or a great idea and then come across it and say to yourself...

Eve: I had that idea a couple of years ago!

Mattie: Rollerblades were my idea. JUST KIDDING!

Eve: Post-It Notes was mine.

Mattie: You're the one!

Eve: Oh well, what are you going to do?

Mattie: Remember that whatever you come up with, you'll want to place your own unique stamp on the idea. Always be positive and wrap it around your current career. All your hopes and dreams will tie-in together.

Eve: A perfect example is the business called DreamDinners.

com, which we talked about previously. I can't believe how much money I spend on groceries because I live right next to a Vons grocery store. If I need something all I have to do is run next door and buy it. The groceries add up fast! But with DreamDinners.com you've got as many meals as you need for the week. All you do is thaw it out and place it in the oven. They're now all over the country.

Mattie: Oh yeah, it's all over the country and under different names. Other people have come up with their version of the same idea and have made it their own business. Last year when I had so many wonderful, gracious people bringing my family meals one neighbor brought us five frozen meals prepared just as you have described. That was fantastic and they were delicious.

Eve: Oh, and you can season the meals and add extra ingredients if you want. The idea is perfect for someone like me who doesn't cook. Here's two Dream Dinner gals realizing what they love to do and figuring out the need. Now they are successful and have financial freedom. How many times have you been on a vacation and wished you could be on vacation forever? Maybe you could. Explore. Investigate. Ask, "Who would have thunk it?"

Mattie: It might not be a specialty of yours but it might be something that hits you between the eyes, something you see as an opportunity, a need you can fulfill. For example, you're on vacation and you notice an item or a convenience is missing in the hotel room. You say to yourself, "Gosh, if they only had this it would be so much easier." I notice or miss things like that and say to myself, "Well now, if I could be the person to supply this then I could sell it to the hotel and become a hundredthousandollaraire!

Eve: A hundredthousandollaraire, just imagine! Well those are the moments, those brilliant moments when you think, "Why didn't I go for that?" We've all done it! We've thought of something that would make life better or easier and then somebody else comes out with that similar idea and makes a killing. I think it's about following through with your ideas. It's difficult when you're married with kids and you've got laundry to do, meals to plan, a house to keep clean and you still have errands to run. There's the bank, the post office, all the things you need to get done in one day. "You want me to dream? Excuse me? I don't have any brain cells left for that!" That's another great reason to grab a friend and do it together because you can bounce ideas around, you can be each other's sounding board and more often than not, when one person is feeling down the other is feeling up.

Mattie: I think that has been a huge advantage to our project. We've been able to bounce off of each other. When one of us was down the other one was there to help things through. Partnering was great for me because I was able to lean on you, Eve, and you've been able to lean on me. Some people could do it alone, and that's terrific. Go for it! I just know Eve and I have demanding lives and a lot of children. Together we have eight children.

Eve: Whoo Hoo!

Mattie: That's a lot of love and a lot of people to take care of.

Eve: And a lot of challenges.

Mattie: A lot of challenges. Yet we've been here for each other.

Eve: We really are the perfect poster children for a career move or trying something different and new. Honestly, for me, holding our book in our hands means we're a success, even if we never sell one copy. "Wow! We wrote a book!" Especially looking at our *Forty Schmorty* lives, if we can do it anyone can do it. With everything that has happened to us in the last year, along with all the "stuff" we already had going on, it's possible!

Mattie: I remember my junior year of high school. I took a class called V.I.C.A. this stands for Vocational Industrial Clubs of America. On the very first day of class the instructor wrote the letters "I.A.D.O.M." on the chalkboard. He turned around and asked the class, "Does anyone know what this means?" And of course no one knew. So as he pointed to each letter with the chalk (I remember this so well) he recited, "It All Depends On Me." This has stuck with me for thirty years. No one else is going to make it happen for you. It all depends on YOU.

Eve: And that's something we've always found with music. Nobody cares as much as we do about our own music. Initially, nobody cares as much as Mattie and Eve about this book. Now we can get people excited about it and we can get people to help us, but if we don't have that enthusiasm and we don't have the drive, their excitement is quickly going to go to the next thing.

Mattie: Talking about it and not doing anything about it is only going to make you the person crying, "Wolf!" When I run into people and mention I'm writing a book with my friend oftentimes I'll get an underwhelming response, "Oh, that's good." There are other times when I mention the book and I get the response, "Really? That's wonderful!" For the not-so-enthused it's the old "Talk is cheap." "Oh yeah, well show me the book when you're done."

Eve: "Right, I'm not impressed. Do you know how many people I know who are writing a book they will never finish?" And I want to insist, "But wait a minute, this is important to me! It's really going to happen. Don't you get it?"

Mattie: So make two lists, one contains your passions (don't forget your hobbies) and one is a list of your personal qualifications. This is so important that we've provided a page at the end of this chapter for you to get started with your list. Decide if you will proceed on your own or bring a friend along, "Where two or more are gathered" you can achieve great things. Keep it simple.

Eve: The interesting thing about you and me is that our career, music and singing for a living is what brought us together and we became great friends. Our lives have unfolded through this book. Career is what brought us together and when you think about it, you never know where you're going to meet your soul mate or your B.F.F. (Best Friend Forever). That person is out there. You have to listen to your heart and dream about manifesting what you want. "I will do this, I can do this!" can get you through all the mundane office work or whatever chore you must do. We all still have to do things we wish we could hire someone else to do, but we're doing it on our own.

Mattie: That's a huge point. We didn't meet in college and we didn't go to grade school together or run into each other in the grocery store or in a playgroup. We met through our careers and now we're moving forward and sharing the extension of our career.

Eve: We are transforming ourselves. Here's a quote from Abraham Maslow: "A musician must make his music, an artist must paint, and a poet must write if he ultimately is to be at peace with himself." The reason I continued with my music career is because I asked myself, "Can I live without it? Can I live without music as my career?"

Mattie: That is a great question to ask yourself.

Eve: I stopped performing music for about six months and I was miserable. I knew then, "No, I can't live without music." So that is the path I chose and now, here I am. I didn't see this coming. I believe this is one of the reasons we started this book. I never thought that writing a book could enhance my music career.

Mattie: So why not ask yourself that very important question: "Can you live without cooking, walking your dog, helping an elderly person, sewing, scrapbooking, taking care of children and teaching, fishing…"

Eve: So many great things!

Mattie: There are so many wonderful things that mean the world to so many people who don't have that service provided for them. Are you that person who can make a difference in someone's life? Lighten their load? Ease their burden? Can you make the choice to change your passion into your career and help others in the world? Awaken your passion!

Eve: Find your peace. Like Abraham says, "The peace is inside of you." Be still, listen and ask questions. It's exciting. It's an exciting adventure. You can dream these huge dreams and it's fun to sit down and think about them.

Mattie: And at least you're starting to think about them. You're awakening your passion.

Eve: And once you start writing things down you can begin with baby steps. Start slowly and you'll realize it's possible.

Mattie: Make little notes for yourself on Post-It Notes and stick them everywhere and anywhere so you can see them. What's your intention? What's your dream? What's your goal? What's your passion? And remember to take it one day at a time. Watch what happens!

Eve: There's nothing better than crossing an action item off a list. "Did it!" "Done!" "Complete!" "A finito!" **I**t **A**ll **D**epends **O**n **M**e! So you don't have anyone to blame if you end up staying in a job you hate because you're just doing it for the paycheck. You have opportunities waiting to discover you. Be open to them. You never know. You might write a book about it. We did.

DREAM LIST

Passions/Hobbies	Qualifications

1.

2.

3.

4.

5.

6.

7.

8.

9.

10.

FORTY Schmorty!

FORTY Schmorty!
...life keeps happening

FINAL WORDS

Eve: I think it's very appropriate we're sharing our final thoughts while I am breast-feeding Henry.

Mattie: And I am nursing my own breasts as I'm recovering from the completion of my reconstructive surgery.

Eve: Writing this book has deepened us as human beings and helped us through challenging times. We "walked through the fire" and went from cheerleaders to warriors. It has helped us both become better friends. We've learned so much by just sharing our life experiences together. Mattie makes me want to reach well beyond my capabilities and strive to be better at everything I do. Working on this book has given me so much more than I put into it. I've been so lucky and blessed to be a part of the story.

Mattie: We innocently started this book thinking it would give us something fun to do. We were ready for a transition of some sort to take place in our lives and feeling a strong need to make a contribution. We thought it would be a great idea to help all women in their forties achieve their goals, find happiness, find or redefine self love and generally experience more love in their lives. And interestingly, every time Eve and I began a chapter different situations would come up in our lives and we would feel compelled to talk about them. Eventually we'd get to the intended subject matter. It is our sincere hope this book has enlightened and inspired you and we hope you can take the information and feel better about yourself and your life.

Eve: Embrace being forty and be excited about being forty (and fifty, sixty, seventy). Know that the world really is your oyster. All those clichés you hear are true. Everything happens for a reason and the reason means something different to all of us. I *want* to be proud of being in my forties. I *want* someone to ask my age and I *want* to proudly proclaim, "I'm forty-four! I look good because I feel good. Let's all start an age revolution!"

Mattie: Sometimes when I tell people my real age they're shocked I actually told them my real age. Then I usually get, "You don't look *that* old!" which I think is a very sweet response. In your forties, expect surprises and always expect change even when things are planned. You can always expect a slight bend in the road so try your hardest to take it with a light heart. Know that it is just the way life is. Stay positive and be happy.

Eve: And get excited because you never know what's around the corner. One final quote (author unknown): "Yesterday is history. Tomorrow is mystery. Today is a gift, that's why they call it the present." Be in gratitude.

Mattie: Because after all…

Eve and Mattie: Life Keeps Happening!

About the Authors

Mattie Mills was born in 1960 in Yuma, Arizona. After touring for three years with the international group, Up With People, Mattie moved to San Diego where she continued her entertainment career, writing, singing and producing shows for SeaWorld's Shamu Show, Seal & Otter Show, City Streets, plus various character shows. In 2004, she created, wrote, produced and hosted *Musicuisine*, a local cooking show that had a four-year run on local Time-Warner Cable. Mattie is a voiceover talent for national and local radio and television commercials and corporate presentations. She is lead vocalist for the San Diego-based dance band, The Heroes. In 2007, Mattie was named Honorary Survivor Susan G. Komen Race for the Cure, San Diego. She lives in San Diego, California, with her family.

Eve Selis was born in 1963 in Deming, New Mexico. She grew up in San Diego, California and attended San Diego State University. Eve is an international recording artist, songwriter, touring performer and winner of five San Diego Music Awards, as well as the Jim Croce Music Award for excellence and dedication to music. She recently released her 8th CD, *Angels and Eagles*. Eve is a champion local fundraiser with such charities as the Storefront Homeless Teen Shelter, City of Hope Breast Cancer Foundation, Voices for Children, Everyday Angels, and many more. She lives in San Diego, California, with her family.

For more information please visit our website:
fortyschmorty.com

You can also subscribe to our video podcast:
gorillasoapbox.com